# THE BOY WHO LOVED
# BATMAN

# THE BOY WHO LOVED

# BATMAN

## A MEMOIR

### MICHAEL E. USLAN

The true story of how a comics-obsessed kid
conquered Hollywood to bring the Dark Knight
to the silver screen

CHRONICLE BOOKS

SAN FRANCISCO

Library of Congress Cataloging-in-Publication Data

Uslan, Michael, 1951-
  The boy who loved Batman : a memoir / Michael E. Uslan.
    p. cm.
  ISBN 978-0-8118-7550-9 (hardcover)
  1.  Uslan, Michael, 1951- 2.  Motion picture producers and directors—United States—Biography. 3.  Television producers and directors—United States—Biography.  I. Title.

  PN1998.3.U85A3 2011
  791.4302'32092—dc22
  [B]

                        2011005940

Manufactured in China
Designed by Michael Morris

10 9 8 7 6 5 4 3 2 1

Chronicle Books LLC
680 Second Street
San Francisco, California 94107
www.chroniclebooks.com

# TABLE of CONTENTS

**Part I:** How to Have an Origin Without a Planet Blowing Up, Parents Murdered, Radioactive Spider Bites, Cosmic Rays, Gamma Rays, White Dwarf Stars, Aliens Crash-Landing, a Magic Word, a Magic Hammer, or a Super Serum

| | | |
|---|---|---|
| CHAPTER ONE | *The Secret Origin of Michael Uslan, Comicbookman!* | 13 |
| CHAPTER TWO | *Just Imagine! Team-Ups and Sidekicks!* | 23 |
| CHAPTER THREE | *Paul and Michael . . . Brother, Power, the Geek!* | 33 |
| CHAPTER FOUR | *Batman and Robin's Dirty Secret!* | 41 |
| CHAPTER FIVE | *Batman Begins . . . for Me!* | 47 |
| CHAPTER SIX | *A Campy Batman on TV. "Holy Shit!"* | 57 |
| CHAPTER SEVEN | *The Comic Book Club—No Girls Allowed!* | 65 |
| CHAPTER EIGHT | *Pros and Cons and Con Artists!* | 75 |
| CHAPTER NINE | *"And Then There Were None!"* | 88 |

**Part II:** "You Still Read Comic Books at Your Age?!"

| | | |
|---|---|---|
| CHAPTER TEN | *Good-Bye Smallville! Hello Metropolis!* | 93 |
| CHAPTER ELEVEN | *The World's First College Professor of Comic Books!* | 97 |
| CHAPTER TWELVE | *I Was a Teenage Junior Woodchuck!* | 109 |
| CHAPTER THIRTEEN | *Plan B. A Strange Costume for Batman and Robin, a Strange Choice for Me!* | 119 |

**Part III:** Bloomington to Hollywood: How to Get There from Here!

| | | |
|---|---|---|
| CHAPTER FOURTEEN | *Life Is Not a Comic Book!* | 131 |
| CHAPTER FIFTEEN | *I Know What Evil Lurks in the Hearts of Men!* | 139 |
| CHAPTER SIXTEEN | *Going Backward? Me, Mr. Mxyzptlk, and a Toyota!* | 153 |
| CHAPTER SEVENTEEN | *Raging Bullshit on a "Rocky" Road!* | 165 |

**Part IV:** At Long Last, the Dark Knight Returns!

CHAPTER EIGHTEEN **Ben and Me, the World's Finest Producer Team!** 177

CHAPTER NINETEEN **Blackest Night: The Ten-Year Human Endurance Contest!** 191

CHAPTER TWENTY **Infinite Crisis! The Human Endurance Contest Continues!** 203

CHAPTER TWENTY-ONE **It's the Stuff Dreams Are Made Of!** 217

**Part V:** "Bats" of Luck

CHAPTER TWENTY-TWO **After The Dark Knight, the Brightest Day!** 227

EPILOGUE **The Road Taken, the Road Not Taken!** 232

**Acknowledgments** 247

**Image Credits** 250

## DEDICATION

To the ones who loved me just for being Michael.
And to all who made my journey possible . . .

## EPIGRAPH

"A bat! That's it! It's an omen!"

—Bruce Wayne, 1939
—Michael Uslan, 1959, age 8

PART I:

# HOW TO HAVE AN ORIGIN WITHOUT A PLANET BLOWING UP, PARENTS MURDERED, RADIOACTIVE SPIDER BITES, COSMIC RAYS, GAMMA RAYS, WHITE DWARF STARS, ALIENS CRASH-LANDING, A MAGIC WORD, A MAGIC HAMMER, OR A SUPER SERUM

# CHAPTER ONE

# The *Secret Origin* of Michael Uslan, COMICBOOKMAN!

The Big Bang that 13.7 billion years ago begat all life in the universe and, according to *Justice League of America* #21 and 22, a string of possibly endless parallel universes, had nothing to do with me, my life, or my very existence. For me, the only true Big Bang occurred when Krypton blew up in *Action Comics* #1, page 1, panel 1. That explosion not only rocketed baby Kal-El to earth, bequeathing our struggling planet its very first superhero, a veritable Superman, it also showered us in a stream of glowing green Kryptonite, rocky remnants of that once proud planet, and transformed a normal human boy into a super comic book fan whose character and story would be shaped forever by the all-powerful weekly doses of four-color fantasy illuminating his imagination. My name is Michael Uslan, and that's me.

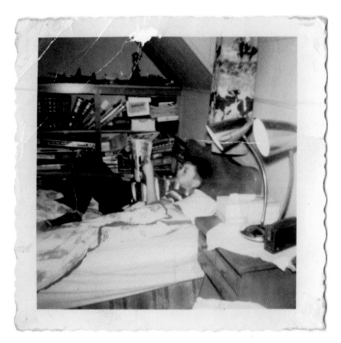

Me in Comic Book Heaven! At age 8, it doesn't get better than this!

My mom may have given birth to me, but my comic books formed me and made me who I am. Published every Wednesday of my lifetime, they were always the next adventure lurking around the next corner of my mind, they provided new vocabulary to my literary arsenal at age eight . . . from "foe" to "origin" to "indestructible" to "invulnerable" . . . and they were the protective secret sanctum Bat Cave where I could escape from the real world and find friends, heroes, and damsels-in-distress who didn't make fun of a boy who read comic books. They were a safe place to curl up, whether in a quiet, out of the way corner of the playground, up in our backyard treehouse, or under my blanket at night with my Cub Scout pocket flashlight.

Who am I? I'm the little kid whose preconceived notions about high school and dating came from reading *Archie Comics*, *Betty & Veronica*, and *Jughead*. I'm the fella who, hearing the word "Kent," thinks superhero not cigarette. I'm the lad who got the "A" on his *Red Badge of Courage* book report, never having read the book but only the "Classics Illustrated" comic book version. I'm the fan who scanned every panel of every story in every issue of every comic book looking for "boo-boos" I could write letters to the editors about and maybe even see my very own name in print in a comic book that has Bruce Wayne's name printed in it near mine. Bruce Wayne? Alfred? Dick Grayson? The Joker? The Catwoman? The Penguin? Two-Face? The Riddler? Batwoman? I knew them all. Personally. I knew everything about them. I knew their secret origins (once I found out from my mom what "origins" were). I knew where the Batmobile was parked.

I knew the name of the street where Bruce Wayne's parents were shot and killed. I knew Commissioner Gordon's first name and Alfred's last name (both of Alfred's last names; there were two— a boo-boo!). I knew every word Bruce Wayne said when, "As if in answer, a huge bat flies in the open window . . . " I knew every trophy in the Bat-Cave and the one real date on the giant penny. Why do I know all his and have a head stuffed with data, details, and delineations that don't matter to you but were all that mattered to me growing up? Why, on the inside, did I never really, actually grow up? The answer is to know me. Yes, my name is Michael Uslan. But that's not exactly who I am . . . really . . . in my secret identity.

I'm the Boy Who Loved Batman.

Wednesday! It was the best day of the week! Better than *The Mickey Mouse Club*'s Wednesday "Anything Can Happen Day." Gimme a break! If you truly wanted to be somewhere on a Wednesday where "Anything Can Happen" it was at a candy store or drugstore on comic book day! Wednesday was the day each week the new comics went on sale all over America. For a kid born in Jersey City, New Jersey, living for three years in Bayonne, New Jersey, growing up first in Wanamassa, New Jersey, and then, starting in sixth grade in Deal Park, New Jersey, just north of the legendary Asbury Park, I found myself embroiled in layer after layer of New Jersey that made me feel like I would never be able to escape my Garden State if I ever needed to. For me the only true escape was to the sacred eight places that sold comic books in and around Wanamassa that were within a human boy's leg power to pedal to on his bike: Wanamassa Pharmacy; Ricky's; Deal Pharmacy; Deal Soda Shop; Allenhurst Pharmacy; Andy's Soda Shop; Flo's, next to the Asbury bus station; and, only as an absolute last resort when all the other places were sold out, that pit-of-terror candy and tobacco store ruled with an iron fist and a tongue of fire by the monstrous proprietor, Old Man Tepid. These were my eight temples to my superhero gods that I faithfully prayed in every Wednesday, poring over the next treasured issue of *Fantastic Four, Challengers of the Unknown, Brave & Bold,* and countless others.

Comic books were 10 cents. The summer I turned ten, I plucked off the "Hey, Kids! Comics!" rack at Wanamassa Pharmacy the new issues of *Superman's Pal, Jimmy Olsen*; *Action Comics*; and *Superman's Girl Friend, Lois Lane*; and handed Mr. Lieberman, the pharmacist who owned the place, a quarter and a nickel. He looked down at my three-prong purchase and said, "That will be thirty-SIX cents, son." I smiled and said politely, no, the comic books are 10 cents. He turned the *Jimmy Olsen* around and pointed to a box at the top that made no sense to me. In fact, I could not . . . and totally refused . . . to believe it. The box that had always said either "10¢" or "Still 10¢" now said "12¢." I stared hard at it, waiting for it to change back to "10¢". It didn't. At age ten, I had my first deflating lesson in a thing called "inflation" . . . something no kid should ever have to know about. I was forced to put back one comic book. I couldn't! How could I leave behind any one of these three issues? I NEEDED them! *Lois Lane* #30 had a mermaid on the cover! In *Jimmy Olsen* #57, he was a human yo-yo for a Martian! A Superman

*Lois Lane* #30 was my first harsh lesson about inflation, while Superman chases tail!

monster made entirely out of Red Kryptonite* was right there on the cover of *Action* #283! Mr. Lieberman forced me to make Mikey's Choice. I surrendered *Lois Lane* because she was a girl. That said, I hopped on my bike and zipped home. My mom, the pillar known as Lil Uslan, was there as she always was whenever I needed her, like Superman was for Jimmy Olsen, only Jimmy had a Superman Emergency Signal Watch and whenever he needed to summon his super pal, all he did was twist a button on it and it went "zeee-zeee-zeee" and Superman instantaneously stopped saving the sun from blowing out, or whatever he happened to be doing wherever he happened to be doing it at that moment, and showed up in the nick of time to save Jimmy. I had no "mommy Emergency Signal Watch" but I didn't need it. She always just knew when something was wrong and always was just there when I needed her. Talk about a superhero! I told her what happened at Wanamassa Pharmacy and as she explained to me about this "worst-thing-than-anything-I-ever-heard-in-my-life" called "inflation," she told me to get in the car and drove me back to Wanamassa Pharmacy before someone else bought *Lois Lane*. She gave Mr. Lieberman 12 cents for me plus an extra nickel for a package of Topps baseball cards with a hard pink slab of gum dusted with some sort of white powder I don't ever want to know about.

My mom saved the day for me at Wanamassa Pharmacy. On the car ride home, I got to thinking about how parents/caregivers don't make out as well as their kids do in comic books. Think about it:

| | |
|---|---|
| Batman's parents, Thomas and Martha | Dead |
| Superman's parents, Jor-El and Lara | Dead |
| Superman's foster parents, Jonathan and Martha | Dead |
| Spider-Man's uncle, Ben | Dead |
| Aquaman's Atlantis mother and Earth father | Dead |
| Robin's parents, John and Mary Grayson | Dead |
| Daredevil's dad, Jack Murdock | Dead |
| Captain Marvel's parents, C.C. and Marilyn | Dead |
| Captain Marvel, Jr.'s grandfather, Jacob | Dead |
| Tarzan's parents, Lord & Lady Greystoke | Dead |

When I read the story "The Last Days of Ma and Pa Kent," that showed Clark's foster parents dying just at the time their son, Superboy, was moving from Smallville to Metropolis and changing his name to Superman, I really did cry. I cried for Superboyman because I didn't know how he possibly would be able to live without his parents. And I cried for me because that one comic book story made me aware that one day my parents would die, too, and I didn't know how I possibly would be able to live without them. Already, my mom had instilled in me the same life lesson that the comic book story of Bruce Wayne becoming Batman then reinforced—once you make a commitment, you honor it, even if it means having to walk through hell before coming out the

---

*What the hell is "Red" Kryptonite? When Krypton blew up, chunks of regular, standard-grade Green Kryptonite streaked through a mysterious cosmic cloud that changed them into Red Kryptonite. Numerous Red Kryptonite meteors eventually struck earth. But don't worry! They bear no danger to us humans (unless, of course, you're just some unlucky asshole who is reading the paper in his house in Connecticut one night when the damn thing plummets through the atmosphere, crashes through the roof, and hits you in the fleshy part of your thigh). But they do affect, change, and transform Superman in unpredictable ways with each exposure, turning him from time to time into a fat Superman, an old man Superman, a baby Superman, and almost any everyday object: a cat, a bird, a rake, a hoe, or whatever object you could find in a "Hidden Picture" puzzle page in the kid's magazine *Highlights for Children*. Red Kryptonite became so popular in the Superman stories that the writers went on to invent Gold Kryptonite (permanently removes Superman's superpowers), White Kryptonite (kills Kryptonian superplant life), Silver Kryptonite (a hoax—like the bottle of snake oil advertised to cure lumbago, consumption, gout, and catarrh), and from time to time as desperate writers needed them, other colors lifted directly from a sixty-four pack of Crayolas.

My parents, Joseph and Lillian Uslan (but just Joe and Lil to anyone who counted), were much better parents than Martha and Jonathan Kent, because my folks were real!

other side. Already, my mother had made me the greatest deal in the history of comic book collecting! Unlike almost everyone else's mom, who either refused to allow comic books in their house or threw them out or surrendered them to those paper drives left over from World War II, MY mom said that IF I kept them stacked neatly in my brother Paul's and my bedroom, and IF I promised to read other things besides comic books (the specific list was books, newspapers, and magazines), I could keep them. The die was cast. Caesar crossed the Rubicon. The fait was accompli. And so, by the time I graduated high school, I had well over 30,000 comic books, dating back to 1936. No, I knew I wouldn't be able to go on if my mom and my dad died. But while that's what young Bruce Wayne thought, too, it was his parents' death that made him vow to become a superhero. It made him Batman. I knew there was some lesson to be learned there, but for the life of me, I couldn't grasp it at age ten.

In sixth grade, when we moved from 915 Raymere Avenue in Wanamassa to a bigger house at 109 Runyan Avenue in Deal Park, I already had so many comic books that from the very first day we moved in, my dad never once got his car into the garage. Instead, my Pop built me floor-to-ceiling shelves around the three walls of the garage and I filled them with my collection. When I ran out of shelf space, I started putting them in plastic Glad Bags my mom had in the kitchen drawer and stacked them up over the entire floor of the garage. You have not

My dad, New Jersey's greatest mason and the best "Old Soft Shoe" dance man and singer since vaudeville died!

lived until you see 30,000 comic books in one room! My dad was just like Pa Kent except better because he was real. He worked six days a week as a mason until he was eighty in whatever weather he faced each day, whether it was 95 degrees with 100 percent New Jersey humidity or bitter, raw cold with snow coming down when he'd light a fire on the job and keep a-goin'. It didn't matter, because every day when he got up before dawn, Pop would pop out of bed with a big smile on his face that said, "I can't wait to get to work!" He LOVED what he did! He was a real craftsman . . . an old-world artist with what he could create with bricks and stone and marble and cement. Both his older brothers, Jack and Irv ("Itchy," as everyone in the family over the age of forty called him: don't ask me; I never even inquired about that, I just accepted it as what was) were stone masons. All his uncles were masons. His father was a mason. My Grandpa came over from Minsk in December 1904 when all the Jewish men who lived in the Jewish ghetto ("*Yahtkigahs en yag zahl*" he would say in either Russian or Yiddish, I could never tell the difference; my dad said it meant, "Yahtkigahs Street near the railroad station") were being rounded up to be sent on a one-way ticket to Manchuria to fight in the Russo-Japanese War. He and the others hightailed it for ports in Belgium or Liverpool to hop a steamship for America, where they planned to make enough money to eventually send for their wives, children, parents, grandparents, aunts, uncles, and cousins. The family name was originally "Uzlian" and was taken from the name of the Jewish *shtetl* about thirty miles south of Minsk where the family originated, and which supposedly was one of the villages used by Sholom Alechim as his model for "Anatevka" in *Fiddler On The Roof*. Uzlian also spawned a Jewish boy who came to be known as General David Sarnoff, founder of RCA and NBC. Grandpa landed at Ellis Island and the official there translated "Uzlian" as "Uslan," and the rest is family history.

On my mom's side, Poppy David and his new wife, Pauline, arrived from Muncacs in Hungary (today, Munkachevo in the Ukraine) via Budapest. Bayonne, New Jersey, where they eventually settled, overlapped in a surprising way with the early history of moviemaking. Named after Bayonne, France, this city was home to one of the earliest motion picture companies in America, owned by the Horsley Brothers and variously known as Nestor Studios and Centaur Studios. They filmed a number of the very first western movies in Bayonne. But Thomas Edison's relentless patent attorneys were closing in on their operation and the weather wasn't cooperating with moviemaking. So under cover of night in 1911, they left 900 Broadway and headed west, not stopping till they got to a sunny village named Hollywood, opening at the corner of Sunset Boulevard and Gower . . . the first movie production studio bigger than a barn. Eventually, the Horsleys' company was absorbed into the new Universal Film Manufacturing Company, now better known as Universal Pictures, originally of Fort Lee, New Jersey, on a site that today is the tollbooth leading onto the George Washington Bridge. Bayonne is also part of Hudson County in north Jersey, which at times over the decades has been compared politically to Chicago. Let me put it simply . . . having grown up in Hudson County, my dad's political philosophy was molded as follows: "Forget Republican or

Grandma Anna (Botwinick) Uslan and Grandpa Sam Uslan in the early 1950s. Had he lived, Grandpa would be 131 years old today. So if you spot him exiting a voting booth in Hudson County, NJ, tell him Paul and I say "Hi!"

Democrat. Always vote out the incumbent. Because by the end of his first term, he has just about mastered the ropes of corruption within the system. Vote for the new guy and that buys us another four-year learning curve before he's then in a position to *schtup* the voters." My Uncle Jack's north Jersey political philosophy was even more hardcore. He used to say, "I believe in two terms for every politician . . . one term in office, then one term in prison." If my Grandpa Sam was alive today, he'd be about 131. I'm told he STILL votes in Hudson County.

When Grandpa and his brothers settled in Bayonne, they wanted to join the Masonic Lodge. Back then, it was exclusive to the Italian masons and not open to Jewish masons. So in conjunction with The Bayonne Hebrew Benevolent Association, they started their own Lodge, the Menorah Lodge, and Grandpa became president in 1917. Their meetings were held above the 33rd Street Club, where more card-playing for big bucks took place than anywhere else in Bayonne but Botwinick's Delicatessen's back room.

The huge Chanukah/Christmas party took place at the 33rd Street Club and was the only time we kids were allowed in. Santa Claus smoked a cigar. I thought that was odd.

Grandpa Uslan always wore the diamond-studded Masonic ring he received as president, whether he was sitting and reading *The Jewish Daily Forward* or chasing corrupt, greasy-palmed building inspectors off his jobs by swinging a mean 2×4. When Grandpa died in 1965, Dad took off his own Masonic ring and slipped on Grandpa's. I wear that ring today and my brother Paul wears Pop's.

Pop . . . Dad . . . Joe Uslan . . . by any name, he LOVED what he did for a living. And when you grow up in a house with that impacting you every day, as Paul and I did, you begin to realize what a wonderful thing it is to see somebody passionate about his work. I thought about all my friends' dads and working moms and wondered how many of them also loved what they did. It was only a guess, but from all the frowns I remembered seeing when they got off the train from Newark or the bus from New York, I figured not many. And I thought that was sad. In the comic books, every superhero loved what he did in his secret identity. Batman loved being a millionaire playboy. Green Arrow loved being a millionaire playboy. The Sandman loved being a millionaire playboy. Iron Man loved being a millionaire playboy. The Green Hornet loved being a millionaire play-boy. The Wasp loved being a wealthy heiress. Batwoman loved being a wealthy heiress. Elasti-Girl loved being a movie star. Tarzan loved being Lord Greystoke. Why couldn't real life be more like my comic books?

# CHAPTER TWO

# Just Imagine!
## TEAM-UPS
### and
## SIDEKICKS!

It was through the world of comic books that I met two of my three best friends in life. Barry Milberg and I bonded on the first day of third grade. One day we started talking comic books and he told me he'd seen a new superhero comic book over at Old Man Tepid's but was fuzzy about the details. He told me he thought it starred four members of the Justice League of America. Then he changed his mind and said the four maybe were Superman's pal Jimmy Olsen as Elastic Lad, Phantom Girl and Sun Boy from the Legion of Super-Heroes, and a monster made of orange rocks. Confused, the minute that school ended, I rode my bike with the Mickey Mantle baseball cards in the spokes over to Old Man Tepid's to investigate.

WANAMASSA GRADE SCHOOL

GRADE 3

1959          1960

Barry and me in our third-grade class photos at Wanamassa School, taken the week we met and became best friends, just like Batman and Superman. I'm on the left.

Going into Tepid's meant taking your life into your hands. You went in only when there was no hope of finding a particular comic book at the other stores within a bike-riding radius of Asbury Park. A man on a mission, I entered the shop and endured the admonishments of Tepid, who, with that little moustache of his and the way his hair fell across the right side of his forehead, looked EXACTLY like that scary picture of Adolph Hitler I saw in *Collier's Encyclopedia.* "Quit reading them comic books, kid!" he bellowed as I sorted through the racks. "This ain't a library, fer chrissakes! You bend it, you buy it! And if you ain't got the ten cents, I'll lock you up in the bathroom in the back of the store!"

I shook like a leaf but survived Tepid's barrage of threats and dirty looks and found the mother lode. Barry was right. But these weren't JLA or Legion of Super-Heroes members. These were all NEW superheroes from Marvel, one of those weird comic book companies that wasn't DC or Dell. This group was called the Fantastic Four, and on Barry's recommendation, after some examination, I gave Tepid a dime for a copy.

*Fantastic Four* #1! And I got "stuck" buying FOUR of them!

He stared at me with his Hitler eyes and *Them*-antennae-like black eyebrows streaked with white, and he stormed over to his comic book rack. He picked up the other three copies of *Fantastic Four* #1 I had been sifting through and raged at me. "You looked at ALL of these! And now they're ruined, boy!" I didn't know I could spoil a comic book by simply looking at it. He demanded that I now buy all four copies and wanted three more dimes or I'd never leave his store and would never see my family again (which was okay by me in the case of my big brother Paul who had already smacked me that morning before I went to school because my toothbrush was too close to HIS toothbrush, which was now contaminated, but I crumbled at the thought of never seeing my mom and dad again). Thank God I had 30 extra cents in my pocket; it was the emergency change my mom had figured I might need some day for an extra milk or chocolate/vanilla Dixie cup. In abject fear, I handed over the rest of my money to this comic book terrorist.

So, fifty years later, here's a "thank you" to my pal Barry and a "fuck you" to Old Man Tepid: today a pristine copy of *Fantastic Four* #1 sells for $52,000—and I have FOUR of 'em!

Barry and I became best friends on that first day of third grade and remain so to this day. He was Jughead to my Archie; Potsie to my Richie Cunningham; Whitey to my Beaver (Whoa!—THAT doesn't sound right!). We spent our childhood laughing (except for that one New Year's Eve we spent in jail in seventh grade). He'd have laid down his life for me, and I for him. Best of all, he "let" me steal his comic books and I "let" him steal my brother's baseball cards in return, teaching us both, at that tender age, much about the art of the deal.

In the best Shakespearean tradition, Barry had a fatal flaw—he threw up on rides. Not every ride, mind you. He could go up and down with no problem. But ONE circle, and he'd vomit. Profusely. Sometimes he did it while he was still spinning, spewing over a wide range of fellow riders and innocent bystanders. Sometimes he'd do it projectile-style. It made me pity the little kid riding in the car in front of him. If the *Guinness Book of World Records* tracked people who did what Barry did, he would be a champion. He barfed on The Beast, retched on The Round-Up, left his vomit on The Comet, hurled on The Howler, spewed on Space Mountain, and upchucked on Ultra-Twister. And best of all, he ALWAYS came back for more. In the words of Metro-Goldwyn and Mayer... "THAT'S entertainment!"

Bobby Klein: Boy Genius, Superfan, Walking Comic Book Encyclopedia, and one of the last earthlings who knows who everyone with the initials "L. L." is in Superman's life!

Best friend number two, Bobby Klein, didn't appear on the scene until fifth grade, and thus, to this very day, he's still thought of and referred to as "the new kid."

Ocean Township School was still pretty new when Bobby showed up. The stairs were showing little wear along the edges. The handrails weren't yet caked in layers of paint. That year, Miss Hall, the kindest teacher in the school and the one who made you want to kind of GO to school each lazy morning, had us working on our "Tour Book of the Southern States." I HATED the geography part and anything that required the use of the words "natural resources" in an essay. But I did love history, thanks to my mom's creativity and make-it-happen energy. At the end of each school year, Ma would find out what Paul and I would be learning the following September in social studies. She would then plot a summer trip to the places we would be learning about—Washington, D.C.;

Jamestown; Williamsburg; or maybe Fort Ticonderoga, Saratoga, and Quebec's Plains of Abraham—so we could BE there and touch History.

Right in the middle of my one-page essay on the importance of Eli Whitney and the sloe-gin fizz, or whatever the hell it was he invented, Miss Hall stepped out into her last name (sorry; fifth-grade joke) and reentered the classroom with this skinny kid who looked like Alfalfa did when he saw that ghost in the Little Rascals' funhouse episode. The rattled boy was clutching a sad brown paper bag that clearly could not have contained a lunch any larger than half a peanut butter and jelly sandwich. No wonder he was so skinny. Someone at home was starving him. These were the days when a person's peanut butter preference was significant. I sized him up immediately, the way only a fifth grader can, and figured he was a Skippy guy . . . someone who could be mistaken for boring, but in reality was just conservative, quiet, and thoughtful. Barry liked Jif. Of course! He was kinda athletic and had what may have been ADD, but back then we more accurately described him as "bouncing around like a kangaroo a lot." I was Peter Pan all the way . . . the superheroic little boy who never grew up.

From the front of the room, Miss Hall formally addressed the class—all thirty-one of us shoehorned into a space designed for twenty—which meant she meant business. "This is a new student, Bobby Klein. He'll be joining us starting today. We have no more lockers available, so who would like to share their locker with Bobby?" We all froze, held our breath, hoping the powers that be, Miss Hall in this instance, wouldn't point her finger of doom at us, since there was NO way a locker could bear the stress of TWO kids. In fifth grade, the average locker was spring-loaded with books, papers, old lunch remnants, dirty gym clothes that, amazingly, developed rigor mortis after just a few weeks, coats, hats, boots, rubbers (the kind you wear on your feet—this was 1961), scarves, gloves, science experiments, extra credit reports, oversized history projects like the pyramid of Ramses made of a mountain of sugar cubes swiped from Perkins Pancake House over a period of five Tuesday-night fried chicken specials, and cemented with white paste that was routinely consumed by Ocean Township kindergartners. We were a generation of kids eating that paste, chewing on our number 2 lead pencils, sitting in classrooms protected by asbestos and lead paint, sniffing wet, jet-black Magic Markers and purple-inked mimeographed spirit masters, while shellacking leaves in our windowless arts and crafts rooms. And sociologists wonder how "the '60s" came to pass. . . .

I felt bad. No one immediately raised his hand to share a locker with this pitiful figure standing nervously like a ten-year-old Don Knotts in front of an alien class in an unknown classroom in a new school. It just does not get worse than that for a kid. And so, I raised my hand—and changed history for both me and for little Don Knotts. We were about to become blood brothers for life. In that second-floor hallway of dear ol' O.T.S. and with Bobby at my side, I dialed my secret fifth-grade locker combination. (I still remember it to this day. It was "6.") As I opened the tinny, skinny door, Bobby's eyes popped the way I only ever saw it happen in cartoons, usually when a wolfish male saw a beautiful, curvy woman. Scotch-taped to the inside of my locker was a full-page color pinup drawing of Superman, torn out of the inside back cover of *Superman Annual* #1. (Value today if no fucking pages are torn out: $2,000. Value today with the pinup missing: $8. I hate me.)

Bobby thought he was the only boy on earth who was totally into comic books and superheroes. Funny, I had always thought the same about myself. He was the first person I met who knew every color Kryptonite came in and what each color could do to the Man of Steel. He knew the names of every person Superman knew whose initials were "L. L." He knew the three best-ever Superman stories: "The Death of Superman," "Return to Krypton," and "Superman-Red/Superman-Blue." Bobby even understood the eternal paradox of comic books—that the stories DC referred to as "imaginary" stories about Superman couldn't exist, because the "real" stories about Superman were, in actuality, also imaginary. Bobby would go on to become known as the boy genius, to get perfect scores on the SATs, to get his advanced degree from M.I.T.—where he double-majored in something like electrical engineering and nuclear physics before becoming a super-intelligent muckamuck of some sort at Intel, where he impressed the hell out of all the other ranking muckamucks by: (1) taking a chip that held 600 bits, bytes, or other forms of breakfast cereal and making it hold 600,000,000 of them; and (2) knowing the names of every person Superman knew whose initials were "L. L."

Bobby and I spoke the same lingo and shared both the same locker and brain. I eventually figured he was okay to invite over to my house to talk, read, and buy comic books together. Bobby's mom worked, so my mom picked him up from his new house in the Siberia of Ocean Township, a town called Wayside. She dropped us off at the Wanamassa stores because we were then within walking distance of three places that sold comic books . . . although one of these was Tepid's. I was too scared to walk in there without my big brother, Paul, but maybe I could with Bobby? I purposefully didn't warn him about Old Man Tepid. I knew Bobby was too nervous a kid to force him to dwell on the horror show that I knew awaited us. The very first second we opened that door, Tepid verbally pounced on poor Bobby, propelling him from New Jersey into a state of shock. Traumatized in mere moments by the unprovoked proprietor, a kind of gurgling Bobby just blindly grabbed the nearest comic book he could reach, paid his 12 cents and fled, swearing never ever to return to this real-life briar patch. It turned out that he had grabbed *Fantastic Four* #15, which featured the first appearance of the Stan Lee–Jack Kirby super-villain known as the Mad Thinker and his Awesome Android (who, in fact, was really not so "awesome," since his head resembled a tall, rocky version of an engorged 1960s television set).

In the "Letter Column" (a comic book term referring to the one to two pages of text in an issue that are devoted to the letters to the editor) in Bobby's *Fantastic Four* #15, Bobby and I read about a new amateur publication called a "fanzine." Fanzines were magazines published by comic book fans for comic book fans on school office mimeograph machines using purple spirit masters which smelled even better than Magic Markers and could give a kid that "am-I-hanging-upside-down-on-monkey-bars-right-now?" dizzying high.

The very first fanzine Bobby and I ever read, *The Rocket's Blast/Comicollector #31*. We had no idea there was anyone else out there in the world who collected comic books and loved superheroes!

Bobby and I were transfixed by these new fanzines with titles like *Alter-Ego, Etcetera, Flame On!, Aurora, Ymir, Star-Studded, True Fan Adventure Theatre, On the Drawing Board, The Comic Reader*, and *Batmania*. We were developing an unquenchable thirst to learn comic book history and to add more and more old comic books to our burgeoning collections and my dad's bursting garage.

A fanzine called *The Rocket's Blast/Comicollector* (RBCC), the brainchild of a young, mysterious Charles Foster Kane-like fanboy with the moniker of "G. B. Love," featured oodles of ads selling old comic books. Our jaws dropped as we flipped through the pages. *Fantastic Four* #1 was now selling for seven and a half times its original cost—a stunning 75 cents! *Hulk* #1 was now going for a brain-numbing $1.25, while *Fantastic Four* #12 ("The Fantastic Four Meet The Hulk") was 50 cents. I took my accumulated allowances, broke open my official A&P "Eight O'Clock Coffee" bank, mined the living room couch cushions and the seats in my parents' Pontiac for lost coins, Scotch-taped ten quarters to a chunk of cardboard I clipped from the back of Pop's "Portland Cement" pad, and sent them off to one Marc Nadel in Brooklyn, New York, the high-rolling seller of these comics.* For two of the longest weeks of my young life, I waited for the mailman every day, longing for my treasures. Finally, a package addressed to me appeared in the mailbox like the prize in the bottom of a box of Cracker Jack. In return for my $2.50 in quarters, Marc mailed me his *Fantastic Four* #1 (current value: $52,000), *Hulk* #1 (current value: $35,000), and *Fantastic Four* #12 (current value: $6,000).

While Bobby and I now virtually lived in the garage with our comic books, Barry preferred to stay outside and play in my parents' car, pretending it was Dick Tracy's cop car or the Batmobile or TV's Supercar (filmed in "Super-MarionetteVision"!). Forced to

*In 1980, Marc Nadel actually tracked me down at my office at the United Artists movie studio in New York City. Not knowing if he should strangle me or kill himself, he instead became my friend, which he still is, although I have not returned his comic books, which we both agree I purchased fair and square in 1964. I asked him what he did with that $2.50 that he so desperately needed at that time. He was an artist. He used the money to buy a Venus Paradise Color-by-Numbers set, a box of Crayolas, a package of colored pencils, and a set of Colorforms. I asked Marc what they were worth. Current value: nuffin'.

choose between comics and cars, Barry always chose cars. He was so into cars, and I was so not. Barry collected Matchbox cars, built models of classic cars, and was famed in Wanamassa as the first kid on the block to race slot cars. Bobby couldn't have cared less about all this. He was cloistered away in his basement trying to turn toy atomic ray-guns into real atomic ray-guns like something out of *MAD Magazine*. I think he wanted to be the first kid on the block to be the last kid on the block.

Knowing he was dealing with two non-car kids, one day Barry pulled an ace out of his sleeve. "Hey, did you guys know there's a couple of old comic book stands at Collingwood?" And so, Bobby and I went slot-car racing with the impishly smiling Barry.

The Collingwood auction and flea market was like a museum, except that you could buy anything you saw there, and nothing ever cost more than $4. In 1964, it was the place to shop for N. Y. World's Fair memorabilia—from the 1939 fair. It was the one place in New Jersey you could still find Sarsaparilla and Postem. And old, OLD comic books. The flea market way back then was nothing like the first-rate place it is today. Back then, it was dingy, dirty, and, yes, even disturbing. We quickly realized the clientele shuffling past us lacked an impressive number of teeth and had all the homey charm of the backwoods of Kentucky. The air smelled of aging french fry grease, sausages, and a whiff of Secaucus pig farm and Fragrance de Exit 12 of the New Jersey Turnpike.

One of the guys selling magazines and comic books was a Jack Weston look-alike, who sweated like no human being I had ever seen. His glasses, too tiny for his chubby-cheeked face, kept sliding down before he pushed them back up onto the slick bridge of his nose. He was not quite as ornery a cuss as Old Man Tepid, but rather possessed the aura of the gaunt, twitching guys with stringy hair, scars, and pockmarks who tend to operate the rides at traveling town fairs. Every Friday night, he hauled box after box of roped-up bundles of ancient comics across the state line from New York and poured them out over a rotting card table left over from some suburban mahjong game. Another table was just barely hidden from sight around an L-shaped, man-made corner of the stand that was supposed to separate the comic books from the porn. The operative words here are "supposed to." It was at this magical place at this magical time that Bobby and I saw our first Golden Age comic books and our first naked lady. The comic books were bound with thin rope. So was the naked lady bending over on the cover of *Gent*. It wouldn't be until 1982 that I would learn her name. Bettie Page. What a name! What a day!

This was "It!"—the if-you-were-lucky, once-in-a-lifetime act of discovering a silver mine, striking oil, finding the Holy Grail, and uncovering the Ark of the Covenant! It was the jackpot of jackpots! The prize of prizes! The comic book equivalent of stumbling upon the Fountain of Youth! Hundreds of old comic books for a nickel apiece! The owner figured that since the magazines were old, they had no value, and he thought he was putting one over on us kids by charging 5 cents for a worthless piece of four-color pulp. They smelled old. They turned my fingers black as I thumbed through the stories of World War II–era superheroes, cowboy stars, spacemen, mystery men, jungle heroes, monsters, zombies, aliens, soldiers, spies, and detectives. The ads at the back of the comics were almost as good as the fantastical adventures: Charles Atlas ads for booklets that would teach you how to stop bullies from kicking sand in your face at the beach; Vacutex blackhead remover; Lavoptik Eye Wash; "X-ray" Specs ("Kids! See Thru Her Clothes!"); 101 Roman Soldiers; the Magic Art Reproducer that would allow you to draw exact copies of the Mona Lisa; "Be Taller Instantly" magic shoe lifts; and the ultimate "must have" for any respectable thirteen-year-old boy, the whoopie cushion.

That first day our discoveries included *Superman* #2, *Police Comics* #1 (introducing Plastic Man), *Captain Marvel, Jr.* #1, *Archie* #2, *MAD* #1–22, 20 percent of all the titles Marvel published from the late '40s to the late '50s when it was known as Atlas, including *Gunsmoke Western, Kid Colt, Rawhide Kid, Two-Gun Kid, Navy Action, Army Action, Navy Combat, Army Combat, Spy, Marvel Tales, Astonishing Tales, Tales to Astonish, Tales of Suspense, Strange Tales, Journey into Mystery, World of Fantasy, Amazing Adult Fantasy, Amazing Fantasy* (introducing Spider-Man), *Amazing Adventures, Uncanny Tales, Mystic, Mystery Tales, Captain America's Weird Tales, Young Men*, and *Men's Adventures*. Then we found *Prize Comics, Black Magic, Daring Mystery, Jumbo, Jungle, Boy Comics, Captain Battle, Captain Battle, Jr., Daredevil, Crime Does Not Pay, Crime and Punishment, Knock Knock* (from 1936), *Xmas, Whiz, Master, Wow, Zip, Tarzan, Turok, My Little Margie, The Jaguar, The Fly, The Double Life of Private Strong, Kaanga, Konga, Gorgo, Fightin' Five*, and the embarrassing *Clint Curtis & the Road Knights*. Anyone in the business of publishing comics was supposed to know that the ink in the lettering bleeds a bit on the cheap pulp paper it's printed on and therefore you NEVER print any words where there is an L next to an I because those letters ALWAYS manage to accidentally form a U. This is why you will never, ever find the words "flick" or "flicker" in a comic book. "Curt" Curtis would have been SO less nasty than "Clint" Curtis! Current value? Priceless.

From that day until the very day we left for college, Bobby and I scoured the territory from Asbury Park to Long Branch rounding up bottles redeemable for cash deposits, hoarded our respective allowances, and cut back on the necessities of life—Pez, Topps baseball cards, freeze pops, Bonomo Turkish taffy, Fruit-Stripe gum, Wacky Packs, and Buckaroo pinball games on the boardwalk. ALL our money went into old 5-cent comic books.

Thank God we didn't invest in real estate!

Hot Rods and Racing Cars #79. A perfect example of why you're NEVER supposed to use the letters "L" and "I" next to each other in a comic book!

LEFT: The Uslan family, summer of 1954, at 11th and B Street in Belmar, NJ, three blocks from where Bruce would form his E Street Band. There's Dad giving us his best "Tony Soprano" look, Mom holding Paul's left arm to prevent him from punching me again (he was a leftie), and me utterly unhappy at having been smacked by Paul, who looks like a cross between "Butch" of *The Little Rascals*, older brother "Wayne" of *The Wonder Years*, and Satan!

ABOVE: Spring 1954 on the Atlantic City boardwalk with my big brother, Paul.

LEFT: Mom and Dad in the 1930s in the Catskills. How cool is Pop? How hot is Mom?! Every kid should have one photo proving to them their mom was once hot!

# *Paul* and *Michael*...
# BROTHER, POWER,
# THE GEEK!

My brother, Paul, was challenging to raise as a kid. He had a good heart and an energetic personality and brains, but was a hellion. Before any doctor identified ADHD, Paul was on hyper-drive. He reminded me of the horse in the movie *The Misfits*, with Marilyn Monroe and Clark Gable. Our parents recognized that there was a little demon in that bottle that needed to be broken free without breaking Paul's spirit. Sometimes that job took a whip (dad's belt strap, which left an imprint on Paul's tushy one night when he was misbehaving in our hotel room in Atlantic City), sometimes a rope (Miss Polonius, Paul's second- AND fourth-grade teacher, lost it one day when she couldn't keep him in his little second-grade chair, and so tied him to it with a rope; her parole should finally be coming up next year), and sometimes with just the right calming words by that little kid's version of a Horse Whisperer, our mom.

Our parents met when my dad was thirteen and Lil moved in across the street from him on 31st Street in Bayonne. Within days of his carving their initials into a telephone pole between their houses, they started going steady. They married at twenty-one, struggled their way through the Depression, then lost a baby boy at childbirth, rendering my mom sick for a year as she shrank to eighty-five pounds and nearly died. Taken care of by Joe, her parents, her sister Clara, and her loyal, loving brothers, Ernie, Bernard, and Alfred, Lil fought her way back to health. Dad worked hard to support his growing family. Mom raised us day by day, hour by hour, in the trenches, through happy times, sad times, good times, bad times, plays, recitals, parent-teacher conferences, class chaperoning, AND kissed boo-boos and made every hurt go away. Protective? Absolutely. Overprotective? Gimme a break . . . she was a Jewish mother from a generation with vestigial Depression memories.

BALTIMORE ORIOLES — Runners-up in the Ocean Township National League race were the Baltimore Orioles, shown above. Sitting, left to right, are Michael Uslan (bat boy), Mike Stokhamer, Ralph Specht, Kenneth Kennedy, Tom Kelly, Arthur Fink. Standing, left to right, are Larry Braslow, Steve Brockel, Paul Uslan, David Calvert, Wayne Lopez, Paul Sherman, Robert Fink. In background are Manager Robert W. Calvert and Coach Edward J. Kennedy. Coach Herbert Brockel and Ira Dorfman are missing from picture. (Pic by Jones.)

Okay, so maybe big brother, Paul, was the All-Star baseball pitcher . . . but I was BAT BOY!

Though Mom was a *macher* in the PTA at Wanamassa School, Den Mother for Paul's Cub Scout Troop, librarian at Ocean Township School, and a member of service organizations like The Link, it was Dad who showed up at every Little League baseball game Paul or I played. I always felt bad for him. Paul was a superstar athlete in every sport he participated in. He was the most dangerous All-Star pitcher in the major league in Ocean Township's Little League. Batters feared him. He won games, saved games, and seemed to be Superboy to all his teammates. I did the only thing I could think of to try to be a superhero to his team. I became their bat boy. I LOVED my title! MY name "Bat Boy" SHOULD have been used as Batman's sidekick's name because Bat Boy is way better than Robin. It's all so simple! It should've been me.

Yep, Paul was great in baseball. On the other hand, I sucked, even in Pee Wee League. The only thing I liked about it was the fathers taking the team to Carvel for chocolate ice cream cones with chocolate sprinkles when we won. One of my Pee Wee League coaches was an asshole. He was, to me, like Batman's villain Blockbuster. Bigger than Batman, stronger than Batman, scarier than Batman, Blockbuster was a screamer, intimidating to everyone smaller or weaker than he was . . . like I said, an asshole. After every game, away from the ears of the parents in the stands, my coach would call together those of us who had struck out and tell us we looked like clowns and were worthless. I felt bad for my dad that he had to come and watch me play Little League when he could be at Paul's game, beaming. Or anywhere else. Now I knew how Superman felt when he had to be Clark Kent. Bruce Wayne had the same kind of thing, but he was so rich he didn't mind being considered nothing special. After that Pee Wee League season, I never played again. I developed a hatred for all team sports. My coach had destroyed all my self-confidence and enjoyment of playing. And I no longer wanted to endure the embarrassment of being superstar Paul's awful little brother. I was sparing Paul and especially Dad shame they didn't deserve. And it was all really okay for me, as I retreated into a happier world filled with boys and men who were far more athletic than the other kids in the neighborhood and school. My world was made up of superheroes. In MY world, I had adventures with a guy who was faster than a speeding bullet . . . more powerful than a locomotive . . . able to leap tall buildings in a single bound! I survived by seeking refuge in my comic books.

Visiting Aunt Clara and Uncle Phil Hyman and our cousins in Bayonne in the summer of 1956, Paul was racking up his usual number of reprimands, which often spilled over to me because I was either in the middle of or on the receiving end of Paul's chaos. Guilt by association. Most big brothers have little use for their little brothers. Paul was not like that. He found a good use for me . . . as a human punching bag. I needed at all times to be aware of the direct line between Paul's fists and my shoulders, chest, arms, and back. He never swung at my head or below the belt. Below the belt, he kicked. As to my head, his favorite torture was to pin me down and drool over my face, nineteen times out of twenty managing to suck back into this mouth his lengthening string of spit. For the sake of variety, sometimes he would just come over and fart on me for no reason.

But before you get the wrong picture of my brother, it was Paul who, while he felt free or even obligated to wallop me, protected me from anyone ELSE ever doing so. It was Paul who taught me how to inhale helium out of a birthday party balloon so I could sing like the Chipmunks, and who turned me into a celebrity whenever I had croup by making a freak show out of it. He charged his friends a dime each to enter my sickroom and listen to me wheeze like the hee-haw of a real donkey. (Come to think of it, I never got my cut of all those dimes!) And it was my big brother who had me hop on his back and led me into the world of comic books for the first time. We were at Irv's candy store on Avenue A in Bayonne. Inside was an entire wall, floor to ceiling, of comic book racks! I had never before seen a non-Harvey or non-Archie comic book and, clinging to Paul's back, my eyes and mouth must have been as open as they had ever been in those first five years of my life. What a picture we made! Paul picked out three comic books and told me I could pick two. He showed me two different issues of a DC comic book called *Strange Adventures*, both of which were terrifying. One cover had walking, talking human gorillas on it in spaceman/army uniforms. I was fascinated! There was something so powerful and frightening about gorillas that were acting like humans and could conquer us or eat us or put us in zoos or make pets out of us. The other cover had a guy trapped under water, and Paul read me the title, "The Man Who Couldn't Drown," and told me the

It LOOKS like him, it sounds like him, but despite what Paul says, this guy on the cover of *Strange Adventures* #68 is NOT Aquaman.

guy would drown, but only if he was in air like us. I asked if he was super like Superman whom I knew from TV. Paul told me this guy's name was Aquaman. It wasn't. Paul lied. But as with everything he ever said, I believed him. This *Strange Adventures* was not about Aquaman, but was just a scary comic book about a scary guy. Paul's explanation had me confused for years as I kept swearing to Bobby Klein, who thought I was nuts, that Aquaman's origin was as a prisoner in a tank of water, while Bobby knew Aquaman's origin was that his mother came from Atlantis and his father was a normal American guy. I said HE was nuts and that that's the other underwater super guy, the Sub-Mareener. (I didn't know how to pronounce Mariner correctly until Mrs. Kent, our English teacher in tenth grade, made us read "The Rhyme of the Ancient Mariner" and, to score some brownie points with her and maybe get "extra credit," I brought in an issue of Sub-Mariner comic books to show her and she was appalled and told me to "put that thing away.") What a frickin' mess! Thanks a lot, Paul!

I want to be fair and balanced here. Paul's final pick that day was a DC comic book called *Showcase* #4, which just so happened, in one of those one in a billion cosmic coincidences that happen here and there in the universe, to be the comic book that introduced the modern-day Flash to the world, thereby single-handedly starting what would become known in later years as the Silver Age of Comics—the reemergence of superheroes who had been so popular during World War II's Golden Age of Comics. Apparently, after the war the world had no further need for superheroes, and the comic book industry languished. *Showcase* #4 would mysteriously disappear from my piles of comic books by 1962, its whereabouts unknown for decades as it continued to become more, and more, and more valuable.

*Showcase* #4: The Silver Age of Comics begins! The Flash returns! And this comic book soon vanishes from my collection.

Meanwhile, it was time for my own two picks as Paul boosted me up onto his shoulders so that I could reach Irv's top rows of comic books. The two I picked were *Sugar & Spike* #2 (remember the hit

TOP: Winter 1954 on Avenue B in Bayonne, NJ. Paul just got slapped on his right wrist by Mom for doing something—probably EVERYTHING —he shouldn't, as I smile broadly at Dad! BOTTOM, LEFT: Every family has one kids photo that's handed out to every relative. This was ours. Paul is pointing at the camera and telling me to "Smile, Mikey!" It was one of the rare times that I did what he told me without getting into trouble. BOTTOM, RIGHT: Paul as The Devil. He claims this was Halloween 1953. I claim it was every day!

movie *Look Who's Talking*?—this was *Look Who's Talking* before there ever was a *Look Who's Talking*) and *Detective Comics* #236, which featured not the Batmobile everyone knew and loved, but a starkly different version of it in the form of an armored urban Bat-Tank. It was an image I would never forget. (Amazingly, this obscure vehicle, used just once in the history of Batman comics, reappeared in the movie *Batman Begins*. What a coincidence!)

Back in Asbury Park, Mom started taking me and Paul to get our hair cut at Red's Barbershop on Asbury Avenue in between Freddie's, home of the greatest thin-crust pizza ever concocted, and Hoerner's Drive-In (NOT the movie kind, but the kind Dad would drive us to, where waitresses in short skirts would roller-skate out to our car and serve us hamburgers, hot dogs, and ice cream off a tray that attached to Dad's window). Paul showed me what was on the slovenly table in between the seats at Red's for people waiting to get clipped—a pile of old, old comic books. In an unsteady wooden chair next to that slovenly table at Red's, I read coverless, yellowing comic books about weird superheroes with odd names like Dr. Mid-Nite, who flung blackout bombs at bad guys, and Fighting American, who was saving democracy from commie super-villains named Hotsky-Trotsky and Poison Ivan, and fun superheroes called Captain Marvel and Billy Batson, who was a kid who had a magic word, Shazam, that changed him into the adult superhero, Captain Marvel. Red's Barber Shop had originally opened me up to a thing called Harvey Comics and a whole bunch of brand new friends to share funny, happy adventures with: Casper the Friendly Ghost; Wendy the Good Little Witch; Spooky the Tuff Little Ghost; Hot Stuff the Little Devil; Baby Huey; Little Lotta; Little Dot; Little Audrey; Little Max; Sad Sack; and Richie Rich (Donald Trump in short pants at age eight). I didn't know it at the time, but years later I found out that Harvey Comics had been asked by the Boy Scouts of America to make a comic book about a young black fantasy character. They decided back then that they had a great idea! They would create a black version of Casper the Friendly Ghost and call him "Jasper the Friendly Ghost." Mercifully, for me, for them, and for civilization, it never saw the light of day on the newsstands.

Separated from me by four years, Paul was attending Wanamassa School (just through the woods behind our house) without me. There were far too many kindergartners for Wanamassa School to hold. This is why they call us "baby boomers." After World War II, all the soldiers came home and, Boom!, their wives began booming out babies faster than the chocolates coming down the pipeline in the candy factory Lucy and Ethel were working in on *I Love Lucy*. So we had to attend kindergarten in a spare room at Ocean Township Police Headquarters with our beautiful blonde princess of a teacher, Mrs. Birkenmeier. Though she was twenty years my senior, I was in love with her that whole year. I still tingle every time I unearth my kindergarten report card and see her words in green ink printed so neatly in box letters, "Michael has no trouble putting on his boots by himself, but even though he can do it himself, he always asks me for help putting on his rubbers." Dear God in Heaven!

Not long after that memorable first trip into the land of comics, I witnessed something that I could never have imagined in my wildest five-year-old dreams. There I was in 1956, playing happily in our living room with my bag full of puppets, including Monkey and Tiger (wasn't I genuinely creative in making up names for them?). I always had to keep Monkey and Tiger separated by standing between them. If I didn't, before too long, the monkey would be trying to punch the tiger, and the tiger would be looking to spank the monkey. I kept them arm's length apart as the three of us looked out our front window and saw my brother, late getting home from school, and now playing catch by himself on the front lawn with his baseball mitt and a hardball. He'd toss the ball up as high as he could and catch it. Until the Ocean Township Police Car pulled up. No siren, no lights. I was awestruck as a policeman slowly got out of the car and walked halfway up our lawn to talk to Paul. He spoke to him for about five minutes. Next thing I witnessed was the cop walking my brother over to the police car, opening the door, and making him get in. I couldn't believe what I was seeing! Then, I watched as the police drove off with my brother. Quietly, and with the biggest smile, I went back to playing with my puppets. I never said a word to my mom about what I saw. But at age five in Wanamassa, New Jersey, I learned there is a God.

# CHAPTER FOUR

# BATMAN and ROBIN'S DIRTY SECRET!

To this very day, I still wake up screaming on many a fitful night amid nightmarish visions of flames, devilish laughter, and Bobby's father, Mr. Klein.

He had had ENOUGH!

A Fort Monmouth scientist, Mr. Klein had just read The Book. No, not the Good Book. One far scarier than tales of a vengeful God. *Seduction of the Innocent* declared an all-out war on the American comic book and promised to blast every superhero into eternal oblivion. Ask any real comic book fan, someone who knows the history of his cherished hobby, to fill in the following blank: Who are the worst villains in history? Hitler, Genghis Khan, Attila the Hun, Lex Luthor, and _____." The answer will always be that Joker, Dr. Fredric Wertham, the bane of every fanboy's existence and author of the book in question.

LEFT: An awkward moment in the Batman/Robin relationship. Uh . . . er . . . well . . . uh . . . so how 'bout them Yankees?

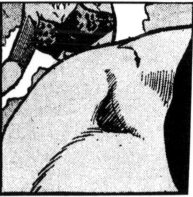

*In ordinary comic books, there are pictures within pictures for children who know how to look.*

*A girl raped and murdered.*

LEFT: Comic books are a communist plot to subvert the youth of America! Comic books cause juvenile delinquency! Comic books cause outbreaks of homosexuality! Comic books cause asthma! Read all about it in *Seduction of the Innocent.*

ABOVE: *Seduction of the Innocent* is like the "Hidden Pictures" puzzle page in *Highlights for Children* magazine. . . . Hidden in this picture is a ho.

Dr. Wertham was a shrink with the Lafargue Clinic in Brooklyn in the '50s when the country was not simply alarmed, but gripped with paranoia occasioned by the dramatic post–World War II rise in juvenile delinquency. What terrible scourge . . . what evil communist plot could cause the youth of America to grease back their hair, don threatening black leather jackets, ride souped-up motorcycles, grow goatees, become beatniks, and even worse, use horrifying new language with alien words like daddy-o and splitsville in front of parents, teachers, and even clergymen? Dr. Wertham had the answer! Almost single-handedly, he caught the culprit in the act! It was COMIC BOOKS! And under the glare of TV cameras and reporters' flashbulbs wherever possible, he set out to destroy them all! Let freedom ring! He would again make America safe for Americans and would de-program teens and preteens in the process. In the era of Senator Joe McCarthy, another witch hunt was underway.

Wertham had interviewed nearly one hundred juvenile delinquents at his clinic. Each one eventually admitted under prodding questioning by the good doctor that at one time or another he had read a comic book. AHA! THEREFORE, concluded Dr. Wertham, comic books CAUSE juvenile delinquency. I wonder what would have happened if he had instead asked the boys if they had ever eaten a pickle? Wertham's claims grew into even more remarkable pronouncements: Girls who read Wonder Woman were doomed to become lesbians. And boys who read the adventures of Batman and Robin all knew what Wertham referred to as Batman and Robin's "dirty secret". . . that the Dynamic Duo— the Caped Crusader and the Boy Wonder—were homosexuals. The secret clues were all right there in the panels of the comic books! How could anyone miss them, wondered the Doctor? Robin was bare-legged, and the way he was drawn running showed him spreading his legs. He was a "ward" of Bruce Wayne. His most conclusive evidence that they were homosexual lovers was their very names, Bruce and Dick. I can't help but wonder what he would have said about the presidential ticket of Bush and Dick in 2000?

Weirdest of all, Wertham claimed that comic books caused asthma. This, of course, was logical because children were staying indoors to read them instead of playing outside in the fresh air. By 1955, towns and cities across America like Jersey City and St. Louis were organizing comic book burnings. Had it not been for the advent of rock 'n' roll in the '50s, which quickly and successfully diverted the attention of society from burning comic books to breaking and melting Elvis records, comic books quite probably would have soon ceased to exist. Senator Estes Kefauver, who had Presidential aspirations and had launched the Congressional investigation into comic books, making sure to have TV cameras present at all key hearings, found bigger witches to hunt.

It seemed that every adult was getting spooked by all this mis- and dis-information. But not my mom. She knew that comics helped me learn to read before I was four, strengthened my vocabulary, and ignited my imagination. Here's my statistic to counter Dr. Wertham: I read twenty times more comic books than Paul did, yet I got into twenty times less trouble than he did. So, my mom's deal was that as long as I kept them neat and promised to read books and newspapers, too, I could go on reading and collecting comic books. She didn't seem at all worried that I would transform into a juvenile delinquent, a homosexual, a commie, or an asthma sufferer.

But at that moment, the heat was on in Wanamassa. Comic book collections were being ferreted out of bedrooms and closets and basements and attics and garages all over town. Kids' sacred stashes were being uncovered. Siblings were ratting out siblings to their parents. But all this was nothing . . . absolutely nothing . . . compared to what was about to happen to Bobby Klein.

Mr. Klein snapped. No, I don't mean he snapped at Bobby. He snapped. Snapped, I tell you! Like what happens to Dr. Bruce Banner when he gets mad and Hulks out, or to Dr. Bruce Gordon when the moon comes out and he transforms into Eclipso. I can't tell you what the precipitating event was, but who cares? What matters is what he did. He took one of those fireplace shovels and, in front of horrified me, catatonic Bobby, and his traumatized brothers Dennis and David, began shoveling Bobby's comic book collection into their fireplace! Try as I may to suppress it, I can picture it now in crystal-clear detail. I watched helplessly as his comics went up in flames with ashes and embers swirling all around . . . *Amazing Fantasy* #15 (first appearance of Spider-Man; current value: $227,000); *Amazing Spider-Man* #1 (current value: $50,000); *Amazing Spider-Man* #2–12 (I have to stop!); *Fantastic Four* #1–14 (including the first appearance of the F.F., the Silver Age Sub-Mariner, Dr. Doom, and Willy Lumpkin, the Fantastic Four's mailman who tried to join their team by showing them his best superpower . . . he could wiggle his ears good); *Tales of Suspense* #39–50 (including the first appearance of Iron Man); *Strange Tales* #101–119 (including the first appearance and origin of Dr. Strange); *Tales to Astonish* #27–50 (including the first appearance of Ant-Man, the Wasp, and Giant-Man); *Journey into Mystery* #83–101 (including the first appearance of Thor); *Avengers* #1–8 (including the first appearance of the Avengers and the first Silver Age appearance of Captain America); *X-Men* #1–8 (including the first appearance of the X-Men, Magneto, Quicksilver, and the Scarlet Witch); *Incredible Hulk* #1–6 (including the first appearance of the Hulk); *Strange Tales Annual* #1; *Sgt. Fury and his Howling Commandos* #1–13 (including the first appearance of Nick Fury). Total value: One ZILLION Dollars!!! In one super-villainous act, Mr. Klein burned them all to cinders!

In April 2008, Bobby's son, Jeff, was married just outside Geppi's Entertainment Museum in Baltimore. Bobby's dad was long gone, but I saw Mrs. Klein at the wedding. It was the first time I had seen her in more than twenty-five years. I couldn't help myself. I asked her if she remembered the Black Wednesday that Mr. Klein burned Bobby's comic books at the stake. She did. I then told her, as a matter of fact and not to be mean or disrespectful, the dollar amount that pile of ash would be worth today. The look on her face was exactly the same one Bobby, Dennis, David, and I sported during the comic book holocaust. As she was leaving the reception to return to her apartment in New Jersey, she kissed Bobby good-bye and handed him a check in the amount of $250. She told him she was sorry for what his dad had done so many, many years ago, and regretted that this was all she had to try to make good for those war crimes. Bobby nobly told her it was no big deal and to keep her check. I went over and kissed her. The mothers and fathers of kids in the '50s were NOT the Wicked Witches of the West who had liquidated their children's comic book collections after all. They were really Glindas with big hearts. They had merely been duped in those halcyon '50s by the self-proclaimed "great and powerful" Wertham of Oz.

# CHAPTER FIVE

# BATMAN BEGINS...

## for Me!

Reading comic books as a kid was just like going through school—every few years was another graduation. In Ocean Township, they made us "graduate" from kindergarten. Then at the end of fourth grade, the Wanamassa kids graduated from Wanamassa School and the Oakhurst kids graduated from Oakhurst School so we could go en masse (which is how baby boomers always moved) to Ocean Township School, which went to eighth grade. When Ocean Township kids like my brother graduated from elementary school before 1965, they went to Asbury Park High School, but starting in 1965, we went to our very own, spanking new Ocean Township High School.

In comic books, you were always graduating from one book to another, from one super-hero to another, from one age-appropriate level to another. Almost every baby boomer comic book reader had a nearly identical experience to his peers. I started my comic book reading with Richie Rich, Little Max, and Casper, and then moved up to Archie, Little Archie, and Cosmo the Merry Martian, before Paul turned me on to Superman. From Superman, the normal progression back then was to Batman. DC Comics, which published both Superman and Batman, was aware of this and wanted Batman to share in the heftier popularity Superman enjoyed. This is why in the '50s, the publisher began a character-destructive program to turn Batman into a clone of Superman. In fact, in some stories, like the stunningly crappy "The Superman-Batman of Planet X," they gave him the superpowers of the Man of Steel, including flying! While I admit that Batman's billowing, scalloped Bat-Cape looked cool in those flying scenes,* it was such a basic violation of his character that even as a little kid, I knew it was wrong. Same thing when they turned Batman into a Bat-Genie in another story. GURRK! A chart might be help-ful here:

| SUPERMAN | BATMAN |
|---|---|
| LOVE INTEREST: Snoopy reporter Lois Lane | LOVE INTEREST: Snoopy reporter Vicki Vale |
| YOUNG BEST FRIEND: Jimmy Olsen | YOUNG BEST FRIEND: Dick Grayson |
| FEMALE VERSION: Supergirl | FEMALE VERSION: Batgirl; Batwoman |
| MISCHIEVOUS IMP FOE: Mr. Mxyzptlk | MISCHIEVOUS IMP FOE: Bat-Mite |
| PET DOG: Krypto the Super-Dog | PET DOG: Ace the Bat-Hound |
| SUPER-GORILLA: Titano the Super-Ape | SUPER-GORILLA: Bat-Ape |
| VILLAINS: The Toyman, the Prankster | VILLAINS: The Riddler, the Joker |

And on and on.

When I officially graduated to Batman, I was eight. Oh, I had read some Batman comics since the age of five, but they were tougher, darker, and scarier than the safer, brighter ones about Clark Kent, the super Boy Scout, who appeared five days a week on TV's *Adventures of Superman*. Every day, the announcer said something like, "Superman, who can change the course of mighty rivers—bend steel with his bare hands." I asked Paul what that meant. I was five, for Chrissakes. And he told me there was a famous circus strongman who fought in a cage with a pet grizzly bear he captured in Germany. "So?" I asked, utterly baffled. "Mikey," Paul said shaking his head in disgust and frustration,

---

*Especially when drawn by best-Bat-Cape-artist-ever, Dick Sprang, who, for entangled legal rea-sons, was never allowed to sign his own name on any of his wonderful art. Bob Kane was legally entitled to be credited on all Batman comics. Like a legion of other superb Batman illustrators most people never heard of, Dick Sprang became known in the industry as a "ghost artist."

"that's the guy they're talking about on Superman—Ben Steel with his bear, Hans." Of course I told everyone I knew about this and swore it was true, and they laughed and made mincemeat out of me!

Now, though, in 1959, I suddenly felt that Batman made more sense than Superman. It was hard to believe in a man who was invulnerable, indestructible, invincible, and all those other "in" words, but easy to believe in a guy who gushed blood when he got stabbed or shot by super-villains. Batman was human. I could identify with him more than I ever could with Superman, the Hulk, or the Human Torch (whom Dr. Wertham referred to in his book as "The Human Torture"). Batman had no superpowers. His greatest super-power was his humanity. His origin story was utterly primal. It transcended cultures, languages, and borders, generation after generation. I mean, his mom and dad get shot dead right in front of his eyes! Over their bodies, in the belief that one person can make a difference, Bruce Wayne sacrifices his childhood and swears to get the guy who did this . . . to get ALL the bad guys. When the bat flies through his open window and he sees it as an omen, becoming a human bat in the process, it's all so powerful! And what about those super-villains? Batman had the best rogues' gallery in the superhero business. No one can rival him. In all Superman's movie serials, TV shows, and feature films, he's faced Lex Luthor how many times? ALL the time, it seems! And his other adversaries? Toyman? Weak. Prankster? Boring. Terra-Man? Gimme a break! He wears a cowboy hat and rides a flying horse! Stupid. Metallo? Boring. Braniac? Okay. You got me on that one. I've been waiting since 1976 for him to show up in a movie.

But now look at Batman's baddies:

Universally known as the Clown Prince of Crime, the Joker was inspired by the joker in a deck of Jerry Robinson's playing cards, and was then influenced by the look of actor Conrad Veidt in one of Bill Finger's favorite movies, *The Man Who Laughed*. While it appears that the Joker and The Batman are polar opposites, they are terrifyingly close to the same thin line, which, but for a twist here and a turn there, could have sent Bruce Wayne over onto the dark side. Interestingly, it's Batman in the guise of a monstrous demonic human bat who is the good guy and the clown-faced Joker who is the homicidal maniac and master of evil, evoking for me Edgar Allan Poe's short story "The Cask of Amontillado," in which the carnival masks the underlying horror. When I was growing up in the '50s and '60s, under the Comics Code Authority, the industry's self-censorship board created to ward off the

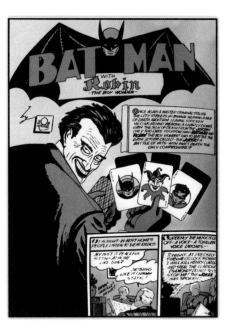

The greatest super-villain ever created in the history of comic books! Introducing the Joker in *Batman* #1, with thanks to Jerry Robinson and Bill Finger.

feds after the hoopla of *Seduction of the Innocent,* the Joker was reduced in stature to a bad clown who made jokes when he robbed banks, and was far removed from the original concept and from today's version of a totally deranged killer.

It was that very same engine of creative destruction, the Comics Code Authority, that forced DC to retire from comics for years any Bat-villains who seemed too gruesome or menacing, including Two-Face and the Scarecrow. It also meant the demise of the Catwoman, because she was all the bad things comic book characters were now not allowed to be: a female in a major role; a possessor of no fewer than two exaggerated body parts; a sexy, stacked, bad girl who carried a whip and wore a dress slit up to what my dad would refer to as "her *pupic*," suggesting a topic that would give Dr. Wertham over-heated conundrums, erotic S & M. If nothing else, the Catwoman should have put to bed all those nasty insinuations and all those catty rumors the Doctor spread about Batman and Robin! Clearly, there was a "thing" between Batman and Catwoman, starting on day one. Their first dramatic encounter was laden with comic book sexual tension. She was merely called the Cat back then, and she wore no mask or villain costume. It wasn't even until *Batman* #3 that she sported a little cape and a fashion disaster of a mask . . . a huge cat head that fit her like a space helmet and hid those lips, those eyes, that hair. Back in the early '40s, Robin was miffed at the end of their first run-in with Catwoman. Batman and Robin were just about to capture her. Robin was straining to grab her and almost had his hands on her when Batman "accidentally" tripped, thus allowing the sultry, seductive Selina Kyle—which would turn out to be her real name— to slip away to strike another day. (By the time the *Batman* TV show debuted in 1966, a "run-in" with Catwoman would be referred to as a "CATaclysmic CATegory-One CATastrophe," which, to me, a true-blue Batman fan, was the first campy sign that the end of the earth was nigh.)

Meanwhile, Bruce Wayne's relationships with normal women like his two former fiancées Linda Page and Julie Madison, plus Vicki Vale and Silver St. Cloud, went nowhere fast. He terminated all of them without batting an eye. Could you imagine Superman's reaction to all this? Superman was the superhero who would stop fighting General Zod to help an old lady cross the street. He was the ultimate power on earth and could have any woman on the frickin' planet, but he wound up in the '50s and '60s saddled with Lois Lane and Lana Lang, two unquenchable snoops who were normal good girls, but royal pains in the ass always trying to prove Clark Kent was really Superman. Half his lifetime as Clark Kent, one of these two annoying girlfriends of his was sneaking up behind him, clutching a pair of scissors to cut his hair. Why? If the scissors broke, they would know for sure that he had super-hair and thus must be Superman. Jesus! Even between the ages of eight and twelve when I was buying,

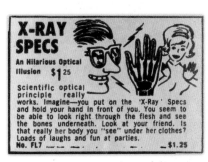

What pubescent male comic book reader did NOT order a pair of X-ray Specs? I put them on and never again would see cheerleader Ronna Berman in the same way!

collecting, and consuming every single issue of *Superman*, this did not sit right with me. I pictured in my wildest fantasies having my pretty classmates Maureen Scott and Jeanne Burns trying to cut my hair whenever I wasn't looking. I mean, ALL the time! Look, I was a very nice boy, but for sure after maybe a year of this, if I were Superman, I'd just turn around and fry them to cinders with my Heat Vision.

It wasn't until seventh grade that it occurred to me that Superman also had X-ray vision and could see through anything except lead . . . walls, vaults, clothes, girls' locker room walls. For a brief time, this concept diverted my attention from Batman back to reading Superman. It got so bad that in desperation, I finally cut out an ad in *Adventure Comics* for X-ray Specs and sent in my $1.25. Now these were advertised as glasses that would give a boy the equivalent of X-ray vision—and they would really work! Really! The ad said so! Not only that, but BEST of all . . . the ad showed a drawing of a guy wearing them and looking at a passing girl and—By GOD!—he could just see through her dress! Even BETTER than that, the ad said . . . right there in black print . . . "See thru her clothing!" If they PRINTED that, it HAD to be true! There was only one bad part—waiting for my X-ray Specs to arrive in the mail. I tore home from school day after day to hit our mailbox before my mom got there and exposed my secret identity. I felt dirty . . . filthy . . . bad. It was GREAT! But the darn wait was eternal! I imagined all the missed opportunities already . . . all those girls' gym classes where all us boys knew they were forced to take showers afterward. The stress was almost unbearable. What was all that bullshit about . . . "Not rain nor snow nor even hail would ever stop the U.S. Mail"? Where the hell were my super-glasses?!? And then, finally, my X-ray Specs came on what was, to that moment, the most exciting day of my life.

I tore open the thankfully innocuous brown package. The FIRST problem was that I had had the idea that these new glasses would very, very subtly replace the glasses I'd been wearing part-time since third grade. These X-ray Specs didn't look like the ones in the drawing in the ad. They were more . . . uh . . . conspicuous. First, they were made out of the same kind of plastic as the 101 Revolutionary War Soldiers I also got from an ad in a comic book. I checked, and even though the names of the companies I ordered my soldiers and my specs from were different, they had the exact same address in Brooklyn. Very suspicious. They would be hard to pass off as plain old REAL glasses. But the second problem with them was a whopper! The lenses in the frames had crazy whirling circles on them . . . reminiscent of every *Twilight Zone* when Rod Serling said, "You're about to enter a dimension not only of sight and sound but of mind." How the hell could I go to school

Cheerleader Ronna Berman. Now do you understand why I sent away for the X-ray Specs?!?

and stare at the wall of the girls' locker room without SOMEBODY catching on? I had to test the water first even more surreptitiously.

I drew up a list of strategic targets, with backups if needed. I ambushed cheerleader Ronna Berman first, lining her up after cheering practice with the sun behind me. And through her ridiculously bulky cheerleader sweater, I thought that possibly I may have sorta maybe somewhat seen a shadow of something round enough to be either a boob, an Ocean Township Varsity Letter O, her wallet in the pocket of her blouse, or . . . not a lemon, not a tangerine, certainly not a grapefruit, maybe an orange? Like the NASA scientists trying to discover whether or not there is water on the Moon, I had lots of ideas, but no conclusive proof whatsoever! It was a hard lesson for a boy who had just thrown away $1.25, had all his immediate hopes and dreams dashed, and for the first time ever, accepted the fact that in the real world, nobody was born with or could acquire a superpower.

But if Batman could live, and even thrive, without a superpower, certainly so could I. Other things worked nearly as well as superpowers. The Dark Knight (a shortened version of Batman's actual alternate descriptive title, the Darkknight Detective) owned a utility belt that had capsules running all around it containing everything Batman ever needed at any time to escape from any deathtrap in which he found himself. By the mid-'60s, every item had been labeled with the word Bat. It had been cool when it was just the Bat-Cave, the Batarang, the Batmobile, and the Batplane. But then it started to get out of hand with the Bat-Wings, the Bat-Copter, and the Bat-Jet. And then the damned floodgates opened, coinciding with the development, production, and broadcast of the campy *Batman* TV show: the Bat-Boat, the Bat-Phone, the Bat-Poles, Bat-Cuffs, the Bat-Cycle, and even Bat-Shark Repellant. Batman's comic book editor, Julius Schwartz, finally put a stop to a lot of this nonsense when he, along with writer Denny O'Neil and artist Neal Adams, returned Batman to his darker roots. He passed a new edict—no longer would writers working for him be lazy and rely on a utility belt that contained everything to allow Batman to defeat any foe at any time. Now, those capsules would be specifically defined. I wasn't the only one growing up. Batman was, too.

If you were a collector and had to buy every comic book that starred Batman every month, you better have had a paper route or some other way to pull down a lucrative income from Wednesday to Wednesday. In addition to *Detective Comics* (which had not only launched Batman in issue #27, May 1939, but had also launched the name of the company that published it, DC Comics) and *Batman* comics, the Caped Crusader also appeared in: *World's Finest Comics*, where issue after issue he teamed up with pal Superman; *Justice League of America*, where he teamed up in one adventure with all the ranking DC superheroes; and *Brave & Bold*, where he teamed up with a different DC superhero every issue. (In terms of the new dark tone, his best partnerships were with the spooky Deadman and his worst were with the comical, incongruous Metal Men . . . for God's sake, it could just as well have been Batman and Mr. Potato-Head fighting the Penguin.)

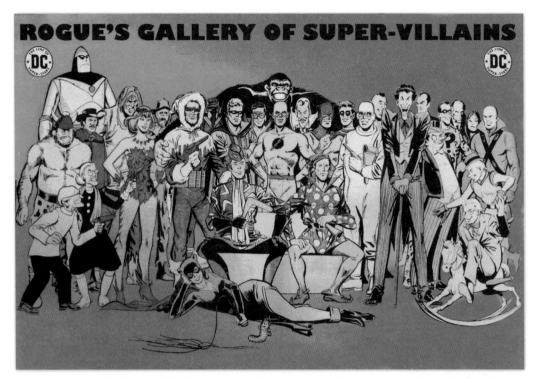

**ROGUE'S GALLERY OF SUPER-VILLAINS**

In this great pinup of DC super-villains by artist extraordinaire Carmine Infantino are nine infamous Batman villains. Can you spot them all?

I always had the Penguin on my B list of Batman villains because he was just too silly with all his birds and umbrellas for a serious Bat-Fan like me. The Riddler was also on the B list for being similar to the Joker, but not as good. Mr. Zero made my B list, but he dropped down to my C list when he changed his name to Mr. Freeze and went over the top. He had a lot of company on my C list: The Terrible Trio—consisting of the Fox, the Shark, and the Vulture—seemed too unrealistic. But that was before I entered the movie business and met the three of them in real life. The Firefly was wrong at the core because in New Jersey we didn't know from a "firefly." It was called a "lightning bug." Now THERE'S a name for a great Batman villain! Blockbuster was dumb and strong. So what? So were half my brother's friends. Killer Moth might have been put to rest with two large-sized mothballs. Ho-hum. To earn a place on my D list, a super-villain had to be a combination of silly, stupid, corny, and unworthy of the Masked Manhunter, another comic book sobriquet for Batman. My D villains were: the Mad Hatter (If I didn't like birds and umbrellas, why on earth would I want to read about a villain with hats?); Tweedle Dee and Tweedle Dum (not only were they "Dum," they were stupid; I hated them—they were for babies, and I was ten!); and Bat-Mite. Oy! What can I say about a mischievous interdimensional imp who pops in to play tricks on my hero, like turning him into a baby . . . Bat-Baby? Okay, so it was cute when I was eight, but by the time I was ten, I wanted to see Bat-Mite dead.

Remembering how strongly I felt about Bat-Mite, years later in college when I started working for DC Comics and my first assignment was answering kids' fan mail to Batman and Superman, I was able to sympathize with one very young reader who wrote a letter to Superman in crayon. It read: "Dear Superman, I love your comic books. I hope Jimmy Olsen falls off a cliff and dies. Love, Jerry." When my boss wasn't looking, I took one of those preprinted fan-response postcards with Superman's picture on it. I filled out the kid's address and then added the following note: "Dear Jerry, Me, too. Love, Superman." Some nights when I flip on *Seinfeld* reruns and I see Superman on his refrigerator, I wonder if he was THAT Jerry.

As to the A list, besides the Joker and Catwoman, that list stars Two-Face, a mesmerizing, gruesome, complex psychopath; the Scarecrow; Hugo Strange (I related to him in those Coke-bottle glasses until science learned how to make eyeglass lenses thin); Man-Bat (a different take on the "Dr. Jekyll and Mr. Hyde" theme than what Stan Lee was doing with it on his Incredible Hulk); Ra's al Ghul (whose original story arc with Batman is one of his most classic, plus it features Ghul's ravishing bad girl, Talia, who, due more to the word "bad" than "ravishing," became another flame of Batman's); the Gorilla Boss of Gotham City;* the Composite Superman (who is half-Batman, too, and it just pissed me off SO much that they didn't call him the Composite Batman!); the Reaper (don't make me spoil the story for you; go read "Night of the Reaper" from 1971's *Detective Comics* #237!); Joe Chill, Lew Moxon, and Boss Zucco (without these three gangsters, there would have been NO Batman or Robin!); and the Outsider. (Reading the Outsider's plot lines was like watching a '30s or '40s cliff-hanging movie serial where chapter by chapter, the identity of the villain was hidden from the audience. Finally at the very end, after twelve to fifteen weeks of watching and waiting, they would reveal the big surprise. That's how the secret of the Outsider played out for more than a year in Batman's comics. Often, he was nothing more than a disembodied voice left on a tape recorder.)

Being the comic book buff I was, my high school notebooks were filled less with class notes than with the superhero

As a kid, I wanted to create a superhero with insect powers, but all the good insect names were taken: spider, fly, bee, wasp, yellow jacket, hornet, tarantula, scorpion. I was left with the Cricket! Sounded better than the Cockroach!

*I loved the movies *King Kong*, *Son of Kong*, *Kaanga*, and *Plan 9 from Outer Space*, which featured a gorilla who wore a fish bowl with a 1950s TV antennae on top of his head. Gorillas in comic books are the best! And yes, my favorite Flash villain is Gorilla Grodd; my favorite Superman villain is Titano the Super-Ape from Krypton, who had Kryptonite vision; and my very favorite member of the super heroic Legion of Super-Pets is Superboy's pet, Beppo the Super-Monkey.

and cartoon drawings of a daydreaming boy. Winning me the most fame and acclaim from my school peers were my fifty pages of caricatures of Superman, Batman, the Hulk, and Spider-Man (I really felt for Marvel artist Steve Ditko; those intricate webbings on Spidey's face mask were really tough to draw!). After a while, though, I started writing and drawing my own comic books. I began by doing parodies of my favorite Marvel comics to entertain my friends. The Fantastic Four became the Funny-Farm Four; Daredevil turned into Queerdevil (not that there's anything wrong with that); Sgt. Fury and his Howling Commandos spawned Sgt. Fooie and his Blithering Idiots; and Shang-Chi, Master of Kung Fu, became Yuck-Fou, a comment on just how behind the times the comic book portrayals of Asians were circa 1967.

The first page of my script for *The Cricket*. If I read aloud Bobby Klein's and my comic book writing in seventh grade, it sounds exactly like an episode of the *Batman* TV show!

Way back in seventh grade, I had created my very own original comic book superhero whose powers were based on magnified powers of insects. I needed a great insect name for a superhero, but the pickings were slim. There already were Ant-Man, the Wasp, Bee-Man, Yellow Jacket, the Green Hornet, Spider-Man, Tarantula, the Scorpion, the Blue Beetle, the Beetle, the Gray Grasshopper, Mantis (never caught her praying, however), the Fly, and Firefly. I was left with the Cricket and resolved to make him great. I wrote a script as a daily comic strip for newspapers and sent it out. A truly nice guy from the Sacramento Union newspaper in California liked what I did. He was an old-time comic book fan, particularly of Captain Marvel. He and I began corresponding and he was wowed by my already extensive knowledge of comic books from the '40s and '50s. Turned out he was a cartoonist, and he agreed to draw the comic strip. We prepared a couple of weeks of samples so that with the backing of his newspaper we could try for national syndication. I was on my way to fame and fortune as a comic strip writer until I made one little, fatal mistake. He requested a photo of me for the packet being prepared to pitch "The Cricket" to potential buyers. So I sent him my seventh-grade school picture. Big boo-boo! I can only guess that based on my knowledge of old comic books he had assumed that I was one of them full-fledged adults. When he realized he'd been communicating and working with a thirteen-year-old boy, the Cricket met an immediate and untimely end. My obsession moved back to Batman and, apparently, his moved on to the Zodiac Killer in San Francisco, where his heroic work on the case would one day be recognized and hailed.

# CHAPTER SIX

# A CAMPY BATMAN on TV. "HOLY SHIT!"

As I've pointed out, I used to write letters to the editors whenever I'd spot a boo-boo in a comic book. And they were all over the place. But the biggest boo-boo I ever saw was one that Batman co-creator Bob Kane confirmed to me was the biggest error in any Batman comic book. In this particular story, a bad guy threatened to blow up the Bat-Cave, this in an era before either kids or superheroes knew the concept of "terrorist." Batman and Robin were forced to set up an X-ray scanning machine in the Bat-Cave to check the daily deluge of letters and gifts they were sent by their adoring public. In this instance, the script indicated that one package they opened was a huge stuffed bat that a fan of Batman has sent them. When the artist read that, he drew the scene as he interpreted it and showed them scanning not a stuffed bat, but a stuffed baseball bat. Bob Kane had heard of corked baseball bats,

LEFT: This was what Batman creator, Bob Kane, told me was the biggest error ever in *Batman* comics!

but never a stuffed baseball bat. I did not think this was the biggest boo-boo in the history of Batman. I thought that occurred the day in January 1966 when they made my Batman into a new thing called "high camp." They made people laugh at Batman. And that just killed me. In 1966, after months of anticipation, I kept ABC Channel 7 on every second I was home in the hopes of catching yet another teaser commercial for the upcoming new *Batman* TV series. Finally, one night in January *Batman* premiered, and I was simultaneously thrilled and horrified by what I saw.

I was THRILLED because Batman was on TV! Not since George Reeves's *Adventures of Superman* had there been a great comic book superhero on the small screen. And somebody was spending a ton of money on this! It was in color! The sets were elaborate and expensive. The car was cool! The animated opening looked like Bob Kane's Batman comics. Frank Gorshin was terrific as the Riddler.

BUT ... and in a world of big buts, this was the biggest one of all ...

I was HORRIFIED when I realized that the world was laughing at Batman. Not with him. AT him. They had him talking in stilted dialogue and purple prose. The actor playing the Joker, Cesar Romero, refused to shave off his moustache, so the Joker had white greasepaint covering a frickin' moustache! Appalling! There were "Bat" labels on everything, including a thick Bat-Pole labeled "Bruce" and a thin Bat-Pole labeled "Dick"! They had Batman dancing "The Bat-Tusi," fer Chrissakes! And then, there were those "POW," "ZAP," and "WHAM" signs every time they hit a villain or vice versa. Oh, the ignominy! In the interests of high society's new pop art craze, Batman was sacrificed on an altar of Andy Warhol, Roy Lichtenstein, and the "in" crowd at the Peppermint Lounge or Cheetah Club in New York. Batman desperately needed his own superhero to rescue him from this doom, and I was powerless to help him.

Immediately, things started to happen. Lots of things. I could divide them all into three Bat-Categories (Oh God, they have ME doing it now—halp!) inspired by the 1966 movie, *The Good, the Bad and the Ugly*. First, "The Good."

That summer, I started my first job other than going for coffee for my dad and all the men on his masonry crew. I was a Junior Camp Counselor for Oakhurst Day Camp on Monmouth Road in Oakhurst, New Jersey, right smack across the street from the church that had that infamous sign "Come to Ch_ _ch. What is missing?"

My group was made up of thirty-one boys ages four and five, by far the largest in camp, and so big that the owner Greg Sariotis added a second Junior Counselor, Marc Summerfield, to help manage these kids, most of whom could not yet put their underpants on by themselves, never mind swim or catch or throw a ball. I loved every second of this job and, through this experience, I learned two important life lessons right from the first Wednesday I worked there.

Wednesday was Barbecue Day. It was my job to get the thirty-one kids seated outdoors around a big red table for our group, known, in the best tradition of Archie comics, as

Freshman Boys. Marc and I passed out the paper plates and plastic forks and cups that all the kids used for lunch, plus the napkins they never bothered using even once. Then we went up to the barbecue cooks and got the food to dole out. We gave each camper a hot dog with mustard and optional sauerkraut, a wad of baked beans, a clump of potato salad, a glop of cole slaw, and some sort of liquefied sugar called "fruit juice." Once the kids were finished ingesting or inhaling their delectable barbecue lunch, I had to keep them seated and still at the table . . . next to the playground . . . for half an hour before taking them swimming. YOU try to keep thirty-one four- and five-year-old boys seated quietly at a table for thirty eternal minutes! I contend that it is a physical impossibility that goes directly against the laws of nature. EXCEPT that . . . I stumbled upon a mystical way to do exactly that! The *Batman* TV series was on the air and had captured the imagination of every boy in America (except me). It was a huge fad, and my campers were always playing "Batman-and-Robin-Against-the-Bad-Guys" on the playground. The biggest five-year-old boys always got to play Batman. The smaller five-year-olds got to play the Joker, the Riddler, the Penguin, and Mr. Freeze. The four-year-olds were always stuck having to be Robin. Every time my back was turned, one big five-year-old was smacking one small five-year-old and yelling "POW!" as he hammered him. I KNEW that "Pow!" "Zap!" "Wham" shit was bad! Here was yet another reason to ban it! (My God! I sound like Dr. Wertham and the Comics Code Authority rolled into one!)

Greg Sariotis ordered the Batman playground games stopped cold. I then realized that if they couldn't play a Batman game, the kids might like to hear a Batman story. By the age of fourteen, I had already read close to a thousand Batman comic book tales, so it wasn't like I had to dig for material. I began to spin Batman stories around the big red table after the barbecue. And thirty-one four- and five-year-old boys were hypnotized and didn't budge for thirty minutes. I started making the stories interactive, pausing at big cliff-hanging moments amid deathtraps and doom for the Caped Crusader, and

The original Columbia Pictures movie serial from the early 1940s returns to the big screen in the pop '60s! Five and a half hours of *Batman and Robin* and Bobby Klein and I sat through nearly all of it, devouring popcorn, soda, and thirty pounds of Dots, Chuckles, Chocolate Babies, Milk Duds, SweeTarts, JuJuBees, Good n' Plenty, and Bonomo Turkish Taffy in the process!

asking the kids to tell me what Batman did next to escape. Before long, they were telling more of the story than I was. I had 'em in the palm of my hand. And thus, I learned my first life lesson from being a junior counselor—if you want to sell someone something, you must be passionate about it and be able to communicate your passion. This is EXACTLY what a movie producer has to be able to do to sell a studio on his film project and get them to pony up the bucks to develop and produce it. And this is why "pitching" is my favorite part of producing. While pitching makes many of my producing brethren so nervous that they want to throw up, I can't wait to get into the roomful of studio execs and tell my story, because when I walk into their offices or conference rooms, I don't see the same execs that other producers do. I see my Freshman Boys from the summer of '66 . . . a room full of four- and five-year-olds sitting around a big red table (or a campfire if I'm pitching a horror film like *Constantine*).

Another "Good" that resulted from the *Batman* TV show was the reaction to the new hit series by a movie theater in New York City that brought back to the big screen the original 1943 black and white *Batman* movie serial for a five-hour showing . . . all fifteen chapters without stopping! That was a huge thrill for me and Bobby Klein, and we convinced our parents to let us take a bus from Asbury Park to New York City to see it. The "huge" part of the thrill died after about three and a half hours of watching the credits and, at the beginning of each twenty-minute chapter, a five-minute recap of the chapter we had seen just fifty seconds earlier. At the five-hour mark, the repetition and cheap budget wiped out our last thrill. Batman had a paunch and his cloth costume fit about as well as my grandpa Sam's suit after he lost all that weight and had to rely heavily on his suspenders to hold up his pants. Robin had a head of hair on him that was a cross between Bomba the Jungle Boy and Marty Allen of the comedy duo Allen and Rossi. Robin wore the exact same mask I had worn that past Halloween, which I had bought at the Wanamassa Five-and-Ten Cent store for 29 cents.

Of the Good, the Bad, and the Ugly, "the Bad" parts of the *Batman* TV show included all those things that bothered me the most, like the way they put Batman's yellow circle chest symbol too low on his torso. There was a reason that in comic books they called them CHEST symbols and not "Just Barely Above the STOMACH Symbols!" I had serious issues also with Batman's eyebrows being painted in blue over the eye-slots of his mask. One of my top pet peeves, which I've campaigned against (though ultimately to no avail . . . sigh . . .), is painted eyebrows and molded nipples on my superheroes.

And what about "the Ugly"? To me there was nothing uglier or campier or more cloying and annoying than Robin's pop culture version of a Tourette's syndrome display when he continually shouted "Holy _____!" (Add in any word you feel like. It was like playing "Mad Libs.") It was not until the huge San Diego Comic-Con in July 2009 that I finally got some closure to my intense feelings about this. I had agreed to appear on a panel about the Joker with my dear friend, Joker co-creator Jerry Robinson. At the last minute, I was informed that someone special would be joining that panel . . . Adam West, star of the 1966 *Batman* TV series. I had never before actually met Adam, but there was a bit of bad blood circling the perimeter. Back at the New York ComiCon of July 1980 when Ben Melniker, Bob Kane, and I had announced that we were moving forward with a dark, serious Batman movie (if you possess one of the super rare "1980 Year of the Batman" buttons DC Comics gave out to everyone in that crowded room, you have a valuable prize in your hands today!), I was locked into the idea that to honor Adam, we should offer him the role of Thomas Wayne, young Bruce's father, who is gunned down in a critical origin scene. But before we knew it, the papers were filled with statements attributed to Adam that he still wanted to play Batman or a character called Uncle Batman and deriding a dark, serious approach to Batman as the wrong, violating way to go. Unfortunately, the PR was not considered helpful by people and companies about to invest in our film, and never at any time did anyone speak to us directly on behalf of Adam before making statements to the press. The powers involved in the film were miffed and told us to forget his having any role in it. I was sad, because to me there was no reason any of this needed to go south. Over the years, I had the opportunity to meet Burgess Meredith, Cesar Romero, Frank Gorshin, and Lee Merriweather who played, respectively, the Penguin, the Joker, the Riddler, and Catwoman, and I enjoyed meeting each of them. Now, finally, I would meet Adam West.

The large ComiCon hall was jam-packed, SRO. When Adam came in and sat to my left, he made a preemptive strike and said how honored he was to be sharing the stage with the exalted and legendary comic book artist Jerry Robinson, and then laid some similar words on me and my work, pointing out that there will always be room for totally different interpretations of Batman, with no one of them necessarily being right or wrong. I immediately returned this gentleman's favor and explained to the crowd that for two minutes, I was going to silence the movie producer Michael and allow the twelve-year-old fanboy and Bat-Fanatic Michael to surface, and I turned the microphone over to him/me. I told the assembled group that I couldn't believe I was sitting next to the ultimate Batman of the 1960s . . . the star of the *Batman* TV show . . . and to explain how excited I was, I said I needed to say something to Adam West I'd been waiting thirty-three years to say. With a great big smile, I turned to Adam and proclaimed, "Holy Shit!" The place went nuts. Everyone was laughing and, as Adam stood up and gave me a hug and pat on the back, the place broke into rousing applause. And everything was right with the world.

But that doesn't mean that back in 1966 I liked the POW! ZAP! WHAM! bursts of comic book lettering that flashed across the screen whenever the Dynamic Duo was engaged in a fight with the super-villain of the week and his usually weak henchmen. Okay . . . I admit it . . . I liked it the first two weeks. But it got boring fast. And then the most terrible thing in the universe happened. The media adopted those words as icons standing for the whole of anything pop culture and comic books and superheroes. And I mean ANYTHING! From that black hole of a moment, any and every article written about comic books or comic book–based movies, or anything related would always have a headline preceded by those three words, "POW!" "ZAP!" and "WHAM!" It popped up again and again in the most incongruous places to the consternation of fans everywhere and annoying the shit out of me every single time: "Pow! Zap! Wham! New *Batman* Movie To Be Dark, Serious"; "Pow! Zap! Wham! *Dark Knight Returns* Brings Grit to Comic Books"; "Pow! Zap! Wham! *Watchmen* Graphic Novel Brings Sex, Death, and Destruction to Comics"; and my own personal favorite, "Pow! Zap! Wham! *The Dark Knight* Erases Memory of *Batman* TV Series."

Before school was out in 1966, I had seen one too many "Pows!" and snapped! That night, a blue-collar kid from New Jersey swore an oath just like young Bruce Wayne had and defined his mission in life from that moment on. Someday, somehow, I would eliminate these three little words from the collective consciousness of the world culture: Pow! Zap! and Wham! I would restore Batman to his true and rightful identity as the Dark Knight . . . a creature of the night stalking criminals from the shadows as he was originally intended to be by his creators, Bob Kane and Bill Finger . . . a man without superpowers whose greatest "super" power was his humanity . . . a master detective who survived and thrived more by his wits than by his fists. And, by God, after so many decades fighting in the trenches, and thanks to many people who believed in that same cause, when *Batman* and years later *Batman Begins* and *The Dark Knight* arrived in theaters, I believed I had done just that. 2012's *The Dark Knight Rises* would be the icing on the cake.

# CHAPTER SEVEN

# The Comic Book Club–
## NO GIRLS ALLOWED!

It all began innocuously enough. Bobby and I had this particular Wednesday off from seventh grade because it was a semi-major or semi-minor Jewish holiday (Paul used to tell me we could sum up every single Jewish holiday like this: they tried to kill us; we won, let's eat!), and since it seemed like half of Ocean Township School was Jewish, it was closed for the day. I had already sat in services at Temple Beth Torah for hours with my family and was allowed to "escape" after the Torah reading and the rabbi's sermon. We were conservative, but this was Wednesday and there were new comic books to buy at Wanamassa Pharmacy so I was a little less conservative than usual. I met Bobby there and we, yet again, induced Mr. Lieberman to let us snap open the wired bundle of new comic books and magazines delivered by the distributor, if for no other reason than to get two annoying twelve-year-olds out of his hair.

ABOVE, LEFT: Family time, March 1959 celebrating Mom's birthday, Dad's birthday, and Mom & Dad's anniversary with my parents, Paul, Cuz, Aunt Clara, cousins Glen and Bruce, and yours truly. We had little money but lots of love and great times together!

RIGHT: Cuz, me, and Paul on the basketball court Dad built in the backyard of our pink Cape Cod house in Wanamassa, NJ. In case you didn't believe I was a comic book nerd, note the "Davy Crockett" T-shirt, the pair of clamdiggers, and the fashionable brown socks and Buster Brown shoes!

Biking back to my house, we poured out our four-color treasures onto my bed in the bedroom I shared with Paul, who was already up there with our cousin, also named Paul, pouring out his high school black market purchase of a couple of issues of *Playboy*. Cousin Paul was the son of Aunt Clara and Uncle Phil Hyman. They called him "Paul," but Paul and I and our parents called him "Cuz," short for "Cousin," so no one in our families would get our two Pauls mixed up . . . except THEY called MY brother Paul "Cuz," also to avoid confusion from their own perspective. This worked successfully as long as you knew that when our side of the family was with their side of the family we called their Paul "Cuz" while their side of the family called our Paul "Cuz." It was easy to keep straight provided you knew who came from what side of the family. Simply put, that's how we avoided confusion in our family. And I'm not even dealing with "Cuz's" friends in high school who called him not "Paul" Hyman or "Cuz" Hyman, but rather "Buster" Hyman, a joke I did NOT get until 1967.

Bobby and I both knew it was "wrong" for them to be looking at *Playboy* and that the two Pauls would wind up in BIG trouble. But, who were we to talk? That past New Year's Eve, Barry, Bobby, and I had been busted for throwing water balloons from Barry's front yard onto the roof of the house across the street, which just happened to be inhabited by a cross between the Addams Family and a secret Nazi Bund. It was my first ride ever in the backseat of a police car as they chauffeured us to our former kindergarten classroom, now solely a police station again, and made us sit on a bench until one of us agreed to call our parents to come get us . . . on NEW YEAR'S EVE! All our folks were out celebrating, and we were terrified to drag them into this for every reason a twelve-year-old boy can imagine. I knew that my mom and dad were with my Uncle Lou and Aunt Dora Solomon, who had driven down all the way from Long Island. I spilled the name of Paul Samperi's restaurant to the desk sergeant, who leaned over his tall desk, exposing a massive pot-belly that made Barry laugh and get in even deeper trouble. Paul Samperi's was a fancy restaurant in Colonial Terrace, yet another part of Ocean Township. They called my father away from his table for the phone call, and it turned out the cop knew my dad well. "Joe, sorry to bother you on New Year's Eve, but I got your kid here at headquarters," he said quite matter-of-factly. Dad sighed deeply, "What did Paul do?" "No, his name is Michael," said the officer. "No," Dad corrected him, "it's Paul." For the next four minutes, all my poor father did was repeat the words, "No, you mean PAUL." He finally went back to the festive table where my very worried mother took one look at him and knew something was amiss. "What's wrong?" she asked. "It's the Ocean Township Police. They picked up Michael and have him at Police Headquarters. I have to go get him," said Dad. Mom quickly corrected him. "No, you mean Paul." "Uh, no. They have Michael," Dad said again. "No, you mean Paul," Mom held firm. For the next four minutes, all my mother did was repeat the words, "No, you mean PAUL."

So when Paul and Cuz tossed me and Bobby and our comic books out of my bedroom so we would stop haranguing them about their *Playboy* magazines, we began to fanta-size about a place where we could read our comic books in peace. (Bobby hadn't been deterred by his dad's incineration of his collection, and by this time, he had rebuilt a decent collection.) The tree house wasn't a good choice, because we couldn't house our collections there open to the elements. And we wondered how we could find more boys who were into reading comics so we could really discuss each character, each issue, each story . . . maybe even trade 'em or swap 'em for comics they had that we didn't. Shazam! We would start a Comic Book Club!

The Comic Book Club first drafted Barry and Jeff Mendel. Barry was as much into comics as Bobby and I were into cars. But we indoctrinated him and inundated him with them as best we could. We ultimately made him and everyone read the Bible . . . OUR Bible . . . the only real book we ever read about the Golden Age of comic books, Jules Feiffer's *The Great Comic Book Heroes*. It reprinted, in color, stories of superheroes we heard about but had never read. It was a revelation. From *Batman* #1, there was that very first Joker tale! Finally, the Joker we always wanted to see, not the puzzle-dropping clown he had become. The visual contrast between the clown and the killer aspects of the character as portrayed in the '40s was frightening and surprising, and the mood was atmospheric and scary.

The Joker is unarguably the best villain created in the history of comic books! Credit my pal Jerry Robinson, Bob Kane's earliest ghost artist, and Bill Finger, writer extraor-dinaire and co-creator of Batman. I met Finger twice in 1964, ten years before he died penniless, supposedly suffering from alcoholism. The first time was on my very first tour of DC Comics, a tour that was conducted every Tuesday afternoon for lucky fans able to make their way to 575 Lexington Avenue in New York. That meant me and Bobby

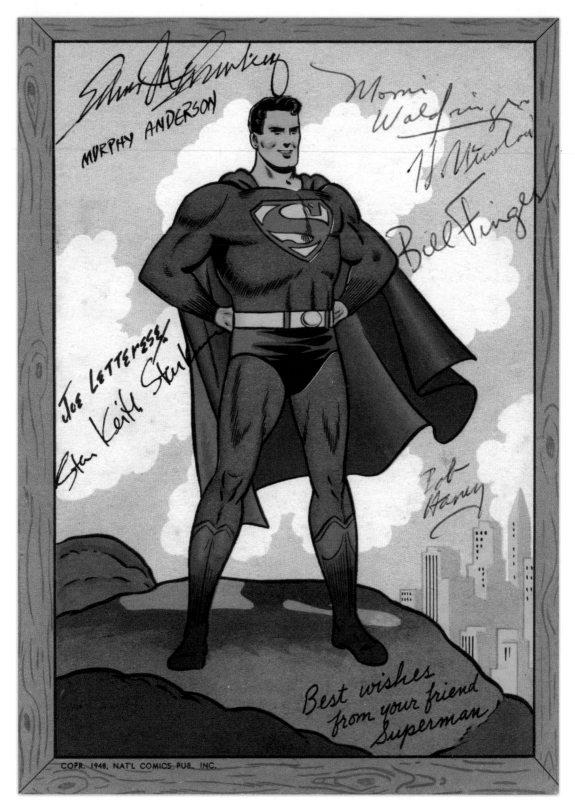

My Superman pinup from my first DC Comics tour, signed by Bill Finger, Batman's co-creator!

and Barry. It was the thrill of a lifetime! They showed us the entire spread and gave us lots of free stuff, all of which I saved forever! The production manager, Sol Harrison, took big pages of gorgeous original art, placed them on a huge paper-cutter, and started chopping them up into tiers to give out to us. I begged and pleaded until he gave me full pages plus an entire original Superman Sunday comic strip by artist Wayne Boring. We met all the writers and artists sitting in the production bull pen and we were given pin-ups of Superman and Batman to get signed. I watched each artist at work, and then got autographs from one of my favorite Silver Age artists, Murphy Anderson. Another man I met was very nice and a real comic book writer. He signed his name, "Bill Finger," on my Superman pinup. Then one of the editors noticed that I had brought with me my Golden Age copy of *All-Flash* #25. This was Julius Schwartz, editor of *Flash*, as well as *Justice League of America*, *Batman*, *Detective Comics*, *Green Lantern*, *The Atom*, and *Hawkman*. He asked me if I was a real Flash fan. When I assured him I was, he led me to his office to meet and get an autograph from Flash scripter John Broome, and then showed me an old, yellowing, bound volume of Golden Age *Flash Comics*, right back to *Flash Comics* #1! I felt faint from the excitement! The oldest Flash comic book I had ever been able to find was #105, and I had been starting to disbelieve there were any before that number. It turned out there were 104 of them, but those 104 had been published long, long before the Flash was revived in his own comic book in 1959, picking up where the old numbering system had left off. At the end of the day, all I could do was kiss Barry's mom. Mrs. Milberg had chaperoned our entire Comic Book Club to New York for this best-ever experience at DC Comics.

The growing membership in the Comic Book Club was impressive, indeed! Jeff Mendel always had secret comic book boxes in his bedroom closet that he opened, like a vault, only on rare occasions and with paranoid precautions. He claimed to have the best and rarest comic books ever made, but he made us wait nearly a year before he showed us his gold mine, allowing the legend that was his collection to build and build in our young, impressionable minds. And when he finally chose to lay it out for us, it really was first class—the first *Thor*; very early *Fantastic Fours*; a big, thick, 25-cent *Black Cat*; and the best collection I ever imagined of comic book titles starting with the letter A—*Amazing Adventures*, *Amazing Adult Fantasy*, *Amazing Fantasy*, *Alarming Tales*, *Astonishing*, *Action*, *Adventure*, *Adventures into Weird Worlds*, and *Adventures Into the Unknown*. Like all of us, he owned a copy of Dell's *Tales from the Tomb*, unquestionably the scariest comic book ever made! At least for nine-year-old boys. In the post-Wertham era we lived in, post-*Tales from the Crypt*, post-*Vault of Horror*, and post-*Haunt of Fear*, the Comics Code Authority ruled the roost in the comic book industry, the way the Hays Office did the movie industry. And, man! Were they ever STRICT! It was as if our Principal, J. Anthony Covino, were on that board, personally deciding what was okay to publish and what was not. The rules were stringent: no use of the words horror, terror, or crime on the covers; no exaggerated drawings of any part of the female anatomy (in fact, play down the role of women generally in these stories); never refer to drugs; never show a bad guy hitting or in any way disrespecting a police officer; no sex, no violence, no nudity, no cursing. And absolutely no walking dead!

DC Comics had a great, powerful, vengeful superhero back in the Golden Age of World War II. He was the Spectre, the ghost of a murdered detective, created by Superman's co-creator Jerry Siegel, with artist Bernard Bailey. Eerily, the Spectre became a founding member of the first superhero team, the Justice Society of America. Typically, the Spectre would turn assorted murderers into wood and then buzz-saw them, or would turn them into glass and then shatter them. The title of the comic book in which his nightmarish adventures took place? *More Fun Comics*. Somebody at DC Comics had a sick sense of humor. After World War II, the Spectre vanished as the Golden Age came to an end and his comic book title bit the dust. But now in 1964, DC was on a hot streak bringing back its defunct Golden Age stars and putting a new creative spin on them. The genius behind this, and DC's architect of the Silver Age of Comics, was Julius Schwartz, the editor who had revealed the history of *Flash Comics* to me. Julie had started the Silver Age by reviving the Flash very successfully. He followed that up with Green Lantern, the Justice Society of America (now to be called the Justice League of America), the Atom, Hawkman, Dr. Fate and Hourman, plus Starman and Black Canary. With all these old superheroes returning to publication, I began what I assumed was a one-man write-in campaign to get Julie Schwartz and DC to bring back the Spectre. For a while, I wrote him a "Letter to the Editor" every day. Julie was a curmudgeon, but he appreciated a loyal and passionate fan, so he always sent me a one- to three-sentence response on a little note that had "From the desk of Julius Schwartz" printed at the top. He kept telling me to go away . . . nicely. The Spectre CAN'T come back. He's a dead detective returned from the grave and the Comics Code has specifically banned the walking dead from comic books. That's when the upstart I was even when I was only thirteen or fourteen wrote him back a two-line letter: "The Comics Code bans the walking dead? What about Casper the Friendly Ghost?" A month later, a note from the desk of Julius Schwartz arrived in my mailbox. All it said was that I'd be pleased to know that the Spectre would be returning to comics along with Dr. Midnite in the upcoming sixtieth issue of *Showcase* comics. My mom was right. If I set my mind to something and never give up, I can make it happen.

After Barry and Jeff Mendel, our next Comic Book Club recruit was the son of our seventh-grade English teacher, Mrs. Eleanor Stiller, one of two teachers responsible for my life's quest to bring a dark and serious Batman to the silver screen. Robert Stiller was younger than the rest of us, so Bobby Klein and I composed a "Comic Book Club Entrance Examination." If he could pass it (and it was tough!), he was in. He passed with flying colors. Thank goodness! I had been prepared to get him in no matter what he scored, because I owed it to Mrs. Stiller. Robert's mom and her sister-in-law, Rita A. Friedman, were not only my seventh- and eighth-grade English teachers, respectively, they were the two most influential people in my life outside my family. It's directly due to their influence on me that there even exists a series of Batman films today. Forget

A great teacher can make a difference in a child's life! Meet Mrs. Ellie Stiller, my seventh-grade English teacher, and Mrs. Rita A. Friedman, my eighth-grade English teacher, who made all the difference in mine!

Superman and Spider-Man . . . nothing on earth can match the power of a great teacher!

Back in November 1963, seventh-grade English class was underway and Mrs. Stiller, as she often did, started walking up and down the aisles while she spoke. The discussion was about our reading assignments, James Hilton's *Lost Horizon*, a book that I would push as reference material for the opening of the movie *Batman Begins* in years to come, and George Orwell's *Animal Farm*. I was preoccupied. I was secretly reading the latest issue of that new comic book I loved so much, *The X-Men*, hiding it behind my big green notebook. As a result, I failed to see Mrs. Stiller sneak up behind me and tug it out of my hand, catching me red-handed. As she held it up, all of my Section 7-9 classmates started laughing. Mrs. Stiller turned to them and said, to my everlasting shock, "If I were you people, I wouldn't laugh. Michael is the best creative writer in this class. And I have a hunch these comic books spark his imagination and build his vocabulary. If I were the rest of you, I'd start reading some of these." The class shut up in more shock than I was. Mrs. Stiller, my teacher, my muse, my DEFENDER.

It was she who opened my eyes, trying to convince me that I had a creative writing talent that I had a responsibility to nurture. She encouraged me to do this and agreed to work with me all year on my writing, provided I wrote every chance I got that entire year. By the time I reached eighth grade, Mrs. Friedman became my creative writing guru and urged me to write about something I was familiar with. My first creative writing story for her was a short story that could have been translated into a comic book tale found in DC's *My Greatest Adventure* or in Marvel's *Amazing Adult Fantasy*. Mrs. Friedman admitted through the laughter she had a hard time controlling that the title of my tale was quite catchy, "I Was Trapped in a Giant Peanut Butter and Jelly Sandwich!" It was a subject I felt I was familiar with . . . I LOVE peanut butter and jelly! The story detailed that time I was being chased by a giant peanut butter and jelly sandwich, which caught me and stuck me between its two slices of bread in a spread so sticky I couldn't crawl out. The ending was pure O. Henry:

"So I pinched myself. And guess what happened. The thing bit my head off!"

The End. Howzat for a surprise ending? Expecting just a routine ending like, "I woke up!" Mrs. Friedman LOVED it! I was surprised. After all, she was the English teacher infamous for her merciless red marking pen. She was TOUGH! A taskmaster! A slave driver! Her reputation preceded her. On the first day of class, she actually had the nerve to dictate to us her set of "Standards," which we had to copy and turn in as we made her "Standards" our own. Her graduating students always knew their English, literature, grammar, vocabulary, and punctuation better than anyone else in our school and, I think, in America. She was the Ancient One, the all-wise, all-knowing Queen of Diagramming Sentences.

Mrs. Friedman loved my peanut butter and jelly opus! However, she suggested I edit my story title down to a simple, more dramatic, "Trapped!" She busted my writing chops at every opportunity. She refused to allow me to be a lazy writer who might think I could just scribble out words and expect them to be perfect and untouchable. She taught me discipline as a writer and forced me to rewrite and rewrite and rewrite. She provoked me, challenged me, and convinced me I could make writing my life's work. When each student in her class was informed he had to team up with another student to do a collaborative project in connection with our reading of Robert Louis Stevenson's *Treasure Island*, I joined forces with Jeff Mendel, the wittiest kid in the class, to write a parody of that book and the thousands of footnotes in our classroom annotated version. We handed it in to Mrs. Friedman, fully illustrated. The following Monday, she announced that it was the funniest thing she had ever read and asked Jeff and me to get up and read chapter one to the class. English period was just before lunch. Everyone was laughing so hard and so long (unashamedly, Jeff and me, too) that we ran out of time to finish the chapter. I was worried about the gorgeous redhead in row one, Ellen Genick, who was laughing so hard she seemed unable to suck in any oxygen and was dropping to the floor next to her desk. So Mrs. Friedman said any student who wanted to skip lunch or recess could stay and hear the rest of the chapter. The entire class passed on lunch and recess. It took us another twenty minutes to laugh our way to the conclusion of our recital. Every day thereafter, Mrs. Friedman turned over the last fifteen minutes of the period to Jeff and me to read another chapter. That was probably what won Jeff his ultimate "Wittiest" class title and me, the Creative Writing Award at eighth-grade graduation, which was sponsored by Ocean Township's weekly newspaper, the *Home News*. That award meant everything to me. But it was the other award I won at graduation that made my mom cry and tell me it was the most meaningful of all to her. It was called the "Character Award." Fair enough . . . I WAS a character. My mom felt it stood for more than that and treasured it for the rest of her life.

RIGHT: My final draft of *Trapped!* (Note: The original title before Mrs. Friedman's red pen edited it down to its proper essence was the far more *National Enquirer*–type title, "I Was Trapped In a Giant Peanut Butter and Jelly Sandwich!")

# Trapped!

I never approved of peanut-butter and jelly, but my mother forced me to eat it every day last week, until it was popping out of my ears. Disgusted, I threw the one I was eating away. Then from the garbage can, the sandwich got up and shrieked, "You threw out a peanut-butter and jelly sandwich. For this act of crime, you must be thrown to the giant sandwich!" Before I knew it, I was being dragged to the outskirts of town, and put in front of an enormous door! When it opened, a prodigious piece of rye bread came my way. An instant later, I was surrounded by some sticky, yellowish, substance. Then I realized! I was trapped! Trapped in a peanut-butter and jelly sandwich! But I didn't worry! I knew it was only a dream. So I pinched myself. And guess what happened. The thing bit my head off!

Wonderful ending, Mike!

Mike Nolan 8-6
Sept. 28, 1964

Welcome to
the 1964
New York
Comicon Booklet!

From
Barnaby Bubnis
68 Walnut Ave.
E. Farmingdale
L.I. N.Y. 11735

ATOM

# COMICS ON PARADE

This ComiCon is the one that lets you do more than dream of Super Heroes; you can be one for a whole evening! There will also be the alter-egos of many famous heroes. So be looking for Clark Kent and Peter Parker with their glasses!

And don't forget that those National Covers go for the best Costumes of the evening. So hop onto the floor where everyone can see you and decide what the best costumes are.

Have a ball and enjoy yourself with the new friends that you've made and be prepared for a special surprise. You'll like it, I'm sure!

BLUE BEETLE

CHARLTON

---

# PROGRAM I

9:30 A.M. - Convention opens. Registration, 4th floor lobby.

11:00-1:30 - The Golden Age of Comics   Panel Discussion
Jerry G. Bails, Moderator
Otto Binder, writer for Fawcett, Prize and National
Bill Finger, writer for National, Timely and Quality
Gardner Fox, writer for National, ME and Big Shot
The early years will be covered by these pros that have helped to create some of the greats of the Golden Age of Comics.

3:00 P.M. - 6:00 P.M. - Exhibits, Trading, Buying and Selling
There will be old comics, new comics, foreign comics and fanzines galore on exhibit. See the covers that you can win. And there will be a pro-cover too! Special tables to trade your comics and fanzines! Dealers will be there to sell some very old and rare comics!

7:30 - 10:00 - The Costume Party ---- The Colorful Evening of Heroes! Meet your favorites in the flesh! Shake hands with Doc Strange! Wrestle with the Ape! Say hello to Wonder Man! And in the middle of the program, a great surprise for all!

---

# PROGRAM II

12:00 -- Serial Showings
"FLASH GORDON CONQUERS THE UNIVERSE"
We will show the first six chapters and then break for an hour. This will give you time to trade somemore and buy books from the dealers again. Happy Trading and Dealing!

3:00 -- Serial Showing
The last six chapters of Flash Gordon.
( We are sorry that the other serial was not sent to us at this time. But efforts will be made in the future to insure the delivery of the proper film for the Cons. Hope that Falk's character, one of the leading newspaper and comic book strips of the 30's and 40's, was satisfactory.)

7:30 -- The Alley Presentations for 1964.
Announcements will be made of the winners and they will be asked to accept at this time. Due to some difficulty the Alleys were not delivered to the hotel and we will have to sent them to the winners at some later date.
PANEL DISCUSSION: COMICS AND FANDOM: WHERE DO WE GO FROM HERE?
Paul Gambaccini will moderate a panel consisting of Murphy Anderson, Roy Thomas, Jim Warren and Rick Weingroff.

We hope that you enjoyed your stay at the Con and look forward to having you with us in the future. We will publish a photo-offset book about this Con and all persons attending will be sent one at a later date.   Comic-ally yours,   DAVID A. KALER

---

# ALLEY AWARDS 1964

BEST ADVENTURE HERO COMIC BOOK
SPIDERMAN
BEST EDITOR
STAN LEE
BEST WRITER
STAN LEE
BEST PENCIL ARTIST
CARMINE INFANTINO
BEST INKING ARTIST
MURPHY ANDERSON
BEST SHORT STORY
"DOORWAY TO THE UNKNOWN"   FLASH #148
BEST NOVEL
"CAPTAIN AMERICA JOINS the AVENGERS"   AVENGERS #4
BEST GIANT COMIC
SPIDERMAN ANNUAL #1
BEST HERO  SPIDERMAN          BEST VILLIAN   DR. DOOM
BEST GROUP  FANTASTIC FOUR    BEST CHARACTER  THING
BEST FANZINE   ALTER EGO #7 by ROY THOMAS

The alleys are selected annually by the members of Fandom. A ballot is sent out each year to the fans for them to select the best of the year's efforts on the part of the companies, pros and the fans themselves. Will your vote be counted in the next Alley contest?

---

# BILL FINGER

Bill Finger was born on February 8, 1914, in Denver, Colorado. His family moved to New York City when he was very young and Bill grew up in the atmosphere of his father's tailor shop.
He wanted to be an artist, but his parents wanted a doctor in the family. But Bill was forced to leave college because of the Depression. He spent a few years at various small jobs, but he wanted to become a writer for the longest time.
Then one night he met Bob Kane at a party. Later when Bob needed someone to write a strip named Rusty and his Pals, he called on Bill. This successful collaboration led to their dreaming up the costume of Batman and the development of Batman as a Doug Fairbanks-Sherlock Holmes type of hero. National then hired Bill to write the origins for Green Lantern and Wildcat. During the middle Forties he worked for Timely on Captain America and also wrote the first All-Winners Squad story. During the Fifties Bill wrote for Quality on Blackhawk and did the famous Manhunt issue for this group. Action, color and human interest are always found in Bill's work. Pick up the Challengers and see what I mean.

# PROS AND CONS AND CON ARTISTS!

Comic-Con gets some 135,000 people crowded into downtown San Diego. The summer convention is sold out months in advance. If they had the space, there's little doubt more people would show up there than showed up at Woodstock in '69. The crush of people became so great that the Con had to negotiate with the San Diego Padres and Major League Baseball to ensure there would be no Padres game next door while the convention was in progress. That worked out well, because now Comic-Con parties and shows have taken over the stadium, too. But it wasn't always like this. "Return with us now to those thrilling days of yesteryear . . ."

LEFT: The attendees' mimeographed official booklet from the 1964 New York ComiCon, the first comic book convention ever held.

In one of those early mimeographed and stapled fanzines with bulging circulations topping two hundred in some cases, Bobby Klein and I found mention of a meeting planned for July in New York City. It was being called a "comic book convention" or ComiCon, for short, or the Con, for shorter. There had never before been a real ComiCon, and we LOVED the idea! We would actually meet face to face (or in some cases, pimple to pimple), people just like us who were totally immersed in the world of comic books and superheroes. We might even make some new friends who shared our obsession. We could buy, sell, and trade old comics! We could attend panels and learn all about the history of comics and debate or discuss what was currently happening in comic books! We could see, touch, and maybe even read comic books from the Golden Age! Superhero movie serials from the '30s and '40s would be played at night! The first ever auction of comic books would take place! Strangest but most fun of all, in a last minute wacky idea, every attendee was invited to make his own costume based upon his favorite superhero and show up Saturday night for a costume parade! Semi-valuable prizes would be awarded by the judge, the legendary Otto Binder himself!

I even asked Otto Binder to autograph his bio for me. I was a true fanboy before the term was even invented.

Otto Binder's beautiful daughter, Mary, named after his other creation, "Mary Marvel," but to me at almost age 14, more like "Dream Girl!"

Who was this Otto Binder? Bobby and I had met the man a few months earlier. Those first fanzines Bobby and I read were filled with articles about one of the most prolific comic book writers in history, a professional in the mainstream comic book industry (collectively referred to as "Pros"). This particular Pro was the primary writer of *Captain Marvel* and the *Marvel Family* in the '40s and '50s, having created the delectable Mary Marvel. He had also written the Golden Age tales of Captain America, the Young Allies, and Marvel's earliest superheroes from Sub-Mariner to the Human Torch. He later journeyed to DC Comics to re-invent Superman for the Silver Age of Comics with his creations of Supergirl, Brainiac, the Legion of Super-Heroes, Lori the Mermaid, Krypto the Super-Dog, the Phantom Zone, Lucy Lane, Super-Monkey, Titano the Super-Ape, Jimmy Olsen's Signal Watch, Elastic Lad, and so much more.

This was Otto Binder, who sometimes used the pen name Eando Binder, a nom de plume that originated when he and his brother Earl ("E and O" Binder) wrote classic science fiction books and stories together. He lived in a New Jersey town called Englewood. Bobby and I contacted him and arranged to go up one Sunday to interview him. We had no idea where Englewood was in relation to Asbury Park, but figured the state was so tiny, everything had to be within an hour of everything. As usual, we conned my parents into giving up their Sunday to drive us on the "longer than an hour" ride to North Jersey. And that glorious, exciting, WOW-of-a-day would change my life!

Bobby and I prepared for this interview like it was a super combination of our final exams and our year-end history project. We reread every fanzine we could find that had anything to do with Otto, Captain Marvel, Superman, or the birth and growth of the comic book industry. We finally wrote out two hundred questions, which we figured ought to cover us adequately in an interview. Now, I wasn't the Human Torch, but let me tell you, when my mom and dad drove me and Bobby up to Otto's house, a domicile known in comic book pro circles as "The House That Captain Marvel Built" (based on the years of comic book script checks Otto received for writing a zillion Captain Marvel stories), and I walked in that front door, being warmly greeted by the lovely and demure Mrs. Ione Binder, I met their blonde, pretty, almost fourteen-year-old daughter, Mary (yep, named after Otto's earlier creation, Mary Marvel), and my body heat rose to the point I was sure I was about to burst into human flames myself! Yes, she was gorgeous. Yes, she seemed sweet. Yes, she seemed bright. But at last, here was the one girl on Earth

19621 NW 4th Avenue
Miami, Florida
April 30, 1966

Dear Mike:

Thank you for your recent letter, which was very welcome . I look forward to the issue coming up. Please send a copy to:

    Charles McHarry, Columnist
    N. Y. Daily News

Please check this, a s I am not sure whether the New s was the source of the enclosed clipping, sent to me recently by my sister-in-law, who is not too dependable in such matters. At any rate, I wish you would point out to Messrs McHarry and Krawitz the following errors in their otherwise very informative article:

(1) Occupation--Billy Batson was a newsboy for only one issue. At the end of the first issue he accepted a job offered him by Sterling Morris as a newscaster-- a job which he still held 13 years later. As TV came in, Billy became the David Brinkly of the forties, which he now appears as today. (Brinkly really is Billy Batson, you know.)

(2) Age--I always thought of CM as about 22 physically; mentally the same as Billy, 12. Not 35! Only the actor was 35--or perhaps 45.

(3) Base--New York. Quite obviously.

(4) Traits --And here is the BIG difference, which Fawcett's stupid lawyers never brought out, much to their discredit: CM was the "World's Mightiest Mortal." He was not immortal, superhuman, nor impervious. Originally he couldn't even fly. He just got there by one means or another. Later, when the publisher pressured us enough, he sort of flew, but this was never too important to the stories. Captain Marvel was just a big kid who got pressured into a ll sorts of situations from which the only escape was to fight, punch, and if necessary fly his w ay out. This was just incidental to the plots, never essential. What was essential w as the fact that he did it all by magic, not by being an extraterrential character. He got all his traits from mythology, not from Nietzschean theories about supermen. He was our answer to the Nazi philosophy then sweeping the world. An overgrown kid facing impossible situations. NEVER a superman. Hitler and Goering were supermen. Captain Marvel was just a big, stupid American kid. It is too bad tha t Fawcett's lawyers never realized this. God knows, Will Lieberson and Wendell Crowley and I tried to tell them this, but they never listened. And now, twenty years later, a columnist comes out with the same banal description of the World's Mightiest Mortal.

(5) Creator--Unimportant, except to give credit to Bill Parker. Bill created the whole thing; I had no more to do with it than Lawrence Olivier had to do with Hamlet! I never created anything. I just drew pictures to illustrate Parker's stories . I made the graven images, like Aaron; like Aaron, I guess I get the blame, even if they don't spell my name right.

Well, Mike, I guess that's the true story. It has been all screwed up as time went by. Or perhaps it was screwed up when it started; I often think so. I only know for sure that I took a big chunk out of my life to devote to the dear old Captain, and when it was all over I didn't even get a wave of the hand from the publisher, who made millions on it.

But let's try, once more, to get things right. If you can't set these charac-

---

Otto Binder put me in touch with so many creators, artists, writers, and editors of the Golden Age of Comics. In seventh grade, I began a weekly correspondence with C. C. Beck, co-creator/artist of Captain Marvel. SHAZAM!

---

ters straight, I don't know who can. Seems to me you have more information on the subject--and all quite impassionately held, than Otto or I have. Write them--and let me know how you make out.

    Yours,

    *C. C. Beck*

    C. C. Beck

PS: Due to unforgivable negligence on the part of my file clerk (me) I seem to have lost your last letter to me and also the letter from the young artist who so admired the Mr. Mind series. Do you have his name and address handy? I believe I gave them to you.

Please send them to me so that I can tell him that his search for originals is fruitless. All my contacts at Faw cett's tell me that absolutely no art rema ins on file.

This sound s pretty fishy to me, but that's what they tell me. And that's w hat I'll have to tell him.

    C.C.B.

*How do you like this typewriter? It can't even space correctly! Like Otto, I spell poorly enough by myself— but this typewriter makes things even worse,* one in our very own, non-parallel universe, who did NOT look at a teenage boy who read and loved comic books as any sort of nerd, geek, or loser whatsoever! I mean, her FATHER was a comic book writer, her Uncle Jack was a comic book artist, and she had grown up since birth amid these funny books. I had to do the mental equivalent of pinching myself to make sure she was real, so I worked up the nerve to actually ask her a question as a test. "So . . . you, like, KNOW that Captain Marvel appeared in *Whiz Comics* as well as in *Captain Marvel Comics*?" I probed. In some melodic tone just above a whisper and without a trace of hesitation, Mary responded, "Uh huh. And *America's Greatest* and *The Marvel Family* . . . and it ISN'T *Captain Marvel Comics*, it's *Captain Marvel Adventures*." Though only thirteen, I now knew this was the only girl on earth qualified to be my wife some day and, even though she seemed to be an "older woman" (she wasn't . . . just seemed so to an awkward thirteen-year-old boy), I would find a way one day to impress her and win her heart. Before her dad even came down the stairs, I knew I would first have to win his respect so that he would like me and let me hang out with him and, thus, see her again. This important interview had just become lots more important to me. I glanced at Bobby to gauge his reaction to Mary and judge the competition I would face, but Bobby's focus was purely on meeting Otto and talking comic books. I had forgotten how immature I had been, too, when I was only twelve and a half. My field was clear to Mary!

Then Otto came down the stairs, a big grin complementing his ruddy cheeks and gray hair. He greeted us warmly and invited me and Bobby up to his comic book sanctum in the attic he had taken over and remodeled into his writing room. With a quick good-bye to my parents, who were relieved to know they were leaving their kid all day with a man who not only wrote comic books for a living but was clearly a normal and respected member of his community with a lovely wife and daughter, and then with a fond adieu to Mary who, I was disappointed to discover, would be remaining downstairs with her mother, Bobby and I ascended into comic book heaven.

We were there for ten hours. With cues from our two hundred questions, Otto brought to life the history of comics. Before there were comic books, there were pulp magazines about heroes of the Depression like the mysterious Shadow, who was the real inspiration for the creation of Batman, and Doc Savage, who was the primary inspiration for the creation of Superman. He revealed to us that there had at one time been movies called "serials" that were like the individual chapters of a comic book and the theaters would show one chapter per Saturday before the big feature film, leaving the heroes in cliff-hanging, deadly situations. The intervening week would give kids time to figure out how the heroes might escape. And these heroes included none other than Captain Marvel, Spy Smasher, Superman, Captain America (all guys Otto wrote), Batman, Blackhawk, the Shadow, the Green Hornet, Flash Gordon, Buck Rogers, the Phantom, Congo Bill, and the Vigilante. And though my dad had explained to me that before TV, all the programs were on the radio and you just listened to them instead of looked at them, it was Otto who told me the radio shows included Superman, the Shadow, the Green Hornet,

Otto Binder takes Bobby and me around New York ComiCon and shows us what the original comic book art looks like and explains how comic books are made.

Archie, the Black Hood, Doc Savage, and the Blue Beetle. Otto regaled us with stories about how the comic book companies like DC Comics and Marvel Comics and Harvey Comics and Archie Comics all came to be, and how and by whom the great comic book heroes were created, starting with Superman and Batman and Captain Marvel. He transported me and Bobby back to the days of World War II and showed us how the early comic books were created, written, drawn, edited, inked, lettered, colored, printed, and distributed. He unlocked a time machine so we could journey back to the Golden Age of Comics and get to know all the comic book characters of Fawcett Publications, including the entire Marvel Family, which, surprisingly, did not simply contain Cap, Mary, and Captain Marvel, Jr., but also an Uncle Marvel, three Lieutenant Marvels, Freckles Marvel, and even Hoppy the Marvel Bunny. Otto made us understand what "lawsuits" were, and then detailed the time Superman hired a lawyer to sue Captain Marvel, claiming Cap was a copy of Superman (so at age thirteen, I could already regale my parents and teachers with stories about something called "copyright infringement"). Superman said Cap kept copying everything he was doing in his comic books. Captain Marvel said that wasn't true, but even if it had been, Superman was just copying everything Popeye had done first, and if the judge would care to look back a few thousand years, he would find that a benevolent Hercules FIRST did everything ALL the superheroes were now doing. Otto then made a serious point. Neither he nor his artist pal C. C. Beck, the co-creator of Captain Marvel, EVER copied Superman and that Superman AND his lawyer were . . . let me get the legal term accurately . . . "full of crap."

At that moment, who should walk up the steps and into the room but Mary Marvel . . . er . . . I mean, Mary Binder . . . carefully balancing a tray of tuna fish sandwiches and sodas for the three kids talking comic books in the attic. I remember that Mary's blouse was turquoise and she wore a necklace with one pearl on it. I couldn't tell you what Bobby or I were wearing that day, or if Otto was in a tie or his bathrobe. But being as hungry as I was at age thirteen in more ways than one, I DO remember the tuna fish and the color of Mary's blouse.

My folks kept checking in by phone, only to be politely but emphatically told to stay away! We were still only at questions 67 and 68 out of 200. My folks were later to report that they had visited every diner in Bergen County that Sunday and that my dad hit a personal best for consuming the most cups of coffee and servings of rice pudding in a single day. As night began to fall, Otto started to pile on the gifts atop our four shaking,

WHAT THEY'RE DOING TODAY...

MARY MARVEL...

CAPTAIN MARVEL— PARKING CARS IN LOT OF CHEESY NIGHT CLUB OWNED BY...

...FORTY-YEAR OLD BILLY BATSON, WHOSE CUSTOMERS COME ONLY TO SEE...

C·C BECK 1965

6 SHOWS NITELY... NEVER A COVER OR MINIMUM

When I asked C. C. Beck in 1965, "Whatever happened to Captain Marvel and The Marvel Family?," he sent me this.

outstretched arms. He gave us copies of his actual comic book scripts for Superman, Superboy, Jimmy Olsen, Lois Lane, a Legion of Super-Heroes story, and a Bizarro tale, all of which he personally inscribed to us. He handed each of us an original Captain Marvel tie clasp from the Golden Age and a copy of his most famous science fiction work, "I, Robot," the amazing story of Adam Link, the first robot to be accorded human rights. And he gave us the book he did for NASA as a technical writer. Then came the GOOD stuff. . . .

Otto Binder gave me and Bobby stacks of Golden Age comic books he had duplicates of, including: *Captain Marvel Adventures* #9 (Mary was right!) with the first full-blown comic book story he ever wrote about Captain Marvel, "Captain Marvel, Saving the King"; *Captain Marvel, Jr.* #1; and tons of *Whiz Comics* and *Master Comics*. By that time, my folks had shown up, refusing to be put off any longer. Maybe we had only gotten to question 157, but nonetheless, Bobby and I felt we had just left the comic book version of the Great Library of Alexandria and had just come back down the mountain after receiving the Ten Commandments from comicbookdom's Moses. Our knowledge base had increased a hundredfold. Otto promised to put us in touch with dozens of writers and artists and editors from the Golden Age of Comics, many of whom still lived in New Jersey or New York. We were starstruck. We were enlightened. And at the age of thirteen, although I had no way of knowing it, I had just taken a giant step forward on my life's path to bringing my vision of Batman to the movies.

Bobby and I wrote polite and enthusiastic thank-you notes to Otto and Mrs. Binder as soon as we got home, and we got a letter back from Otto complimenting us on our behavior and love for comic books, which may have restored his faith in the younger generation. And then came his nervous plea. He was working at DC Comics for a rough, tough editor who was, let's just say, not particularly well liked by most of the people who worked for him nor by many of his peers. Mort Weisinger, as editor, guided Superman successfully . . . even triumphantly . . . through his Silver Age renaissance, but not, apparently without some human collateral damage. So Otto had reason to fear inadvertently incurring the wrath of his boss. In his letter, Otto said he hoped that anything Bobby and I had heard or gleaned from our marathon session with him about the Superman/Captain Marvel lawsuit . . . such as his statement that neither he nor C. C. Beck ever copied from Superman . . . would be kept as a strictly private thing between us and not shared either with fellow fans or in print. By this time, Bobby and I looked at Otto as if he were the uncle we always wanted so, of course, we wrote Otto back that we were old enough to keep stuff secret, and he, with gratitude, sent us yet more stuff to add to our exploding collection of old comic books.

Although I'd have an ongoing correspondence with Otto, and then with all the legends behind the comics he put me in touch with, especially C. C. Beck, I wouldn't see him again until the day he and Bobby and I would be sitting and drinking in a bar in a sketchy New York hotel.*

My mom was appalled! Traumatized! If she had been a Gentile, she'd have been sick to her stomach. But she was Jewish, so she was "nauseous." It was a hot and humid July day in downtown New York City. After an unceasing campaign by me to cajole her and my dad into sacrificing the usual family weekend BBQ, my dad and mom found themselves walking me and Bobby into the lobby of a fleabag hotel not far from the down-and-out Bowery, where squeegee guys in their squeegee fog were offering to squeegee not only my dad's car windshield, but the lenses of my eyeglasses as well. I don't know where Paul was that weekend. He would have been seventeen, so for sure he was back home getting into some kind of trouble. We weren't there at the Broadway Central Hotel for any family gathering or any Fourth of July fireworks, but for the world's first ever comic book convention, where nearly two hundred of us would gather to meet, greet, and otherwise hobnob with our fellow comic book wizards. But don't kid yourself! The fireworks were just starting!

We had to step over an unconscious drunk in the lobby in order to check in, and my mom totally freaked! Maybe a hundred or a hundred and fifty years before, this hotel had been some real classy joint. But now, with scuzzy roaches crawling over the walls and under the leaky ceiling, I thought we had done what Rod Serling warned us about every week, "You've just crossed over into 'The Twilight Zone!'" My mom knew better. This wasn't the Twilight Zone. This was Hell. And her precious child was out of here right this second! Bobby looked at me in horror as if he knew his life was about to end. There was absolutely nothing I could say to my mother at that moment that could have calmed her down or gotten her to back off her edict that we were leaving. Luckily, by age thirteen, I knew the politics of my own family. I did the one and only thing I could do as my one and only chance of staying to attend this world's first Comic-Con. I appealed to the Supreme Court . . . aka, my dad. Even though he, himself, had never read a comic book, he had that understanding that bonds male friends or a father with a son. My dad

---

*For a fascinating and heartrending book on Otto and his family, don't miss *Worlds of Wonder: The Life and Times of Otto Binder* by Bill Schelly.

turned to my mom, talked her down, and somehow managed to get her to agree to let us stay and go to the convention with the idea that this would be a big, funny adventure for the whole family. And YOU don't think superheroes really exist?!? You can have your Thomas Waynes and Pa Kents and Uncle Bens and Uncle Marvels. I had Joe Uslan. My dad. My hero.

As my folks took all our luggage and headed to their not-exactly-deluxe room (I don't know what they were expecting for $9 per night), Bobby and I were set free to go conventioneering. With a last concerned shout from my mom, "Don't touch any-thing!," we were off. As we walked by the sketchy bar in the skeezy lobby of this Bow-ery hotel, we noticed that at this late hour of 9:20 A.M., Otto Binder and another man who looked vaguely familiar were sitting at the bar. We called out to Otto and waved. He beamed when he saw us and yelled, "Mike! Bobby! Come on in!" and we sat at the bar between the two men. Otto asked us what we were drinking. We said Cokes, but I have no doubt we would have been served anything we had asked for. The bartender looked like Long John Silver from the *Treasure Island* movie, only without the parrot and the pirate hat. (I couldn't see his leg.) Otto told us he would take us around in the conven-tion and show us the best old comic books and actual pages of original art drawn for comic books before they were reduced in size, colored, and printed. He also let us know that he would be the judge of the costume parade they were starting Saturday night. And then, he asked us that amazing question, "Boys, how'd you like to meet the creator of Batman?" Bobby and I were positively dazzled. Even razzle-dazzled. We shook our heads in vehement yeses. Otto pointed to the man drinking next to us. "Mike, Bobby . . . meet Bill Finger!"

We knew that Bill Finger had co-created Green Lantern and Wildcat in the Golden Age of Comics. We knew that he wrote many, if not most, of the Batman comics we read growing up. But the only name we had ever seen as a creator/artist in any Batman comic book before 1964 was Bob Kane. We had read some interviews with Bob Kane in comic books and fanzines and we did not remember him mentioning Bill Finger.

The story isn't clear-cut. But it appears that Bob Kane created a superhero originally called Bird-Man. Soon, he changed it to Bat-Man. The guy wore a red-based costume and a plain domino mask and sported real bat wings. Bill Finger then made a few sugges-tions. He thought that if the guy were going to be based on a bat, bats come out at night and the costume should be dark . . . blacks, blues, grays. He thought boots and gloves would make for a better look. Since Superman was the only superhero being published at that time, the second superhero should be different. Superman had superpowers. This guy should be normal like many of the heroes in the pulp magazines and on dramatic radio programs. He urged Bob to change the bat wings into a cape that simply resembled bat wings the way it was scalloped and jutted out. Bill thought Bob could better evoke the image of a bat if, instead of a little mask, he drew over Bat-Man's head a cowl with horns that gave his head a scary bat look. To make it even scarier and more mysterious, he recommended Bob blank out the eye slits. Now, THAT was a cool character! But Bill wondered who he was and what his backstory was. Bob hadn't gotten that far yet. So Bill thought about it all and named him Bruce Wayne and came up with a story about his parents being murdered and Bruce swearing an oath on their graves and becoming Bat-Man after a bat flies into his room like an omen. Later, Bill would add a few more things, namely: Gotham City, the Batmobile, and (with Jerry Robinson) Alfred the butler, the Joker, the Catwoman, the Penguin, and Two-Face. Robin was Jerry's creation with input from Bill and Bob. So was Otto Binder accurate? Was Bill Finger a co-creator of Batman? What do you think?

One interesting postscript is that due to the advocacy of Jerry Robinson, comic book writer Arnold Drake, and others, every year at the San Diego Comic-Con, they present the Bill Finger Award for excellence in comic book writing. Over the years, many people have been awarded The Finger in the comic book industry. (And a few have been given it.) The Award honors a great writer who made a vast contribution to our contemporary mythology.

That first comic book convention was primarily the brainchild of a fan by the name of Bernie Bubnis of New York, who was followed by David Kaler, John Benson, and Phil Seuling. I never knew where exactly in New York Bernie Bubnis was from, but always just assumed it was the streets and playgrounds I saw in the movie *West Side Story*. He may have looked like a con with his greased-back, ducktail haircut, and his black leather jacket, but underneath all the grease and black leather lurked a bright young man who, like us, loved, loved, loved comic books. In 1964 and '65, together with Bobby and 197 other zanies, we unintentionally became the two hundred "Founding Fathers of ComiCons." Not all of us were "fathers," to be perfectly accurate. There were maybe three females there that history-making weekend, including Flo Steinberg, the secretary and gal Friday of Marvel Comics' editor/writer/soon-to-become-a-legend Stan Lee, and La Grande Dame of Comic Book Fandom, the brilliant and irrepressible Maggie Thompson.

Hardly any pros showed up at that very first comic book convention. Why? They were scared. Most of them, as if they were all Dr. Wertham's mid-'50s dupes, assumed that anybody attending a comic book convention had to be a mentally stunted adult or pimply kid with a limit on his IQ. Our very own idols were reluctant if not frightened to interact with us fans. We needed to win them over! We needed credibility! We needed Dr. Jerry Bails! Dr. Bails, a professor at Wayne State University in Michigan, was a co-founder of comic book fandom and became our public face. As a college professor, he brought the desperately needed credibility with the press and the public that was required to gain acceptance as something more than nerds, geeks, or freaks. And Jerry provided exactly that credibility through his combination of articulate college professor and hard-core comic book fan. Only one TV camera showed up that weekend to document what none of us realized was serious history. It was a camera crew from WCBS-TV in New York. They decided to tape what would be the first-ever auction of comic books for a news segment that weekend. They had been tipped off that some demented saps were going to bid as much as $50 or $100 for some old 10-cent comic books. That was a newsworthy story on a slow July weekend. CBS taped the first item going up for bid in that first auction—a copy of *Action Comics* #1 from June 1938, which introduced Superman. The pre-auction estimate was $50 to $100. It went for $40. (A copy sold in 2010 for $1,500,000. Sigh . . .) The CBS cameraman had some technical problems and asked Jerry if he wouldn't mind staging the auction again as if it were happening for the first time. Jerry did it a second time, and then they asked him to do it a third time. Each time, Jerry was getting more and more comfortable and better and better in his newly created role of comic book auctioneer who was really selling comic book collecting and fandom to the television audience. The next item up for bid was the one Bobby and I had targeted to acquire that night. Between us, we had returned enough empty bottles for deposits, saved enough allowances, shoveled enough snow from walkways and driveways, and mowed enough lawns to accumulate more than $20 to bid on and buy *Batman* #1 from Spring 1940. We knew our facts and were well aware that in addition to this being the first edition of *Batman Comics*, it also marked the first appearance of BOTH the Joker and the Catwoman! We figured that $22.50 ought to do the trick. But when the bidding started and quickly got to $20, I told Bobby to stall while I ran to find my dad in the hotel. I found him fast and begged him for $5 so we could get the best comic book ever! He thought

From the original comic book convention costume parade. As the Shadow looks on in the background, Spider-Man hangs from the rusty pipes of the run-down Broadway Central Hotel as he's shot down by the original 1940's DC Comics version of the Sandman with his amazing Wirepoon Gun! That's me in seventh grade dressed up as the Sandman. The Shadow in the background just may be Bobby Klein!

I was not being smart paying so much money for one comic book and was concerned that some adult might be taking advantage of me and Bobby. But my time-is-of-the-essence desperation soaked through and he peeled off a Lincoln and I was back to the auction in a flash. By the time I got back, the bid was $26 but it sounded like everyone else had given up bidding. Bobby and I made our preemptive strike. "$27.50!" I cried out to Jerry. Someone in the audience gasped. Good-bye all our money! Hello *Batman* number ONE!

The damned thing sold for $29.

Some years later, I mowed a few more lawns and finally got a copy. Actually, it was a present from my wife after our first *Batman* movie premiered. She got a great deal on it, too, about fifteen hundred times what that guy paid for it at the first auction at the first comic book convention. Sigh . . .

Another important first at the ComiCon was the costume parade. Fliers were sent out well in advance, encouraging everyone to make a superhero costume for this special festivity. My mom worked with me to create a costume of the original 1939 DC comic book character the Sandman, who wore a green double-breasted suit, a purple cape, orange gloves, a gold fedora, and a gas mask, while packing a Wirepoon Gun. I assumed he was the first color-blind superhero. Together, we made the greatest, coolest, most accurate-looking costume ever! I thought I'd win first prize, and then was certain of it when Otto told me he was going to be the contest judge! Bobby made a costume of the Shadow, and we were ready to rock 'n' roll! A reporter and photographer for the fan-friendly magazine *Castle of Frankenstein* was in attendance to document this unusual event. I sized up the competition and things looked good for me. I forget what costumes were worn that night by fellow fans Maggie Thompson and her husband, Don, or by Roy Thomas, Len Wein, or David Weiss. I do remember a chubby Marv Wolfman dressed in a really great costume of Herbie, that plump lump known as the Fat Fury. Then Phil Seuling and his wife, Carole, entered in super-cool Captain Marvel and Mary Marvel costumes, as Phil struck a classic superhero hands-on-hips pose and looked about at all the superheroes assembled in this run-down ballroom, including Batman and Spider-Man, and proclaimed, "It's a bad night for evildoers!" Everyone laughed, but I got nervous. His costume was amazing! But he had a goatee. Captain Marvel didn't. Phil should've shaved. I was confident Otto would deduct points from him for that. And then, I abandoned all hope like ye who entered here. In sashayed comic fandom *macher* Dave Kaler, in full makeup and garbed in a swirl of blue satin that could have been designed by Bob Mackie for Cher's Las Vegas act. He was Dr. Strange. No, I mean, he WAS Dr. Strange! It was the ultimate, professional superhero costume in a class my mom and I could not equal. When I heard that Dave Kaler would be running an upcoming comic book convention, I never even bothered to make another costume. I was now forever done with Little League AND with superhero dress-ups.

Every year since, even as I near my fiftieth annual comic book convention, I have a very special place in my heart for all the fans who DO dress up in costumes . . . even those 350-pound guys I see dressed like Princess Leia. "What hath we wrought?" We started something fun, cool, and outrageous that has become a tradition rooted in the sheer excitement of our being with a bunch of people who share a love of comics despite being pretty unique individuals. In the days before the Internet, collecting comic books was an isolating hobby. But now, starting with these first comic book conventions and the growing network of fanzines and fanzine readers, comic book collecting became a connection point for people sharing a common interest . . . people who could even discuss the artistic merits of Jack Kirby versus Carmine Infantino and Murphy Anderson. Bobby and I couldn't do that with anyone in Ocean Township or Asbury Park outside the Comic Book Club. For weeks after ComiCon, all I could think of was comics. It crowded out all thoughts of school, girls, the Yankees, anything. There was no room for anything else in my consciousness for months to come.

In 1973, just nine years later, the Broadway Central Hotel and its leaky roof and bulging walls collapsed on itself, burying along with it uncountable roaches, a lot of rats, and forgotten memories and dreams . . . forgotten by nearly everyone, except Bobby and me.

Fan flyers for early comic book conventions. Bobby and I planned our year around attending them! And searching for that NEXT copy of *Action Comics* #1 for $40 or *Batman* #1 for $29!

# CHAPTER NINE

# "AND THEN THERE WERE NONE!"

These are the things I do not remember. I can't remember when it happened. I can't remember for sure who called me. I don't remember where I was when I got the call. I don't remember if I ever asked anyone in an attempt to get clarifying details. I don't remember what was in the note I wrote to Otto and Mrs. Binder. The fellow comic book fan on the phone told me Mary Binder had been with some friends in front of her school the previous morning when a car went out of control and jumped the curb. At age sixteen, Mary was dead.

I remember someone telling me later that Otto was drinking heavily.

I remember an editor at DC telling me that Otto's wife, Ione, spiraled downward after Mary died and that one day when Otto came home from work, he found her trying to burn down the house and finally had to have her institutionalized.

I remember the next call. Otto Binder had had a heart attack and died. And in what felt like the blink of an eye, a Marvel of a family was gone. The last *Marvel Family* comic book Otto ever wrote was the final issue. The cover showed only blank outlines of the Family. The title of his last story . . . "And Then There Were None."

Sadly, the most prophetic comic book cover of all time, the last issue of *The Marvel Family.*

# PART II

# "YOU STILL READ COMIC BOOKS AT YOUR AGE?!"

**TOP:** Me (front row) in my senior year at O.T.H.S. in the middle of the Yearbook staff and our advisor, Mr. Lefsky, who failed to notice how the photographer lined him up in front of the blackboard upon which I had drawn angel wings and a halo! I already owned 30,000 comic books by then!

**LEFT:** Bobby Klein in our senior year at Ocean Township High School cramming before his live TV appearance on *It's Academic*, then a popular *Jeopardy*-style competition between high school teams! Eventually, you can take the "boy" out of "fanboy," but never the "fan!"

**RIGHT:** The greatest French teacher ever created, Miss Blakeslee! Move over Lynda "Wonder Woman" Carter!

# Good-Bye Smallville!

# HELLO METROPOLIS!

If each boy at Ocean Township High School had been allowed by a merciful God to imagine his own perfect fantasy scenario for drooling teenage lust, he'd undoubtedly have fantasized about a young, early-twenties French teacher with a thing for micro-miniskirts, showing up to teach him a foreign language. And she'd have to be statuesque... in fact, a look-alike for Lynda Carter's TV Amazon princess, Wonder Woman, but with long flowing hair down to a perfect butt. If that's not a complete enough fantasy girl, let's imagine she'd be the coolest, hippest chick in New Jersey, if not the world. If that fantasy had had a name, it would have been "April Blakeslee." And it was. And at this moment in time, so many years later, I'd like to pause a moment to say, "She was real," and to personally thank God for having sent her to us in 1968. Amen. Hallelujah!

Every school day, we had French class with Miss Blakeslee. And every day, she'd bop into class in one of an array of short skirts and sit on her desk and teach us French. And every day, Ira Byock, Jeff Mendel, Steve Huntington, and I sat in the front row, desks slightly, subtly angled. It was merely, in the words of Janis Joplin of Big Brother and the Holding Company, "Cheap Thrills." In fact, we had all recently seen Janis as well as Joe Cocker live in concert at Convention Hall. Barry used his press pass to get us in free to both the early and late shows of Janis. He had conned Julie Klein's father, who owned the weekly township newspaper, *The Home News*, into giving him a press pass (actually, I think it was just a laminated piece of paper upon which Mr. Klein hand-printed the word Press) so that Barry could take photographs of local events involving the children of Ocean Township. But to my amazement, Barry was really good. He worked in black and white, and was soon taking fantastic shots of every rock 'n' roll act to play Asbury Park or the newly opened Garden State Arts Center. Janis Joplin was one of the best singers of all time, yet was not the nicest looking woman ever. While pretending to be Barry's photographer's assistant by holding his package of Sylvania Blue-Dot flashbulbs, I learned that looks have nothing to do with sexuality. Barry and I were allowed to stand directly in front of Janis's feet at the center of the stage so Barry could take pictures (for a newspaper, mind you, read only by our parents, grandparents, and Mrs. Butter, Timmy and Faye Hauser's sainted Irish grandmother who babysat for Paul and me, providing my complete knowledge of Irish tunes . . . everything from "Harrigan" to "Has Anybody Here Seen Kelly?"). We could see up close from the way Janis moved her ass . . . her beat-tapping feet . . . her entire body . . . the way she shook her hair off her face without touching it . . . that this was the sexiest woman alive. In the haze of time and the '60s, her opening act . . . or maybe it was Joe Cocker's opening act . . . was Led Zeppelin. Along with the later Concert for Bangladesh and Cream's Farewell Concert at Madison Square Garden, the Concert for George at the Royal Albert Hall, one concert at the Fillmore East and two at the Fillmore West in San Francisco headlined by the Grateful Dead, this was my second favorite concert ever! The best? The Doors. And my date would be the second sexiest woman alive, Miss Blakeslee.

School was concluding for the year and my fab high school days were about to end. Finals were over, but we still had to officially report to some classes for a few days before graduation. So Miss Blakeslee had nothing left to teach (or so I thought) and just sat around bullshitting with her entourage of French Club officers. When she heard we were all going to see the Doors, she went nuts! The Doors was her favorite group! Jim Morrison was her god! She was so jealous of us! And without thinking . . . because if I had thought, I never would have opened my mouth . . . the words just came out . . . "Uh, Miss Blakeslee . . . I have an extra ticket . . . second row . . . center aisle. You . . . uh . . . wanna go . . . . . . with me?" She excitedly said, "YES!" and I have no further recollection of anything until the year 2002. Well, maybe that's an exaggeration, but I was stunned into the frickin' Twilight Zone!

We agreed to meet Saturday night on the Boardwalk, to the left of Convention Hall, at 8:45 P.M. for the 9 o'clock show. When the time came, waiting for me on the Asbury Park boardwalk was Miss Blakeslee in tight, bell-bottomed, button down hip-huggers, wearing water buffalo sandals and a turquoise tank top that made my eyes look exactly like Superman's that instant he first turns on his X-ray vision.

"Shall we go in? It's almost 9 o'clock," she said to me. "NO!" I practically shrieked in a voice I hadn't heard since two weeks after my Bar Mitzvah. I then leveled with her about what I wanted . . . needed . . . her to do. I explained that almost every guy I knew had tickets for this show and that we all got them around the same time and were in the orchestra seats. I wanted to make sure every single one of my friends was already sitting down in Convention Hall before I walked down the aisle to row two with her next to me. Now I was sure I had just screwed everything up with this juvenile confession of mine. "That's so great!" she responded mercifully. And we then waited until 9:07 P.M. before parading in. As we started walking down the row to our seats, she grabbed my arm and held it, as I saw out of the seeming thirty-two corners of my eyes the jaw-dropped, frozen faces of the French Club officers. I prayed that somewhere in the balcony, all the high school Twirlers were gaping at this scene . . . and that all the Cheerleaders were now suddenly crushed that they had missed the chance to date me during high school. That one night I so wished would never end passed in the blink of an eye. That one night, the Doors were the Doors, Jim Morrison was Jim Morrison, and Miss Blakeslee was . . . April. She told me to call her April.

And me? I was the boy-man at exactly the crossroads of my own past and future. High school would dissolve around me that Sunday. Before August ended, I would load up a car and head to college in Indiana, leaving my home, my parents, and my childhood behind. All my friends at the Doors concert would depart, too, some becoming ghosts of times past. I wanted desperately to cling to it all, and I wanted to leave it all behind on the next leg of my journey. So I made a choice. I left it all behind . . . except . . . I never let go of my childhood. Without it, I couldn't make movies, create cartoons, write comic books, or be in touch enough with Me to write this book. And that has made all the difference.

J213  The Comic Book in Society               Syllabus

Michael Uslan, Instructor                     Spring 1972
        (336-6070, 612 N. Grant)


A.  Required Reading - Comics Reference

    Steranko, James:  The Steranko History of Comics, Vol. 1

B.  Recommended Reading - Books (students select one or more of the first
                            three to read.

    Feiffer, Jules,  The Great Comic Book Heroes
    Lupoff, Dick,  All In Color For A Dime (paperback)
    Perry, George,  Penguin Story of Comics (paperback)
    Crown Pub.,  Superman From the 30's to 70's
    Crown Pub.,  Batman From the 30's to 70's
    Alyn, Kirk,  A Job for Superman!
    Harmon, Jim,  The Great Radio Heroes

C.  Required Reading - Comics

    The Forever People (DC)          Spiderman (Marvel)
    The New Gods (DC)                Conan (Marvel)
    Mr. Miracle (DC)                 Special Assignments
    (When not on stands, available through me.)

D.  Course Purpose

    Panelology, the study of comic art, as a legitimate art form will be the
primary purpose of the course.  Comics as a social force as well as a source
of entertainment, escapism, propaganda, and relevance will also be considered.

E.  Mid-Term Paper

    All students will be required to write a paper five or so pages in le
length on any facet of comics of personal interest.  I don't care if it's
about your sexual fantasies of Wonder Woman or the use of cramped foreshortening
as a comic are technique, as long as you are involved in what you are writing.
Please--no plagarism.

F.  Final Project

    Students are to muster whatever creative forces they can to create,
write, and/or draw an original comic strip of any type, using philosophies
and techniques picked up from class discussions or readings.  Super-hero,
sceince-fiction, gothic, wester, war, romance, underground, etc. all are
valid areas.  Collaboration with one or two others in the class is permis-
sible.  The final form should be polished enough to be acceptable to a publication.

AP wires
UPI wires
Louisville Courier J
L.A. Times
Pitts. Gazette
Wash. Post
St Louis. Post
Indy News
Newark Star Ledger
Terre Haute Star
IOS
Herald Telephone
Asbury Park Press

Interviews
WHAS Louisville        KFWB Los Angeles        KBLM San Antonio    NBC- National
KDKA Pittsburgh        WCBS New York           KAUM Houston +      News
KMOX St. Louis         Metromedia -Los Angeles    locals           Jim Gerard ⑥
WBZ Boston             Metro media -South Carolina +   WISH-TV (CBS)  NBC-Indianapdi.
                          Southeast              Indianapolis ⑧    Good Morning
                                                                   Show WTTV ⑭

The opening of the syllabus I created for the world's first college-accredited course on comic books in 1972.
My handwritten notes recorded all the media that contacted me for interviews when the story first broke.

# CHAPTER ELEVEN

# The *World's First* COLLEGE PROFESSOR *of* COMIC BOOKS!

Indiana University, the pride of Bloomington, the gem of the Big Ten, home of the best music school and some of the greatest college schools and courses in America, with a grand tradition in sports from basketball and swimming to soccer and its world-renowned Little 500 Bicycle Race, had a brochure it used to send out to prospective freshmen, titled "The Top Ten Legends of Indiana University." My brother, Paul, was TWO of 'em!

He was the nameless student who poured soap powder into the gigantic landmark in the center of campus, the Showalter Fountain. It featured a reclining naked lady with a group of fish throwing up on her. In the dead of night, Paul filled the churning fountain with soap powder and hopped in and took a bath, using a long scrubbing brush on his back. Unidentified, the local papers branded the mystery scoundrel "Mr. Bubbles" in honor of the unending stream of soap bubbles that overflowed the fountain and filled the entire plaza between the Auditorium, the classy Lilly Library, and the Fine Arts Building. Now it can be told. Paul did it! And he made a clean getaway.

Number two came during a challenge made to him by his Sigma Alpha Mu fraternity brothers. Back then, Paul never passed up a challenge, a dare, or anything that sounded like fun, consequences be damned. This time, he was the nameless mystery man who rode the campus bus up and down North Jordan, better known as I.U.'s resplendent fraternity row, which showcased palatial sorority houses and frat houses from one end to the other. Does a guy riding a bus sound boring? How is that "legendary"? The answers are based on the fact that Paul rode it, stopping off to visit each sorority en route, in a madras jockstrap and a transparent raincoat (the latter, I assume, so he wouldn't catch cold). A Legend!

Paul in college in 1969 with his dog, Charlie.

College is the best time in life to be adventurous and travel when you have virtually no money. I learned that soon after I joined Paul's fraternity and met the *Animal House*–meets–*The Hangover* gang of fraters. And that's what I did starting Christmas vacation of our sophomore year. We had a month off from I.U. One of my pledge brothers had a brother-in-law who needed someone to drive a rental car from Indianapolis to Los Angeles and was willing to pay all gas and tolls. It was a cool 1969 Firebird capable of taking two people comfortably across the country. So five of us went, including me and my roommate, Marc Caplan, and fellow Sammy fraternity brother, Peeper Freemas. (Today, he is an adult and you sure as hell better call him "Ron" and not "Peeper.") We planned on avoiding all costs of hotels and meals by carefully planning the trip around people and places we could mooch off. We crossed the United States at a cost per person of $4.00.

Our college adventure was the first time I had ever been in Los Angeles, and our initial stop was the place I had been dreaming of seeing since 1956 . . . Disneyland! The park had recently been torn up by a group of yippies, the not-as-peaceful version of the hippies, and as a result, Disney had banned all bearded young people from the park. By then, I had a beard to complement my increasingly long hair. Here now was the perfect battle for anyone willing to stand up for what they believed in! Clearly the policy was unconstitutional and illegal and prejudiced against young males, from hippies to the Amish;

protests, demonstrations, picketing, and a legal challenge were called for! But I needed to ride in the Mixing Bowls and on the Flying Dumbos! I had to zoom down the Matterhorn like I'd been seeing on TV since I was five! I had to take the Jungle Cruise and climb Swiss Family Robinson's Tree House! And I needed to board Peter Pan's flying pirate ship to Never Land! Fuck my principles. I shaved my beard off and went to Disneyland! Once inside, I bathed in my childhood, I basked in my dreams, I explored the blurred line between reality and fantasy, and I appreciated the fact that it was all an illusion. Yes, I was now ready for a career in Hollywood. The only question remaining for a blue collar kid from New Jersey who was in school in the wilds of Bloomington, Indiana, was, how do I get there from here?

During my years at I.U., I wasn't the only person contemplating a career in movies or television. There was a girl named Jane Pauley in Kappa Kappa Gamma, who became the Queen of TV news reporting and wound up marrying Garry Trudeau, a major, major cartoonist! There was a guy named Howard Ashman, who would go on to rack up lots of awards for writing the music to Disney's *Little Mermaid, Beauty and the Beast*, and *Aladdin*. Juniors that year were Angelo Pizzo and David Anspaugh, who would write and direct *Hoosiers* and *Rudy*. Seniors were a young actor named Kevin Kline; a playwright named Steve Tesich, who would win an Oscar for his movie *Breaking Away* based on I.U.'s Little 500 Bicycle Race; and Bruce Rubin, who would nab his Academy Award for writing *Ghost*. We were all there at the same time, eventually qualifying as some sort of Hoosier mafia in Hollywood.

It was an interesting time to be going to college, 1969 to 1973, as evidenced by Captain America's dilemma when the president of the United States ordered him onto a college campus post–Kent State to support the National Guard troops facing protesting anti-war college students, their guns pointed at the kids. It was a confusing time to be a Captain America comics fan, but what was intriguing was that it was also a confusing time for Captain America to be Captain America. He was having second thoughts. Who is Captain America? What does Captain America stand for or symbolize? Is he a superhero whose thoughts, philosophies, and allegiance change every four years with the newly elected president and administration? Or does Captain America need to be something that transcends politics? Should he be there supporting U.S. soldiers no matter what? Should he be there supporting the U.S. students who have a Constitutional right to protest peacefully? Yes, it was a dilemma for Cap and for me as his reader. The students at Indiana University's main campus would soon elect a Black Panther as president of the Student Body. Unrelated, Marvel would soon be spinning off its black superhero called the Black Panther into his own comic book title.

Cultures were clashing. Never was that more evident to me than when as an undergrad I was selected to serve as a judge on the Youth Grants Panel of the National Endowment for the Humanities in Washington, D.C. They flew me into the nation's capital for days of evaluating projects submitted to the N.E.H. for funding. The deliberations were intensive and followed a firm set of guid elines, as we judged each project on its own merits. And then, one of the gentlemen overseeing this process came in and addressed us as a group. He made us aware of one project we would be considering that dealt with a very narrow subject with some connection to Whittier, California, and Whittier College, which then-President Nixon had attended. He made a point of alerting us to the fact that this was a project that the president would very much like to see funded, and then left us to our work. At the end of the several days of deliberation, the Youth Grants Panel completed its discussions, debates, and voting process and presented the list of projects we agreed to fund. Before we were dismissed, the same gentleman made a return appearance before us. He was not happy. Not happy at all. He reiterated in sterner tones that, as we may not have understood him the previous time, President Nixon specifically hoped to see his pet project funded by the N.E.H. Since we had not chosen it as one of the projects to be funded, the gentleman was refraining from submitting our list, and we had one more opportunity to reopen our decision-making process and reconsider very carefully the great merit of the Whittier work. He then left us to our "do-over." Some on this panel were left-leaning early '70s protesting students. Some were right-wing Young Americans for Freedom. Some of us considered ourselves totally independent. We were ALL pissed off. Perhaps just a few years earlier, the Youth Grant judges would have smiled and just bent the rules to accommodate a president's request. Not here, not now. Everyone banded together in a united stand that the other projects we had agreed to fund were more deserving than this one. When we returned our verdict, it was clear that it was time for us to leave. The supervising gentleman was angry and offended by our final decision. We all left Washington and returned to our lives, proud of the work we had done and that we had stood up to such inappropriate political pressure. So you can imagine my greenhorn shock when the N.E.H. announcement was made some weeks later, and there in the funded projects was the Whittier one. My cynical dad and jaded Uncle Jack were right. Politics just may be a system favoring the rich and powerful.

In the late '60s and early '70s, generations were being split by a gap as wide as the Grand Canyon. It was a time of great experimentation on college campuses across America . . . in every way imaginable. And if you don't know the kinds of things I'm alluding to, I cannot reveal more due to a Baby-Boomer Pledge we all had to take years ago when we started having children of our own and needed to cover our collective tracks.

During my junior year at I.U., the College of Arts and Sciences wanted to be as daring and experimental as its students had become. It started an experimental curriculum department with the idea that if a student or professor had an idea for a course that had never been taught anywhere, and if he could obtain the backing of a department within the College, he would then have the right to appear before a panel of deans and professors to pitch his course. If his pitch was approved, his course would be accredited, and he would be allowed to teach it on campus. I had already been "teaching" a group of students about comic books for more than a year through what I.U. recognized as "The Free University." I would assemble the class in Dunn Meadow in nice weather for outdoor discussions about comic books from different academic perspectives for one college credit. Fellow campus radio station disc jockey and comic book fan Roger Stern also pioneered the teaching of comic books before he went on to become one of the all-time great writers of comic books from *Superman* to *Spider-Man*. In a stunning coincidence, also at I.U. at that time was Allan Grafman, who would one day go on to become the president of Archie Comics!

I was consumed by the idea of taking a five-pronged academic approach to teaching comic books and getting the class fully accredited as a three credit-hour college course. My syllabus quickly evolved. The first academic discipline involved would be art. Comic books constitute a true American art form, as indigenous to this country as jazz. Next was anthropology. Comic books and the superheroes are our contemporary American folklore, our modern-day mythology. My pitch would be that the gods of ancient Egypt, Greece, and Rome still exist, although today they wear spandex and capes. After all, the Greeks called him Hermes, the Romans called him Mercury, and we call him the Flash. The Greeks called him Poseidon, the Romans called him Neptune, and we call him Aquaman. The third discipline was sociology. Comic books have been published every week since the mid-1930s. Thus, they have been a mirror of our society, reflecting the changing American culture. Our emotions, mores, fads, slang, and, unfortunately, our biases and prejudices, have been reflected through historical events such as World War II, the Korean War, and the Vietnam War, as well as through peace times. Fourth was English. Comic books are literature, from Jack Kirby's *Fourth World Trilogy* to Stan Lee's *Thor*, and even *Classics Illustrated*. Finally, there was psychology. Comic books have had a psychological impact on their readers. If you don't believe me, just ask Dr. Wertham!

And so, forearmed with my syllabus, I approached one of my Folklore professors, Dr. Henry Glassie, and explained my proposal. He got behind it immediately. He concurred that the plots, motifs, and conventional stock characters found in traditional folklore are exactly the same as the ones found today in comic books. At the end of the day, it's still stories of heroes versus villains, dragons, monsters, and sorcerers, with damsels not-so-much-in-distress-as-before. The stories now are merely cloaked in contemporary drapings. It was time for me to pitch this to the committee.

My appointment was from 11:15 A.M. to 11:30 A.M. I put on my Amazing Spider-Man T-shirt for impact. I clutched my collection of comic books and pages of original art. It was too late to do anything about my shoulder-length hair or love beads. As I took one last, deep breath and walked into the dean's conference room, I had some serious déjà vu. Not that I thought I had ever before actually been in this room. It just so resembled in my head the way I had always pictured the Justice League of America's Secret Sanctum: dark mahogany walls; a long, thick conference table; and high-back plush chairs. I could just picture a tiny floating chair to my left holding the seated superhero the Atom. As I entered, the dean looked down at me from over the top of that little pair of half-glasses he had perched atop the end of his nose. With the sound of disgust dripping off every word, he said to me, "So YOU'RE the fellow who wants to teach a course on 'funny books' at MY University?" I knew I was in deep shit.

"Do you have the one where SUPERMAN gets hit by Kryptonite bullets?"

This is EXACTLY what it looked like when I pitched my idea for a comic book course to the dean and professors at Indiana University!

I launched into my pitch, outlining the five disciplines I would use to approach the subject academically and began to explain the theory that comic books were our modern-day mythology. I think the dean let me speak for about three minutes before he cut me off. "Oh, come on! Comic books as mythology? Superheroes as folklore? Really, Mr. Uslan, give me a break," he said shaking his head. His next statement, I was sure, had been written by Fredric Wertham himself. "What comic books are . . . are cheap, maybe lurid entertainment for children. Nothing more, nothing less. Look, I read comic books when I was a kid. I read every issue of *Superman* I could get my hands on. But it's nothing but kids' stuff, and I reject your premise."

What happened in the next three minutes changed my life.

I knew I had to think fast. I was facing certain doom. There really was only one chance.

"May I ask you two questions?" I delicately inquired.

The dean sat back, and with a dismissive wave said, "Ask me what you want."

"Are you familiar with the story of Moses?" I asked. He was really taken aback by my question. He responded with a slow drawl, elongating his word, "Yyyyyesss . . . and so?"

"So would you VERY briefly just summarize for me the basic story of Moses?" I asked with a deadpan face.

He sat back in his chair and folded his arms, all the while grilling me with his penetrating stare. "Mr. Uslan, I don't know what GAME you're playing here. . . ."

"Oh uh. I blew it!" I thought as I abandoned all hope.

" . . . but I will play this game with you," he surprised me and certainly surprised the professors sitting in the oversized chairs normally reserved for Wonder Woman, Hawkman, and J'onn J'onzz, the Manhunter from Mars. And he played right into my trap.

"The Hebrew people were being persecuted, their first-born were being slain," he offered. "A Hebrew couple placed their infant son into a little wicker basket and sent him drifting down the Nile. The basket was found by an Egyptian couple who raised the child as their own son. When he grew up and learned of his true heritage, he became a great hero to his people by—"

I jumped in to cut him off. My turn. "That's great! Thank you very, very much. Now, you said you read *Superman* comics when you were a kid. Do you recall the origin of Superman?" I asked.

"Sure," he replied with some enthusiasm, most likely in an effort to show me how comic book cool he was. "The planet Krypton was about to explode. A scientist and his wife placed their infant son into a little rocket ship and sent him to earth where he was found by the Kents, who raised him as their own son. When he grew up and learned of his true—"

Suddenly, the dean stopped talking. He stared at me for what I was sure was an eternity. And then he said, "Mr. Uslan, your course is accredited."

The professors in the room remained silent, but were clearly blown away by what they had just witnessed. This was a turning point for me, and may have been one for the dean, for now he wanted to see if I had brought any old 1940s *Superman* comics or original art with me. As I laid out what I had, he got very excited. He picked up *Superman #52* and shouted, "I had this one! I remember this! Say . . . do you have the one where Superman gets hit by Kryptonite bullets?!? That was the BEST!"

I love the smell of an old comic book. It smells like . . . victory.

As I scraped together all my materials and left the Sanctum, I was on cloud nine. I couldn't believe that I had pulled it off! I was now the world's first college-accredited Professor of Comic Books! Students who enrolled in my course could eventually get the same number of credit hours as for a history or psychology course. I was on a great natural high as I glided back to the house at Tenth and Grant I shared with Brad Finkle and Scotty Maybaum, behind the pinball parlor. And just then, I heard from my mom. No, not on the telephone, but loud and clear in my head. It was something she had been telling me for years . . . "Michael, you can have the most wonderful creative ideas, but if you don't market them and yourself, no one will ever see your wares. Use BOTH sides of your brain." And so I did. And the next wacky step in my journey suddenly seemed obvious. Wacky as hell . . . but obvious.

When I got to the house, I picked up the phone and dialed Information, getting the number of United Press International in Indianapolis. Back then, UPI was as big a news syndicate as Associated Press is today. I asked to speak to a reporter who covered stories about education in the state. After a brief wait, a man got on the phone, and I proceeded to scream at him.

"What's WRONG with you?!" I yelled. "You people have a responsibility to the public! You're supposed to be our watchdog! How could this have happened without you even knowing?!"

"Calm down, please," said the reporter. "What are you talking about?"

"I just heard that there's a course on COMIC BOOKS being taught at Indiana University! This is OUTRAGEOUS! Are you telling me, as a taxpayer in the state of Indiana,

# Course On Comic Books Is Being Taught At IU This Year

### By B. J. GILLEY

INDIANAPOLIS (UPI) — Comic books no longer are being taken as light amusement for the very young, as **Mike Uslan**, a junior at Indiana University at Bloomington can testify. In fact, he's teaching a course on them this semester.

The course, offered under a policy the College of Arts and Sciences has of allowing development of new studies by students if they can show merit in the course and present material to be studied, is under the supervision of Prof. Henry Glassie of the IU Department of Folklore.

Teaching the course may come easy to Uslan, who is 20 and from Deal Park, N. J., and has been a serious collector of comic books for most of his life. But he said he has put quite a bit of work into getting the course ready. He feels comic books deserve more attention than many people have given them.

"As Time magazine pointed out recently, comic books are very much part of our culture in America and have largely been taken for granted for too long," Uslan said. "I spent quite a bit of time in New York over our semester break visiting the offices of several comic book publishers."

### Criticism Is Unfounded

The publishers were eager to cooperate with Uslan in providing material for the courses, he said. He noted comic books fell in disrepute during the 1950s when a book "Seduction of the Innocent" accused the periodicals of making youngsters prone to sadism and perversions. Although the accusations proved unfounded, many people still look down on comics.

"What I hope to do in the course is present comic books as a legitimate art form in America and show why they should be accepted as a social force, reflecting change around them and the society in which they were created," Uslan said.

Students in the course, which is for two credits, will have to read several books on the history and techniques of comic books, write a paper on some aspect of comic books and prepare their own original cartoon strip, he said.

His syllabus for the course deals with the history of comics—including the development of the Comics Code Authority which serves as a censor board, comic book characters in other media, underground comics, and use of comics for, escapism, entertainment and propaganda.

Uslan said most people have forgotten the amount of propaganda contained in such comics as Captain American during World War II and overlook the way characters have influenced society—from Mickey Mouse watches to concepts of morality.

### Hero Has Pimples

Recently comic books have moved into a new era of relevancy," he said. "Not only are traditional heroes like Superman concerned about bigotry and pollution, but there has also been the emergence of anti-heroes in comic books.

"For example Spiderman is the first 'hero' to have pimples and have a hard time with girls," Uslan said. "He also has to avoid the police because they look at him as an outlaw."

A new series launched by "DC" comics and written by Jack Kirby is really a trilogy similar to "The Lord of the Rings" series by J. R. Tolkien, Uslan said. "It is particularly interesting because of its symbolism and philosophy," he said.

Uslan "learned to read when I was three using comic books" and became an early collector, taking advantage of those assembled by an older brother. He now has a collection of more than 10,000 comics in partnership with a friend who is a junior at M.I.T.

### Valued at $10,000

"We figure the value of the collection is at least $10,000—$1 a book—but I have some that are very valuable, like the first issue of Plastic Man from the 1940s which is worth $100," Uslan said.

His collection includes books from 1936 to the present and Uslan said he has noticed a change in the way comic books are now acquired.

"I used to go to auctions and pick up old editions for about a nickel a piece," he said. "Now there are magazine ads from persons wanting to buy or sell a particular edition and an annual convention for collectors in New York City."

Uslan said he had no definite plans concerning his own collection but he and his partner had sold some of the books to help with the expenses of going to college.

Student in comic course at Indiana University reviews a textbook— an "Adventure" comic of "Supergirl." Instructor believes young can identify with super-achievers.

## Flash Gordon Goes to College

by John G. Rogers

BLOOMINGTON, IND.

Two Indiana University students were discussing their grades. Said one: "I did all right. I got an A in Superman." The other grumbled: "Well, you're lucky. The best I could do in Flash Gordon was a C plus."

Superman and Flash Gordon in a university curriculum? Here at Indiana they are—and very popular, too. There's a list of more than 100 students waiting to enroll in this accredited once-a-week class that delves into all aspects of our comic-book heroes—those doughty fellows who defy danger, gravity, crooks, logic, the odds—and always come out on top.

The comic-book course is conducted not by a faculty member but a 20-year-old student—Mike Uslan of Deal, N.J., in a special experimental project.

Says Rhoda Bunnell, assistant dean of arts and sciences: "In this experiment, we throw away tradition and say that just about everything in the world around us is an appropriate subject for study and scrutiny. Michael Uslan came before our experimental curriculum committee and convinced us that such people as Batman and the Green Hornet are part of an authentic American art form, worthy of study with credit toward graduation.

Uslan, a junior majoring in history, whose ultimate ambition is to be a lawyer, can hardly remember when he wasn't a comic-book buff. In fact, by poring through his older brother's comics, he mastered rudimentary reading before he was 4 years old and in his early teens was a regular visitor to the New York offices of the artists, writers and publishers who turn out the colorful publications.

### Heroes wanted

"They're more than just escapism, adventure, excitement and thrills," Mike contends. "They're a very real reflection of our times and our ways of thought. American society seems to love and crave heroes. Kids find them in comic books. American voters love glamour in their political candidates. And you start finding glamour when you're a kid reading comic books. Unfortunately, many of us are attracted to violence. And there it is—right in the comics.

"But there's more serious stuff. Wonder Woman relates to women's lib—the heroine is making it on her own in a man's world. Green Arrow showed a heroin addict, how he got hooked and how he kicked the habit through all

Informal group gathers around conference table to talk about Batman and Green Hornet. There are 100 more students waiting to enroll in the accredited course.

Instructor Uslan wears T-shirt with Spider-man on chest.

PARADE • APRIL 9, 1972

**ABOVE, LOWER LEFT:** The newspaper story that changed my life! UPI went out with it and it was picked up by papers throughout the world. The "Lois Lane" imitator in the photo? My girlfriend, Nancy, whom I met on the first day of our freshman year at I.U.! **LOWER RIGHT:** My course was covered by reporters from *Parade* magazine, *Playboy*, and *Penthouse*! Nancy is the college co-ed reading the comic book in the photo. She got an "A," of course!

that they're using MY money to teach our kids COMIC BOOKS?! This is horrible! It must be some communist plot to subvert the youth of America!" And I hung up the phone.

It took this poor man three days to find out whether or not Indiana University did have a comic book course, and who the lunatic was teaching it. He finally tracked me down and came to Bloomington to interview me. That interview turned into a story a third of a page long in the newspapers, plus a photo. It was picked up by virtually every newspaper in North America and in a handful of foreign countries as well. Immediately, my telephone started ringing off the hook. I got calls seemingly from everybody I ever knew . . . from other colleges wanting to know how to design comic book courses of their own and where to find good teachers for them, from high schools wanting to develop this as a mini-course for seniors, from TV and radio talk shows around the globe that wanted me to appear on their shows or do interviews, and from major magazines. I.U.'s own Independent Study Division contacted me to reveal that they were being overwhelmed by requests from people wanting to take Indiana University's new course via correspondence. They offered to pay me to adapt my course for correspondence, and when I explained that there was no textbook to cover the educational uses of comic books, they paid me to write the first textbook on comics, which I did so that I could then teach the correspondence course as well as the in-classroom version.

I wound up doing the TV and radio talk show circuit, and by the time my class actually convened for the first time, I had a backlog of media requests. Every class was filled with television cameras and reporters. John Chancellor got to me first from the *NBC Nightly News*, followed by crews from the other networks. I remember the one class in which I had four magazine reporters sitting in the first row: *Family Weekly*, *Parade*, *Playboy*, and *Penthouse*. This course certainly appealed to EVERYONE! When the university first made students aware of it, nearly two hundred students wanted to get into a class that had a maximum enrollment of thirty-five. I needed to siphon out the students who weren't serious or thought it was one of those automatic A courses, so I declared that no student could get in without a personal interview with me.

I was about two weeks into the glorious madness, and just back from having flown to do two major Chicago TV talk shows, when my phone rang one afternoon. The entire conversation is inked into my head like some giant word balloon.

"Is this Mike Uslan?" an enthusiastic male voice boomed.

"Uh, yes," I murmured, not sure whether I was talking to someone in the media or another one of the nut-jobs coming out of the woodwork as fast as the reporters were.

"Hiya, Mike! This is Stan Lee from Marvel Comics in New York!" he declared.

Stan Lee! My god! My idol! Co-creator of the pantheon of Marvel Superheroes!

I call this my "Burning Bush" moment.

"Mike, everywhere I turn, I'm seeing you on TV or reading about you in a magazine! What you're doing is just great for the entire comic book industry! How can I be helpful?" asked Stan the Man.

By the end of the conversation, Stan had agreed to ship me lots of comic books that would be applicable to my course and to send me two guest speakers for the class. Wow! (Which, to be clear, has nothing to do with the campy connotations of "Pow!")

Two hours later, my phone rang again. A monotone adult voice that sounded very much like a real businessman asked me if I was me. I assured him I was.

"Mr. Uslan, my name is Sol Harrison, Vice President of DC Comics in New York. We publish *Superman, Wonder Woman—*"

"And *Batman!*" I cut him off, and knew that was an "oops!" and vowed to myself to shut up and let him do the talking. He did so.

"Our President, Carmine Infantino, and myself have listened to you quite a bit on the radio and read about you in a lot of newspapers, and we think what you're doing there at Indiana University is wonderful for the whole comic book industry. We'd like to meet an innovative young man like you and were wondering if we could fly you to New York to discuss ways we can work together?"

I can still remember my classic reply: "Uh . . . okay."

The next thing I knew, I was on a plane heading back east for my first visit to DC Comics' offices since that afternoon tour with the Comic Book Club when Julie Schwartz had taken me by the hand to show me a copy of *Flash Comics* #1.

Best of all, as the world's first college professor of a fully accredited course on comic books, I made it into *Ripley's Believe It Or Not!* My mother was so proud.

Christopher "Superman" Reeve with Sol Harrison, DC Comics' eventual president, who worked on the color separations for the cover of America's first official comic book, and in 1972 mentored me at DC Comics and in the comic book industry, putting me on the road to write Batman comic books as well as bring a dark and serious Batman to the silver screen.

The *Ripley's Believe It Or Not!* cartoon panel got the date wrong by a good five years: My course was originally taught from 1972 to 1973.

# CHAPTER TWELVE

# I WAS A TEENAGE JUNIOR WOODCHUCK!

There I was, being flown to New York to meet the heads of DC Comics! I couldn't have been more excited! To make it all just perfect, I had traded in my first-class ticket for two coach tickets so that I could take along my girlfriend, Nancy, whom I met and fell in love with on our first day of college at I.U. (She wasn't even unpacked when we met. Literally, as her parents were pulling out of her dorm's parking lot after dropping her off, I was walking up that driveway.) She'd be great to have with me. She was personable and had a killer smile and knew all the right things to say . . . except . . . every once in awhile, her brain would momentarily short-circuit until she'd apply invisible duct tape, and then everything would be back to normal. For example, some famous family quotes from Nancy: "Imagine his shock the next day when he woke up and realized he was dead!" Now she knew and I knew that she was talking about a man's reaction to the passing of his old dog, but to those around us, it was incomprehensible. Or the time she called the president of DC Comics, the legendary Paul Levitz, to ask if he could arrange for an original Batman drawing to be sent to the very ill child of a friend. What she MEANT to say on Paul's voicemail was, "Hi, Paul. I wonder if you can help me? I have a friend whose son is a HUGE Batman fan . . ." But what came out was, "Hi, Paul. I wonder if you can help me? I have a friend whose son is a HUGE fat man." She hung up. Paul still hasn't recovered. For better or for worse, she was coming along to my first meeting with the heads of DC.

It was one of those rare days in the early '70s when I wore a jacket and tie. Sol Harrison, DC's vice president, could not have been warmer or kinder. He was a deep believer in the potential for comic books to be utilized in education. One of the pet projects he wanted me to work with him on was called Edu-Graphics—using Batman, Superman, and Wonder Woman in a series of specially prepared comic books to motivate students to read and then teach them to read with controlled-vocabulary comic book stories that introduced one new word on each page. The pictures reinforced the text. An illustrated glossary at the back of the comic complemented the efforts. These Edu-Graphics were being designed to target two groups: English-as-a-second-language students and what, at that time, were referred to as brain-injured children. Sol took Nancy and me to lunch at a fancy New York restaurant and told us that he and his wife, Gert, had a brain-injured child and had dedicated their lives to helping these children and raising money for all medical research and care efforts. He informed us that the old terms such as "retarded" or "slow" were no longer considered proper and that the new terminology was "brain-injured." Sol and Gert had started the wonderful summer camp called Camp Harrison as a special place these kids could go to enjoy their summers with the proper attention and care. It was a side of Sol that few people in the business ever knew. Sol's silent compassion was carried on by the later heads of DC Comics, with Paul Levitz's behind-the-scenes help for struggling, aging, and ill artists, writers, and editors who were facing huge challenges and crises in their lives. Paul also organized and ran beautiful and dignified memorials for those DC talents who passed on, creating a sense of comfort and joy for their bereaved families and coworkers.

And so, after this magical lunch, Sol took Nancy and me back to DC Comics to go over the details of the job they were offering me. My DC job would involve summers working at their offices in NY, while they would pay me a weekly retainer for my services while I was still in school at Indiana. This was it! The biggest moment of my life since that policeman drove away with my brother when I was five! Sol opened the big hall closet for me to hang up Nancy's coat. I put it on a hanger, and it slid right off onto the floor. I reached down into the big closet and picked it up and placed it over the hanger again. I went to hang it up, and her coat slipped off a second time and onto the floor. As I bent down in that dark closet again to fetch the elusive coat, it happened. Sol said something politely innocuous like, "Having trouble?" And that's when Nancy chose to short-circuit. She smiled at Sol, rolled her eyes, and then the words came out. "Oy! I'm dating a RE-tard!"

"Oh, nononononononono . . .," went through my head like a locomotive. I froze, bent over in that big, dark closet, never ever wanting to leave. How could I ever come back now and face him? This can't be happening! I'm in a dark, safe place . . .

Sol was kind and dearly sympathetic. Without the slightest hint of being upset, he smiled and corrected my girlfriend, "No, Nancy, you're dating a brain-injured fellow," he chuckled. I almost chucked. Nancy's face changed back from horrified red to normal tan.

That is the way that, in 1972, DC began hiring real fanboys, whom they could train and develop into the next generation of DC executives, editors, production managers, colorists, production artists, and writers. We were all young and bubbling over with enthusiasm and feeling like we were the luckiest souls on earth to be working at DC Comics. Besides me (reporting directly to VP Sol Harrison), there was Paul Levitz (who was already writing and serving as editor Joe Orlando's assistant), Allan Asherman (editor/writer Denny O'Neil's assistant), Jack Harris (editor Murray Boltinoff's assistant), Guy Lillian the 63rd (or some number I've forgotten), Carl Gafford, Tony Tollin, Steve Mitchell, and Bob Rozakis (editor Julie Schwartz's assistant and a walking, talking mainframe computer with total knowledge of everything). We were the first of the baby boomers, coming in after an earlier generation of comic book fans were given assignments as writers or artists, and who eventually went on to become top talent like the famed Roy Thomas, Len Wein, Marv Wolfman, Gerry Conway, and Marty Pasko. The "grown-ups" at DC needed something to collectively call the whole lot of us. I'm not sure, but it may have been DC's resident comic book junkie, E. Nelson Bridwell, who borrowed the club name coined by the famous cartoonist Carl Barks in forming a group for Donald Duck's nephews, Huey, Dewey, and Louie, the "Junior Woodchucks." The name stuck. Suddenly, as if I were starring in a '50s horror movie, I was a teenage Woodchuck!

We were all friends. We worked together, had lunch together, hung out together, laughed together, hotly debated hot comic book topics together, shook our heads together over corporate decisions that were being made for reasons we couldn't fathom, cheered every company move we knew in our unified gut would be well received by our fellow fans, and planned sleep-over party weekends for all of us and whatever significant others there were at the time, with my Nancy, Bob's Laurie, and Jack's Kelly leading those femmes fatales. We were as bound as our comic book collections.

My path was becoming clearer and clearer to me! When a door opened that might further my efforts to make a lifetime career out of my passion for comic books . . . even slightly . . . I had to, without hesitation, stick my foot in that door. One foot in front of the other, one open door at a time, might just make it possible to make my dreams come true. If starting out, I had made it my goal to bring the real, dark and serious Batman I loved to the silver screen, I may as well have declared, "One day, I want to jump across the Grand Canyon!" Impossible! The chasm was too far to leap over. But at first I had a slightly more modest goal in mind. My parents knew, and Mrs. Stiller and Mrs. Friedman knew, and Bobby, Barry, Marc, Paul, and Nancy knew that my dream since I was eight years old was to write Batman comics. He was my one true superhero. It was that "being human" thing. When I was eight, in my heart of hearts, I believed that if I studied really hard and worked out really hard, and if my dad bought me a cool car, I could BE this guy! Short of that, I would write Batman comics someday. And here I was, with my foot wedged firmly in the door to the Bat-Cave.

The three big projects I was involved in at DC included working with Sol, a team of researchers from Harvard's Graduate School of Education, and Fred Cahill, a Warner Communications executive. Warner Communications had been a funeral parlor company that acquired Kinney Service, which owned tons of parking garages in New York, and Kinney Service had acquired DC Comics when it was an independent company on the New York Stock Exchange. (And I immediately bought two whole shares of the company so that I could be an owner, and then quickly wrote a letter to the editor of *Wonder Woman* comics, throwing my weight around as such and telling him what to do. That letter was actually published by editor Robert Kanigher in *Wonder Woman* #161 with a follow-up letter in #165.) The plan for the public offering on the NYSE was the cause of the name change to National Periodical Publications from National Comics. After all, they thought, what investor in his right mind would sink his money into shares of a comic book company as opposed to a "Periodical Publications" publisher?*

Our plan was to sell Edu-Graphics to the New York City Board of Education as a supplemental reading program, along with beautifully rendered bulletin board displays and filmstrips. Meanwhile, Sol started sending me out to national teachers' conventions to staff a DC Edu-Graphics booth and to lecture and make presentations to teachers and school administrators.

Sol and I, along with Fred Cahill, went in and appeared before the New York City Board of Education for what would be the second "pitch" of my budding career. And we sold them on our Edu-Graphics program! Comic books had just officially become a teaching tool in schools!

The second pet project Sol had in store for me at DC was what everyone there considered to be his "Fulton's Folly" . . . the Comicmobile. By the early '70s, Comic Book distribution was deteriorating everywhere. Its forty-year mainstay, mom-and-pop candy stores and corner drugstores, were vanishing from the changing American landscape. Those remaining had only limited rack space for comic books and magazines. They cut down on or stopped displaying comic books. It no longer made economic sense for them. In the limited space they had, why sell a comic for 15 cents or 20 cents or even 25 cents if that same space could be occupied by a $1.50 *Time* magazine or a $2.95

*For great stories about the secrets behind the companies jockeying for control of National, check out Gerard Jones's eye-opening book *Men of Tomorrow*, the true story behind *The Amazing Adventures of Kavalier & Clay*, Michael Chabon's Pulitzer Prize–winning novel about the birth and growth of the comic book industry, and ongoing issues of Roy Thomas's *Alter Ego* magazine, which documents the history of comic books.

*Playboy?* 7-11 had become a lifeline for comic book distribution, but out-of-the-box thinking was required. DC tried selling comics in packets of three at big discount stores like Woolco, K-Mart, and Wal-Mart. They invented comic book vending machines and tested them out in such places as Maryland rest stops on I-95 toward Washington, D.C. I stumbled across one of these machines when I was ten and my folks were taking me and Paul to the nation's capital for the celebration of the Civil War Centennial. I marveled at the find. I stared at it as if I were at the first demonstration of the telephone or movie projector or phonograph. I already had every comic book in that machine, but I hit up Dad for a dime and watched as my duplicate copy of *Superman* #149 slowly tumbled out and into my hands.

Known internally as "Solly's Folly," The Comicmobile was Sol Harrison's experiment with new ways to distribute comic books to kids. I drove it up and down the Jersey Shore in the summer of '73 and learned much about why kids buy which comic books!

The Comicmobile was Sol Harrison's brainchild to revolutionize comic book distribution and gather critical market research from readers in the process. It was a big van painted with the DC comic book characters and logo. I was to spend the bulk of my summer driving it around the beach communities of the Jersey Shore, ringing my bell as I traversed street after street, park after park, and beach after beach, selling comic books from my truck the same way the Good Humor Man sold his ice cream. But I needed what to any normal person would be "help" or an assistant, but to me, being me, was a "sidekick." I found mine and, of course, her name was "Robin!" Robin Burke had been a year behind me at O.T.H.S. but was a very bright, very pretty, very talented writer in her own right, and one of the few females during my college years not to judge me for my comic book habit.

We sold tons of comic books that summer and spoke to all our customers, learning that kids selected comic books for, first, the covers, and second, the titles. They preferred green monsters to any other color. They liked their monsters best when they were giant-size versions of smaller animals like rats, insects, and spiders. They liked dinosaurs and gorillas. They thought the word *weird* in a title was far spookier than *chilling* or *unexpected*. They loved seeing Batman team up with the robot group known as the Metal Men or with that cool retro Bill Finger–Irwin Hasen creation, Wildcat. They didn't seem to really know that *Action Comics* featured Superman or that *Detective Comics* featured Batman. The names Lois Lane, Jimmy Olsen, and Supergirl were not as appealing as that mainstay name, Superman.

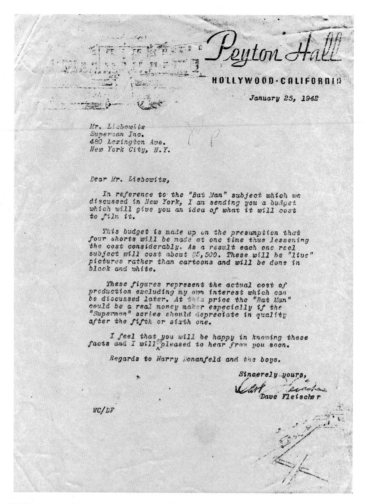

While attempting to restore order to the corporate history of DC Comics by cleaning out "The Closet," I stumbled across the plans of Max Fleischer and his brother Dave to follow-up their immortal *Superman* cartoons with "Bat Man"! Oh, but what might have been had World War II not disrupted their plans!

When I left the Jersey Shore to head back to school at Indiana, Bob Rozakis took over the Comicmobile and headed for the wilds of Planet Long Island. His experiences there mirrored mine. We wrote up a huge market research report for DC President Carmine Infantino and Vice President Sol Harrison. As a result, lots more green monsters and giant animals and insects soon showed up on covers, along with assorted dinosaurs and DC's continuing tradition of gorillas. *Weird* started popping up on DC books with *Weird Mystery*, *Weird Western*, *Weird Worlds*, *Weird Adventure*, *Weird War Tales*, but mercifully stopping just short of *Weird Romance*. The Metal Men and Wildcat returned again and again to the pages of *Brave & Bold* with its Batman team-up stories. In ads and on comic book covers, new readers were cued that it was "*Superman's Action Comics*" and "*Batman's Detective Comics*." The individual comic book titles of *Lois Lane*, *Jimmy Olsen*, and *Supergirl* were combined into one big comic book called *The Superman Family*. As always, Batman imitated it with his own new book, *The Batman Family*.

I designed ads for these comic books based on the title of the then-hit TV series, making them "All in the (DC) Family." DC liked that, and gave me the okay to make up other comic book ads. I made up one heralding their superhero line and their mystery line, and introducing their new adventure line of comic books. That ad was resurrected decades later to introduce DC's newest comic books in 2009.

Another thing I suggested to Sol was a new DC logo that would evoke the familiar one I grew up with, but would tout DC's new slogan, "The Line of Super-Stars." So I drew the classic concentric circles every fan knew with the initials DC in the center circle. Instead of dots on each side, I put little stars. Then I replaced the word *Superman* in the top arc with the words *The Line of* and replaced the words *National Comics* in the bottom arc with the words *Super-Stars*. Sol polished it up and it became DC's new logo, and I was as proud as I could be!

One of the stranger projects Sol planned for me was "The Closet." This was the deep, never opened, "Fibber McGee"–type Closet in between the offices of President Carmine Infantino and Consultant William M. Gaines, who just happened to be the Bill Gaines who published *MAD* magazine and all those great horror comics of the 1950s like *Tales from the Crypt*! Sol wanted me to clean out that Closet, inventory what the hell was in there, put it in some sort of order, and show him anything unusual or special I might stumble across. Fair enough. I slowly unlocked the Closet door and was probably the first person to flip on the light since 1967. Remember the last scene of *Raiders of the Lost Ark* when the Ark of the Covenant is put in a secret government warehouse the size of Utah? THAT was this! And now . . . it was all mine!

It was a disheveled, chaotic, ignored, abandoned history of DC Comics dating back to Day One. As I sifted through George Reeves's Superman costume from the years the series was shot in color to Adam West's Batman costume from 1966, and all the scrapbooks put together by DC's attorney Louis Nizer for their no-holds-barred 1940 through 1953 lawsuit against Captain Marvel, I knew I had struck comic book gold! Corporate records and sales figures and contracts and correspondence littered the place. I pulled Sol in to see what I found in the first ten minutes. He couldn't believe it! I asked him if, as a comic book historian who had written the world's first textbook on comic books for Indiana University, I might be permitted to make notes on what I uncovered from the history of the company; he gave me a blanket okay. I found: the original bankruptcy papers of DC founder, Major Malcolm Wheeler-Nicholson; the curious legal papers setting up a receiver, and the aging pieces of correspondence and assorted legal documents that demonstrated that the Major had had no choice but to sell his company to his printer, Harry Donnenfeld; the in-house DC censorship code predating the formation of the Comics Code Authority; the sales figures for the earliest issues of *Action Comics* and *Superman*; legal cease and desist letters and legal files regarding Archie Comics' *The Double Life of Private Strong* by Joe Simon and Jack Kirby (whose character The Shield was alleged to infringe on Superman), Fox's Wonder Man, Fawcett's Master Man, a barely known character being called Superwoman, and more.

As days turned into weeks, I kept digging up treasure. I found: the documentation of Max Fleischer's 1942 series for what was to be black and white Bat-Man films to follow up his startling, phenomenal Superman cartoons, a Bat-project killed by the advent of World War II; the early 1940s script for the first Superman cartoon, including last-minute hand-written changes; and, most amazing of all, a pile of the strangest comic books I had ever seen and never heard of! They were called "ash-cans." These were mock-ups put together at DC in the '30s through the '50s whenever they were thinking of publishing a new comic book title and didn't want to get beaten to the punch by another publisher. To be able to trademark the title and logo, they had to prove it was used in interstate commerce, so they would make up a few dummy copies with the new title logo on it and mail them to a few employees to secure the title. For a brief moment, I had in my hands such one-of-a-kind gems as pre-1938 *Action Comics*, *Double-Action Comics*, *Action Funnies*, and a dozen more! Sol scooped them up to lock them in his desk drawer for safekeeping as he encouraged me to keep going. Treasures! Treasures! And MORE treasures! As we said back in Indiana, I was in "pig heaven"!

The day soon came when Carmine and Sol let us loose! The Junior Woodchucks were to conceive, plan, design, write, lay out, and produce an official DC fanzine of the highest quality, called *The Amazing World of DC Comics*. And, by God, we did it! Those seventeen magical issues, very rare today, showcased the best of DC—its artists, writers, editors, characters, innovations, and history. We all loved learning about or uncovering the history, and I took every opportunity to sit at lunch with Sol and his best friend and production chief and colorist, Jack Adler, and listen to all their fun, funny, outrageous stories from the birth of the comic book industry. (Sol had been the color separator on the first issue of the first real comic book, *Famous Funnies* #1.) The stories ranged from behind-the-scenes shocking incidents involving the legendary figures who started the various comic book companies to untold tales of shit going on behind the scenes even then in the '70s! One day, I stopped the already-ancient Ira Schnapp when he came up to the offices. He had been a letterer and logo designer beginning in the '30s. He showed me how he took artist Joe Shuster's crude Superman title and turned it into the trademark the world knows and recognizes today. Ira had designed most of DC's logos from the '30s to '60s, but his favorite work was the lettering carved just above the great New York City Post Office behind Madison Square Garden and Penn Station on Eighth Avenue at 33rd Street. I loved senior staffer Gerta Gattel, a tiny yet feisty and brilliant and compassionate lady my grandma's age, who had the keys to the DC Library . . . that vault housing every comic book the company ever published from *New Fun Comics* #1 to the day's releases. This was the top of Mt. Sinai for a comic book fan! This was where Julie Schwartz got that bound volume of *Flash Comics* so he could show me that first issue when I was touring DC at age thirteen. Appreciating my love for comic book history, Gerta allowed me to sit in the library during half of my lunch hour every day so I could start reading every comic book DC ever published. If it hadn't been for the fact that I also cared about my parents, my girlfriend, and my friends, I think I'd still be sitting there today. In fact, Allan Asherman is the lucky Junior Woodchuck who inherited Gerta's job when she retired and, according to my calculations, should just about now be completing his reading of every DC comic from 1935 to 1986 and be well on his way to reading every DC comic book ever, while I ultimately ran out of time and headed back home again to Indiana.

Freshman year at I.U. and I meet the girl of my dreams the first day! For the next four years, everyone I knew kept telling me "You DON'T fall in love with the first girl you set your eyes on in college!"

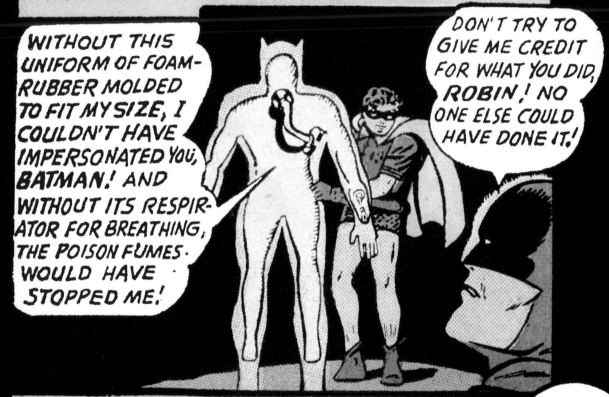

# PLAN B.
# A *STRANGE* COSTUME FOR
# BATMAN AND ROBIN,
# A *STRANGE* CHOICE FOR ME!

Bloomington in the early '70s was paradise. It was doing far better than my poor childhood field of dreams known as Asbury Park. Riots erupted there in the summer of 1970, and it took forty years just to get the old girl back up on her feet. Today, Asbury has done what every great comic book hero has done. Like The Batman, Superman, Captain America, Green Lantern, and the Flash, it has come back from the dead for some new glory days, with its famed boardwalk reviving classic pinball machines that once again scream to me and all my old buddies, "Greetings from Asbury Park, NJ!" Bloomington, on the other hand, has never faded. The campus is one of the very prettiest in America. The landscaping is breathtaking. Many of the buildings are classically covered in ivy. Whenever a building downtown or on bustling, vibrant Kirkwood Avenue is vacated,

LEFT: Batman and Robin already knew! I had to learn the hard way in life. ALWAYS have an emergency Plan "B"! And a Plan "C," "D," and "E" if possible!

Me in my senior year at I.U. while teaching the comic book course.

the next great new restaurant, store, or bar pops up. Three things were the focus of my waning days at I.U. First was my comic book course, of course. Sol Harrison and Stan "the Man" Lee kept their words and sent me guest lecturers. DC's contribution came in the form of Denny O'Neil, the award-winning writer who had helped return The Batman to his dark and mysterious roots in the comics and who had ushered comics into the age of social relevance by making the villains in his stories not just a bunch of costumed crazies, but such issues as pollution, overpopulation, corrupt politicians, deprivation of civil rights, deprivation of women's rights, and other burning problems of the day. Denny and I would wind up becoming friends after his visit to Bloomington. He wrote up my course for a terrific article for *Penthouse* and played a key role in the next step on my path to Hollywood. The two lecturers from Marvel were Hoosier native Steve Engelhart and Gerry Conway. Steve took cosmic philosophies, religious allusions, and science fiction concepts and melded them together into the most mind-blowing stories for a generation of college students. With him, we read the comic book adventures of Dr. Strange as he confronted life, death, the meaning of both, and God himself, along the way finding Eternity. Among his many accomplishments, Gerry had created the Punisher and killed off Spider-Man's love, Gwen Stacy. The TV cameras and reporters came back to my classroom to cover the comic book pros who, Stan Lee aside, were perhaps the first comic book writers to lecture in a college class.

But my college days were not all about comic books. The second focal point in my senior year at I.U. had actually begun the year before and was my other passion—a torch I'd been carrying since my brother had first come home with some new 45 rpm records to play on the family Victrola: "Hound Dog" (flipside "Don't Be Cruel") and "Blue Suede Shoes." I was totally into rock 'n' roll, fueled by my Jersey Shore friend Steve Huntington, who was the walking encyclopedia of rock (and went on to become the voice of Radio Margaritaville). With a collection of a thousand 45s, largely stolen from my brother, I brought the world of "oldies" to the Sammy House. My fraternity brother Larry Hoffman had recently started working at the campus radio station, WIUS. He was doing newscasts, but was desperate to break into disc jockeying. So . . . we plotted an off-the-wall, free-spirited, free-wheeling oldies show that would not only feature music from the '50s and pre-Beatles '60s, but would also showcase our zany writing, acting, and producing talents as we prepared, with music and sound effects, all sorts of fake commercials and elaborate audio comedy sketches plus ad-libbed humor that would test the boundaries of campus radio rules and regulations . . . and there were plenty of those. But this was the early '70s, man! As I've said, a time of great experimentation on college campuses. The head honcho of WIUS told us we were nuts and that the station had a rigid format that had to be followed . . . no deviation. But he didn't know that we were deviants at heart. And so we waited . . . until finals week of my junior year when most of the station's DJs quit to study and take their tests. We made our play. The station manager needed someone on the air with programming to accommodate all the pre-sold advertising that needed to run. He gave us a 9 P.M. to midnight time slot on Thursday night of finals week. And we turned college radio on its head.

People who listened to us back then claim that what we did was *Saturday Night Live* on the radio, years before there was a *Saturday Night Live*. Aping Dick Clark, we named the show *Bloomington Bandstand*. We played up to twenty songs an hour, told anecdotes about the records and the artists, broadcast our comedy bits, and started a service called Date Board, where students devoid of a date for the weekend would call us and give their phone number, their first name, and one adjective that best described them (e.g., "Sexy" Sue, "Studly" Steve, "Uncontrollable" Eunice).

The overnight popularity of *Bloomington Bandstand* and the unparalleled positive feedback from students and sponsors spurred the station management to give us a weekly show.

Denny O'Neil ... Superman and Green Lantern owe him much    ids/Dennis Kagan

# Holy Comics!
## Course a national celebrity

By LeAnn Spencer
ids Staff Writer

What started out as one of the more unusual J-Course seminars has turned into a nationally-publicized course with a taped segment scheduled for showing on WMAQ, Chicago, later this week.

The course, The Comic Book in Society, J213, is an outgrowth of last semester's one credit course. Mike Uslan, junior, this semester's coordinator for the now two-hour course, said the major difference is the social orientation of this semester's course.

The first publicity on the course was an article in The Daily Student,

International (UPI) interview with Bruce J. Gilley, of the Indianapolis UPI office. Gilley's story appeared in local newspapers including the Bloomington Herald-Telephone and the Indianapolis News, Jan. 21.

WISH-TV, Indianapolis, filmed the class and Uslan's collection of comic books.

In two days Uslan's 10,000 comics and I.U.'s Foster Project seminar's story had traveled over UPI and Associated Press wires all over the country.

The phone calls became more frequent and more frequently long distance.

Calls for interviews — some taped some live — came from eight

network asked Uslan if the course could possibly be offered by correspondence next fall.

Publishers in the comic book world soon heard about Uslan and his class. Stan Lee, writer and editor for Marvel Comics, called Tuesday to personally congratulate Uslan on his course and discuss trends in the comic book industry.

DC Comics called and offered to help Uslan in any way they could with his course this semester. The result of that offer was the arrival of Denny O'Neil, writer and creator of Green Lantern and Green Arrow at Wednesday's class (see related story, below).

Uslan said "One more call from

Denny O'Neil, one of the great comic book writers of all time, becomes the first guest lecturer in my comic book course at Indiana University! Denny wrote the landmark *Green Lantern/Green Arrow* series, the Shadow, Superman, Justice League, Captain Marvel, and, with artist Neal Adams and editor Julius Schwartz, returned Batman to his dark roots in the comics. That's me sitting at the table on the right, with Nancy looking on.

And things only got wilder after that. Larry and I started appearing in person on campus, running dorm and fraternity 1950s sockhop parties while broadcasting live. When Larry graduated that year, my college roomie, Marc Caplan, stepped in to become my new DJ partner. It was business major Marc (whose frat nickname was "Used Car Salesman") who realized we could DJ dances all over and charge for our personal appearances. We started to run sockhops by riding up on motorcycles wearing black leather jackets and chains, sunglasses, and greased-back ducktail haircuts.

Marc marketed the hell out of us and the popularity of the radio show, nailing a TV pilot deal and, in the process, upping our price per campus dance to $300 (and that's in early-1970s dollars!). Typically, he'd book us each weekend for one or sometimes two dances. The large amount of money coming in led me to the third defining factor in the last semester of my senior year. This falls into that category of "What was I thinking?!?" I graduated from college in three and a half years. In December of my senior year, I was done. No more credit hours needed. No more classes. No more courses. Done. I completed all the requirements except one ... I never told my parents. I was afraid that they might make me come home or start working or do something equally heinous. By

The original *Bloomington Bandstand* rock 'n' roll oldies DJs, me (center), Larry Hoffman (right; later replaced by Marc Caplan), and radio newsman Eric Heckman (left).

this time, I had stopped accepting money from them for college, as I was rolling in it from *Bandstand* plus what I was making from writing the comic book textbooks for I.U., from teaching the students who enrolled in my course through correspondence, and from my retainer from DC Comics. So it wasn't like I was being a cad. In fact, the only thing different now was that my weekends in Bloomington began every single week on Friday night, and ended every single week on Friday afternoon. My time was spent teaching comics, DJing, hanging with Nancy and with my friends, performing at dances, and one other thing. . . .

Every Friday during my senior year, armed with a yellow pad and pen, I went to the I.U. library, and read *Variety* magazine, the weekly bible for the motion picture, television, and theater industries. I would thumb through every article in search of names of studio executives, agents, producers, and TV programmers, plus the companies they were with. By the end of that semester, I had amassed a list of 372 names. The reason? I wanted to be able to apply for jobs to actual, real, individuals and not just send my resume out to "Human Resources" or "To Whom It May Concern." And so I sat down and started typing out 372 cover letters on my dear old Underwood-Olivetti typewriter. Now, for those of you under the age of forty, a typewriter is a mechanical device a little larger than a keyboard, upon which I would type out—oh, just look for it the next time you visit a museum. You'll see a typewriter there . . . right next to the VCR.

The fastest two-finger typist alive, I banged out all my cover letters, and off they went to Los Angeles and New York. Trying to cover every possible base to get a job in the movie biz, as the then-Prior of the Sammy Fraternity House, I also called the head of our national Sigma Alpha Mu organization, whom I had gotten to know well and admired greatly. He was a swell guy based in Indianapolis by the name of Bill Schwartz. I asked Bill if there were any Sammies in top positions in the motion picture or television industries. He informed me that the president of Universal Pictures was a fraternity brother. I asked him if they had freshman frat applications going back to his era. He said they did. I asked him if he would read this man's to me. He dug it out and called me back a few days later. I took notes on any course, activity, and interest he had that I also had in high school or college. I then attempted to write him a killer cover letter set up almost as a psychological profile of the man. What did I have to lose? I knew nobody in Hollywood. I had no relatives in Hollywood. I didn't come from money so couldn't buy my way into Hollywood. Ten days later, I got a letter back from one of the Universal Prez's Sammy fraters who was then working for him in Universal's publishing division. This man said that Universal's topper had told him to reach out to me and see how they could be helpful. Wow!

That incident made it clear to me that what I had to do was get up off my ass and try to make something happen. I started knocking on every door I could think of. What I didn't yet know was that it wouldn't be long before every one of them would slam in my face. This is the one and only guarantee I can make. In your journey through life, I PROMISE you that doors will slam in your face. So what do you do about it when it happens? I found out I really had only two choices. I could go home and cry about it . . . or . . . I could pick myself up, dust myself off, then go back and knock again . . . and knock again . . . and knock again . . . until my knuckles started to bleed. I didn't know any other way to succeed in making my dreams come true. The dark, serious Batman movies I dreamed of were to be created on a foundation of my own bloody knuckles.

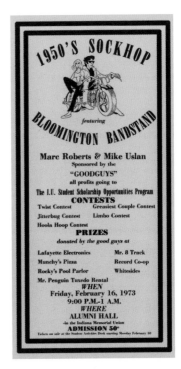

Marc Caplan figured out how to monetize the *Bloomington Bandstand* radio show via live campus sock hops!

I had done very well in college and expected to find someone who would be interested in hiring a creative young man to write movies or cartoons or write for TV and just be all-around "creative." Fat chance. I received two job offers from the 372 resumes I sent out. A top New York talent agency told me I'd make a good agent and that this would open the Hollywood and New York entertainment industry to me. They asked if I'd like to join their agent training program . . . a five-year process to become an agent that would start me in the mailroom for the first two years at $95 per week, before becoming a secretary/assistant, before . . . maybe . . . becoming an agent. Then an important producer of many of the big disaster movies at Universal thought I'd make a good production assistant and suggested I move to L.A. where he'd have me Xerox scripts and go for coffee for $95 per week. I passed on both offers for two good reasons. Number one, I would have starved trying to live in New York City or L.A. on $95 a week. Number two, I had decided to get married. How on earth would I be able to support a wife? What the hell was I going to do? Feeling the comic book business might not be for me, yet having been turned down by 370 people for a creative job in the movie or TV industry, where could I turn? The Vietnam War draft was still on, limiting my choices severely unless I liked the idea of spending the rest of my life in Ottawa. At turning point times like this, the magic word is not "Shazam," but "Plan B!" Back in 1961, I had read all about Batman's emergency Plan B. I read it in one of the all-time greatest comic books ever, *Batman Annual #1*, but that big book merely reprinted it from *Detective Comics* #165, issued a year before I was even born. If something terrible happened to Batman, Robin was to slip into a strange, big costume that was Batman's size and would fit Robin in a Trojan Horse kind of way so he could pass himself off as the real adult Batman so that every crook in Gotham City wouldn't just pour out of the woodwork thinking Batman was disabled or dead. And what was the only way to tell if this was the real Batman or the dangerous Plan B Batman costume with Robin inside it? The chest symbol of the latter had the black silhouette of a robin rather than a bat. Sneaky. Cool. But I thought the red breast on the black robin was a dead giveaway. My version of that emergency plan was devoid of costumes, robins, or bats. My Plan B? I would go to law school.

Now, nobody said getting into law school would be easy . . . especially when I really did NOT want to go, but I just concocted this as a plan that MIGHT ultimately get me where I wanted to go. Amid LSAT review courses and deciding to propose to Nancy, I thought it might be fun to live in Washington, D.C., and go to law school there at Georgetown. So with my fellow law school contenders Cousin Brucie and Roomie Scott, the three caballeros headed to that "other" DC for interviews with an admissions officer at Georgetown Law School.

We got to Washington early enough in the day so that we could have our coat and tie interviews, but then in the car changed back into our torn jeans and torn T-shirts and got in a fast tour of the city. It was nearly 4 o'clock when we got to the Capitol and decided to squeeze in one last attraction for the day. But it was too late for that. The place was closing at 5 P.M. and we had only enough time left to run through it on our own. As we tore around the Capitol, I yelled to Scott and Bruce to keep moving and not to stop to look at anything! What a tour! Walking past an open door, I looked in and discovered an open meeting room of some sort with a lot of hubbub going on inside. I spied a big TV camera labeled "ABC" and lights being carried in and thick cable being run out a window to a truck below. Something BIG was happening in the Capitol, and I was really curious! I walked into the room and went over to one of the TV crewmen milling about and asked him what was going on. "It's the presidential campaign. You heard how Senator George McGovern's running mate, Senator Tom Eagleton, was discovered to have had some psychological problem and electroshock treatment?" the man asked. "Sure," I said. "It's screwing up any chance he has to beat Nixon," I moaned. "Well, tonight at 7:30 P.M., Senator McGovern is gonna broadcast an address live to the nation and he's gonna announce who he's picked to replace Eagleton on his ticket," he revealed. I pulled Scott and Bruce aside and told them we couldn't leave. This was history in the making and a chance for us to rub elbows with it and even meet my idol, Senator McGovern. While he was no Eugene McCarthy or Bobby Kennedy, he was a good man.

If I was generally risk-averse growing up, Scott was risk-less. Just pulling him away from his studies to play pinball was a daily challenge. He saw only the dangers and the consequences: "But what if we're caught?" "But what if the FBI busts us?" "Can't they send us to jail for trespassing in the Capitol after closing hours?" "How can we possibly pull this off?" "We're three college kids in jeans and T-shirts! How will anybody believe we're supposed to be here?" I calmed him down. "First, we ARE gonna do this! We're staying. We're meeting McGovern. And we're witnessing history tonight. Now, it's easy. We just act like we belong here. Let's make the ABC guys think we're with the Capitol's janitorial staff. Let's make the janitorial staff think we're McGovern workers. Half the people in his campaign look like hippies. Anyone else comes in, let 'em think we're with the TV guys. Fit in. Be cocky. We belong here! Let's do it!" I whispered. Bruce was pumped. He knew how to bullshit with the best of us. Scott, I think, was resigned to a future in prison. But since he was now resigned to it, he was cool and ready to give it a go.

At 5 P.M., the announcement reverberated around the Capitol. It was now closed. All visitors must exit immediately. You could tell that the lady on the intercom meant every word she was saying! The doors swung shut and, for better or for worse, there was no turning back. We helped move the chairs in and out of the room (literally!—in order to make us look both busy and official, we'd slowly move the chairs in, then would slowly carry them out . . . a bunch of times) for the TV guys until, without our acknowledging anything, they just assumed we were with the Capitol staff. Then the TV union guys had a dinner break. We had no food. Uh Oh! Just then, the Capitol's custodial staff showed up, surprised that most of their work had been done, and looked hard at us. So we sat closer to the TV guys, hoping the Capitol workers would think we were with them. I asked some of the ABC crew if they had any food to spare. They did, but said we should be pissed that the Capitol doesn't feed us better. Now the Capitol workers saw us eating with the TV crew and were sure we were part of that group. Already, it was 6:30 P.M. What a breeze! We were home free! Piece of cake!

Just then, four big Secret Service or FBI agents with little headsets entered the room. They pulled out handheld metal detectors and started going over the room with the proverbial fine-tooth comb. "We are so screwed!" I thought as I wondered if they'd take us to a local jail or to a federal prison for the night and started to picture what my one phone call to my mom was going to sound like. "Ma? Hi! Now don't get upset! I'm okay! I've got some good news and some bad news. The good news is I'm in Washington, D.C. for my interview at Georgetown Law School. The bad news is I'm being held in a federal prison. But don't worry! They're feeding me." No . . . I didn't think this would sit well with her.

It was now 7 P.M. Those agents were all over that room. But they apparently thought we were McGovern workers and never paid any attention to us. Everyone was convinced we were somebody else without our ever having said anything. In fact, the TV guys asked me to be McGovern's stand-in and sit in his chair while they adjusted the lighting. And then came the first round of serious, level one hubbub.*

*"Hubbub"? What the hell IS that, anyway? Gram used to use that term. Gram had the BEST expressions . . . very colorful and mostly in either Yiddish or Hungarian. When Paul was behaving his absolute worst, she used to say, "Choke a mega shecky." Paul always thought it

CONT.

At 7:15 P.M., in walked Senator McGovern. We shook his hand as he walked by us and said hello. He sat down at the desk set up for his speech, directly in front of the one "pooled" TV camera, courtesy of ABC. Makeup was touched up. Everything was checked out, and then in came the McGovern workers, led by a loud lady. She immediately took charge of everything, double-checked and triple-checked all details, looked over the place and everyone in it, then came walking by Scott, Bruce, and me standing just to the left of Senator McGovern's desk. "Who are YOU?" she said to Scott. He couldn't speak. She stared at Bruce. "And who are YOU?" she demanded. I quickly jumped in to divert the attention from Scott, who was mentally already serving his fourth year in prison. "Hi. Nice to meet you, I'm—" She cut me off so fast she shouldda got a ticket. "How are you here without a badge?!? EVERYBODY here has a badge! Where's your BADGE?!?" I started double-talking, fast-talking, but she kept cutting me off, refusing to allow the bullshit to start piling up. It was true. EVERYONE else the whole time had a lavaliere with an official badge on it. Not yours truly nor my pals, Moe and Larry. "We helped the Capitol janitorial staff move all the chairs in . . . and out . . . and—" "So you're telling me you're with the Capitol? Speak up!" she hissed in my face. "No, you didn't let me explain," I made up. "We've been assisting the ABC guys with the TV cables and—" "So you're with ABC?" she shrieked. "No, what I'm trying to tell you if you'd let me finish so you can understand that if what I'm telling you so you'll clearly know exactly—" And then she cut me off again and yelled for someone named Bob! Just then the TV guy yelled, "Twenty seconds to air!" and the Lady in My Face gurgled a gravelly, grating, "GREAT! JUST GREAT!" threw up her hands, and stormed over behind the cameraman and into obscurity.

As the TV guy yelled "5 . . . 4 . . . 3 . . . 2 . . ." I could hear my jail sentence dwindling away. I edged even closer to the front left corner of the Senator's desk, a hair off camera, just missing the little tiny bit of room I would have needed to lean over and wave, "Hi, Mom!"

A lovely picture of a lovely lady, none other than "Gram" Grandma Miriam Solomon, who came over from Hungary as the greatest cook in America or, for sure, in Bayonne, New Jersey!

meant, "Go sit down, darling." Years later, Uncle Phil told him it meant, "Kiss my ass!" in Hungarian. Then, when Paul did something awful and swore he'd never do it again so he could avoid a smack on his tush, she'd say something in Yiddish that to my young ears sounded like, *"Ich der bubba vega zayda, der zayda gezeida zuhndt."* Our dad eventually explained to us that she said, "If your grandmother had testicles, she'd be your grandfather." I pondered that when I was eight . . . until I was fifty-one. Now I think I get it. Last, when Paul and I were bored and could find nothing to do and no place to go, she'd either tell us to *"Hocken a chynick"* ("Go chop a teakettle," our mom said) or *"Gay cocken offen yom"* ("Go shit in the sea," translated Little Aunt Shirley).

Brucie and Scotty and I watched history unfold as George McGovern named Sargent Shriver as his new vice presidential running mate. When it was over, we had a chance to chat with the man running for president of the United States. We did make it quick. Not willing to tempt the gods any further before our escape route was blocked, we exited with some of the ABC workers out the TV guys' ladder at the window of the room, and bid adieu to the Capitol and Washington, D.C., as giddy as three little boys coming home from the circus they had just snuck into.

Bruce wound up going to Rutgers Law School and Scott went to Case Western Reserve. I held out. I wound up getting a postcard from Georgetown University Law School informing me I was on their waiting list and that they would be back in touch with further information soon. That was thirty-eight years ago, and I'm still waiting. But each day, I check my mailbox just in case the acceptance has finally arrived.

PART III:

# BLOOMINGTON TO HOLLYWOOD: HOW TO GET THERE FROM HERE!

# LIFE *Is Not a* COMIC BOOK!

I ended up attending Indiana University's School of Law in Bloomington, the same place Hoagy Carmichael went. And I don't care how old you are, shame on you if you don't know who he is. Do two things: Google him and then go and listen to the song "Stardust," one of the most perfect songs ever written. Hoagy was my inspiration. If he was a creative guy and went to law school anyway, I could stick it out and do the same. But just before law school started, I had one other thing to do . . . get married.

Nancy and I had a pending problem. We were going to be married, I was going to start law school, she was going to start nursing school, and we had no money. My DJing days were over, I had stopped teaching the correspondence course on comics, and DC ended my Indiana retainer, paying me only when I worked in their New York office in the summer. Student loans became mandatory and were secured at a 3 percent interest rate, but would require me to start repaying them after my first year at a budget-busting sum of $28.01 per month. This was on top of our already high monthly rent of $140 for a deluxe two-bedroom apartment on the perimeter of town (a sum that by the end of my three years of law school escalated to the lofty heights of $150 per month!). We got that new TV thing called cable. They charged us $5 a month, but the picture was now much better, and we got a new free channel that rotated a view of an outdoor thermometer, a clock, and a barometer. All at NO extra charge! What would they think of next? This was all just before the Arab oil embargo that sent the price of gas soaring to a dollar or more per gallon after it had stayed safely under the 39.9-cent mark for years. So what were we going to do to survive financially? In the very words of the Wizard of Oz, "You've forced me into a cataclysmic decision."

I sold 20,000 comic books from my collection. With that money, I bought an engagement ring and our wedding rings (from her Uncle Vic Youkilis, whose family begat Kevin Youkilis, All-Star for the Boston Red Sox—but as a die-hard Yankees fan, like my grandfather, father, brother, and son, I forgive them); took Nancy on a two and a half week honeymoon to London, Paris, and Rome; and then prepaid all three years' tuition at law school.

Our wedding was a memorable affair for all involved, the high point of which came when the rabbi scolded me, before two hundred guests as I was standing under the *chuppah*, because I read comic books.

The service started out lovely enough. There was no what-I-would-call "foreshadowing." Nancy's family had accepted me nicely (except for her Uncle Ned, who thought comic books were stupid, but had never read one). My family was there with my mom and dad with Gram and Aunt Clara and Uncle Phil in the very first row of the cavernous synagogue. Paul was my best man in what would mark the growing up and turning point in our relationship and place us on the road to becoming best friends as well as brothers.

There we were, Nancy and me, strains of "Sunrise, Sunset" wafting among the rafters, as we made our way up onto the elevated dais. The clock was approaching 7:20 P.M. as Rabbi Goldman turned to my wife-almost-nearly-to-be and, with a faceful of smile, beamed, "Nancy . . . I've known you since you were a little girl. Always happy, always friendly, always kind, a down-to-earth, salt-of-the-earth girl who made your parents, Morry and Anne, two wonderful, contributing temple members and community pillars, also salt-of-the-earth people, proud to be your parents. And today you've become a lovely young woman on the precipice of marriage." The rabbi turned to me, and suddenly his smile imploded into a black hole just under his nose. His tone was no longer warm and toasty. Now it was overdone and burnt. Suddenly he reminded me of someone. It took me a second to place him, but then I realized. Fredric Wertham! He looked like Dr. Wertham in a *yarmulke*! Jesus!

"And Michael . . . I don't know you as well. In fact, we just met yesterday in my office . . . ." He was referring to our preparatory meeting, during which I had been hung over from my bachelor party the night before, having thrown up for the eleventh time in the bushes just underneath the rabbi's office window as Nancy was dragging me in to meet him. But I was doing far better than my college roomie Brad, who had gotten so drunk at the Cincinnati strip joint The Tender Trap that he locked himself in the bathroom in the back and threw up. The two problems with that were: A) he had locked himself in the women's room; and B) he had passed out inside. They had to call an ambulance. Cops arrived with it and wound up unhooking the door from its hinges, extracting Brad, and putting him in a straitjacket when he struggled to keep them from taking him away. They took him to Cincinnati General's emergency room, where they gave him a powerful shot while leaving him strapped to a gurney in the hallway. Brad was out like a light for the duration.

But this next morning, I, meanwhile, had turned pure white or sea green (I can't remember which), as Nancy and I were ushered into the rabbi's office. I recall moving his trash can over with my foot so it would be between my legs if I started barfing during my meet and greet with the rabbi. Let's say no more about it except to state officially that the meeting did not go well. Now, in our actual marriage ceremony under the *chuppah*, the rabbi continued to talk at me.

". . . I know, Michael, you come from New Jersey, which has some lovely . . . gardens . . . thus it is called the Garden State. But Michael . . . a man does not spend his days reading and teaching comic books! (Uh oh! Oh, shit! Where was this going?!) A man must leave his childhood behind and become a responsible husband, father, and contributor to his community and his temple! (I turned around and looked at my mom in the front row. She looked like that bulldog in the Tom and Jerry cartoons who wears a red turtleneck sweatshirt and a brown bowler hat and has a cigar butt hanging out of the side of his mouth. I KNEW that look! Odds were now 79 percent she was going to get up out of her seat, march up on stage, and punch this guy in the chops! Nancy's mom was just as steaming and was already plotting to leave the temple the next week. I just looked at them and shrugged before turning back around to face my accuser and my final fate.)

"And so, always remember, Michael . . . life is NOT a comic book," Nancy's rabbi said to me, just before pronouncing us man and wife.

Later, when my brother was in his yoga phase, he would smile a lot (no more hitting!) and say, "Just turn it around, Mikey, and make it into your negative reinforcement!" It was the first time in my life my older brother didn't lie to me. He was positively right! My mom and dad, Mrs. Stiller, and Mrs. Friedman . . . they were the positive reinforcements in my life. But this rabbi, and many people like him, would be my negative reinforcement, prodding, pushing, and driving me forward in an "I'll show him!" endless burst of energy at the times I was low in my long journey.

The moment we returned from our honeymoon, law school started. I hated it. I didn't want to be there, it was all just a Plan B, but now I learned that with every Plan B comes pain. I resented that I could not just waltz into some great creative job in Hollywood, until I learned that there is no entitlement to anything. This seemed like a draw-back, until I realized that 90 percent of people seem to sit back and wait for life to come to them. They are the misguided entitled or simply the nonmotivated of the world. I repeated my mantra to myself over and over that if I'm willing to get up off my ass and cover every base and knock on every door, I can make something happen for me. I can make a closed door swing open. I can make my own "luck," I can make someone's "no" into the next person's "yes." Indiana University was a wonderful place to learn the lat-ter. To me, it was a place where a person never has to accept "no" as a final answer, but can try other means, other people, other methods, until someone somewhere in that giant little microcosm will say "yes." I took that with me when I left Bloomington for New York and Hollywood. It is a critical piece of my personal philosophy.

I quit law school four times in the first three weeks. The first legal catchphrase they taught us was "res ipsa loquitur," which means, in Latin, "The thing speaks for itself." Well, at the end of the first week, I came home to our bright, new apartment, walked right by Nancy, and threw all my books into the garbage can and shouted, "Res ipsa loquitur!" I was done. Without me knowing, Nancy quietly fished the books out of the garbage and hid them until she could talk me down over that weekend, convincing me to go back and give it another try. I was used to being an A student with relatively little effort . . . until I got to law school. I was now in a class with 199 other A students. SOME-BODY had to become the B, the C, the D, and the F students. There was an old adage floating around the school . . . "The A students make the law professors, the B students make the judges, and the C students make the money." If that was true, I would be mak-ing tons of money someday.

I despised the Socratic method, which was actually a recipe for mincemeat made out of first-year law students like me . . . especially me. It was a lose/lose situation. Even if I hit on a right answer, the professor would hammer me worse until he exposed flawed thinking and pounced. I quickly learned to disappear in such classes. There were two ways to do so. Way #1: This method I invented based on Chameleon Boy of the Legion of Super-Heroes. He could turn into anything and blend into any environment. Inspired, I always sat behind the biggest, burliest fellow I could find. Then I started wearing only black and white and gray so as not to attract the roving eye of the professor. I slouched a lot. Way #2: I based this method on yet another member of the Legion of Super-Heroes, Invisible Kid. I ditched some classes. More than some. My nickname quickly became the Phantom. (Kids! DO NOT TRY THIS AT HOME! That's a real disclaimer, everyone. It was a bad choice, but we all must live with our mistakes, eh?) I mean, what was I sup-posed to do when, on the first day of class, my "Commercial Transactions" prof began by saying in exactly the same monotone as Ben Stein, "Welcome to Commercial Transac-tions . . . sigh. . . . This course will be about as interesting as watching paint dry." By the end of the second class, he had me convinced, and I didn't go back again until the final. Instead, I just struggled on my own. My first problem was that I had never really studied previously except the night before a test, and that gimmick was now worthless. If I was to survive law school, I realized I had to learn self-discipline and sit at my desk for up to ten hours at a time and just concentrate and study. The trouble was, without even being aware of what I was doing, I was up looking out the windows, up watching TV, up having a snack, and up making instant coffee I could choke down to try to stay awake. I was everywhere but at my desk. I needed to do something to keep me in place. I took the belt off my bathrobe and used it to tie myself to my desk chair. I couldn't believe how often that caught me trying to bolt. Tied to a chair, I taught myself how to study. Being able to sit still and work was one of the three most important things I learned while in law school. It's a skill that serves me well every day, helped me become successful, and helped me accomplish a lot more than I thought I could.

For me, law school was a probably necessary and definitely painful means to an end. I planned to use my legal education to do something OTHER than be a lawyer. That did not sit well with a large chunk of my classmates, who judged that I was just taking up the space of someone who deserved to be there, who wanted to become a lawyer. To aggravate matters, I wanted to study everything I could having anything to do with entertainment or communications. Some of my classmates loved making fun of the crazy guy interested in entertainment who was enrolled in Bloomington, Indiana, instead of in some L.A. law school. After all, out of a class of two hundred, I was, indeed, the ONLY student expressing an interest in entertainment and communications. My theory was that if I couldn't get in the front door of the creative side of the entertainment industry, then I would focus on becoming an entertainment attorney and use that to get my foot in the motion picture industry door, network like mad, meet the power brokers of Hollywood and New York, and learn how movies are financed and produced and marketed. Then one day, I would sneak in the back door and write and produce movies, television, and animation. THAT was my fully strategized Plan B.

It worked.

But law school was not my biggest challenge. By my second year, Nancy was enrolled in nursing school and we were on exact opposite schedules and both under an absurd degree of stress. Nancy had to be at the hospital by 6 A.M. and was waking up about the same time I was going to bed after studying. The only time our paths really crossed was at dinner when we were both maxed out. It was not much better that first year with Nancy working long, long hours in a Bloomington doctor's office. Thus, four months into our marriage, although we had dated for most of the previous four years, there were lots of arguments and slamming doors and unhappiness with life. And one morning, Nancy decided she'd bolt to a motel and make a dramatic point as to the state of our young marriage. The trouble was, that day I didn't get home till 8 P.M. and had no idea that she had been gone all day. As I walked in the door of our apartment, the phone was ringing. It was Nancy to let me know where she was in case I was by now panicking. I did not let her know I didn't know she had gone. Instead I went for the jugular. Her weakness . . . both our weakness . . . was a Sicilian pepperoni pizza from Noble Roman's, a local Indiana franchise. I told her I had just ordered a large pie and it would be there in twenty minutes, so why not come back to share it with me and we'd just sit and talk things out. It worked! I couldn't believe it! But that didn't guarantee the marriage crisis was over. We talked for hours that night and arrived at the same conclusion. Our marriage was at a turning point. We had no kids, so it would be easy to walk away right at this moment. The hard choice would be to commit to our marriage in the belief we had something special that was worth fighting FOR. But if we were going to choose this option, we'd have to agree to work daily at our marriage the same way we'd work at a job. This was our most important job and needed to be approached like that. It was the right choice.

Nancy had huge stresses at school. Her hands were full as not only a nursing student, but also in her added role as the president of her nursing school class. She was in a year-round program connected to Ivy Tech and Bloomington Hospital that drew a lot of young women from small towns in central Indiana like Paoli, Spencer, Ellettsville, and Gnaw Bone. Her drama began when the class broke up into groups to research and present papers on the topic of how to treat people of different races and religions who are hospitalized under a nurse's care. When one group made their presentation about how to handle Jewish patients under their care, they painted a portrait of the most extreme orthodox person in existence. They had the nurses all taking notes on the need to use two different sets of dishes with these patients and how to pre-tear toilet paper because Jews didn't tear toilet paper from Friday evening to Saturday evening. That's when Nancy corrected them and set them straight—thirty-five small-town Indiana girls in the mid-'70s learned that the classmate they had elected as their president was a Jew. The next period was lunch, and when Nancy sat down to eat with a group of them, she knew something was different. No one was talking, and everyone was staring at her . . . at her head to be perfectly precise. Finally, Nancy called them on it. Embarrassed, they told her that they'd never actually seen a Jew before, but had heard of them. "I'll bet," said Nancy. "Okay . . . what do you want to know?" Slowly, uncomfortably, they helped each other work up the nerve to ask Nancy the one burning question they all had. "Nancy, can we see your horns?" they asked sheepishly. Nancy was thrown, but recovered before anyone realized the impact of their words. She then pulled apart and separated her curly hair so they could all conclusively see that, contrary to what their parents, grandparents, and ministers may have told them, Jews do not have horns. They not only took the shocking news in stride, but seemed relieved to see it for themselves. Like when Rick Jones learned in *The Incredible Hulk* #1 that the Hulk was really just mild-mannered scientist Bruce Banner, an otherwise normal guy. I still sometimes can't help thinking how much easier life would be if it were just like my comic books.

My wedding photo!

GANG WARS, DEPRESSION, AND CRIME--TIMES WHEN THE VIOLENCE OF EVIL WAS MET BY THE VIOLENCE OF GOOD... WHEN THE SELF-PROCLAIMED VIGILANTE OF DARKNESS, THE SHADOW, DEALT OUT HIS OWN BRAND OF JUSTICE ON...

"THE NIGHT OF THE FALLING DEATH!"

SCRIPT: MICHAEL USLAN
ART: FRANK ROBBINS &
FRANK McLAUGHLIN

I HEREBY CERTIFY THE FOLLOWING PAGES TO BE A TRUE RECORD. THE SHADOW.

# CHAPTER FIFTEEN

# I Know What EVIL LURKS IN THE HEARTS OF MEN!

The '70s meant college, Indiana, Nancy, Marc, the Sammy House and my frat brothers, wild U.S. trips, teaching comic books, writing my first books, working for DC Comics, having my first dream come true, DJing my own rock 'n' roll oldies and trivia radio show, performing live, getting married, my first tour of Europe, writing comic books, the return of the New York Yankees to glory, working in the motion picture industry, becoming a movie producer and writer, and assisting in my wife's first pregnancy, NOT necessarily in that order.

Well, if you think I was having a grand decade, you should've seen Batman in the '70s! It was a seminal and sensational decade for him, too. This was when he really began to revert back to his true, grittier nature after a pop spin in the '60s. In fact, when I make a list of my top twenty Batman stories of all time, NINE of 'em are from the '70s:

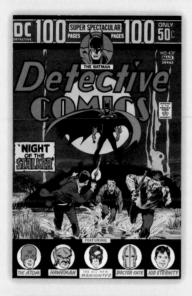

1. **Night of the Stalker** from *Detective Comics* #439, which I read over Thanksgiving 1973, I immediately pronounced to be the BEST Batman comic book story ever written, and since then, nothing has changed my mind. I made Tim Burton read it when we were pitching him to direct the 1989 *Batman*, and you'll see its influence in the opening sequence of the film. I bow before my comic book course guest lecturer Steve Engelhart, and Neal Adams and Sal Amendola, and Archie Goodwin, for this historic work—in which, by the way, there is NO dialogue. Batman says nothing. He doesn't have to. The emotional impact is intense.

2. **Night of the Reaper** from *Batman* #237, which came out around September 1971, became a hot topic in my comic book course about the impact comics could have on an audience and as hard evidence of their growing sophistication in theme and storytelling. This is a POWERFUL tale everyone should read, and it is courtesy of another of my comic book course guest lecturers, Denny O'Neil, and the magic that is Neal Adams.

3. **Robin Dies at Dawn** from 1963's *Batman* #156, which I read when I was twelve, is a Bill Finger, Shelly Moldoff, Charlie Paris opus that moved me to tears when I was a kid.

4. **The Laughing Fish,** a multi-parter starting in *Detective Comics* #475 in 1978, was one of my three most favorite Joker stories ever told, brought to us by the minds of Steve Engelhart and artist Marshall Rogers, who brought style to the Dark Knight.

5. *Batman* #1 from Spring 1940 qualifies in its entirety, but particularly for the very first Joker story (but don't ignore the nearly as great first Catwoman tale), courtesy of Bill Finger, Jerry Robinson, and Bob Kane.

6. **Daughter of the Demon** from 1971's *Batman* #232 kicked off the emergence of Ra's al Ghul and his daughter, Talia, giving us fans the greatest Batman villain created post–*Batman* TV show. From the typewriter and pencils and pens of Denny O'Neil (of course) and Neal Adams (who else?).

7. **The First Batman** from *Detective Comics* #235 in 1956 was one of the very earliest superhero comic books I ever read (or maybe mostly looked at the pictures), which also happened to be the issue that expanded and redefined the origin of Batman himself, making me feel as a new reader that I was getting on board the Batman saga on the ground floor, all thanks to Bill Finger, Shelly Moldoff, and Stan Kaye.

8. **Batman: Year One** took off in *Batman* #404 in 1987 from the talents of Frank Miller and David Mazzucchelli and was a huge influence on *Batman Begins*.

9. *The Dark Knight Returns*, in 1986, was a seminal graphic novel out of the fertile mind and artistry of Frank Miller, as he deconstructed Batman for a brand-new generation.

10. *Batman Annual* #1 from 1961! Manohmanohman!

11. *Detective Comics* #327 from 1964. Not one single story, but the whole look and feel of this entire comic book was just revolutionary and shocking. Gone was the artwork of Shelly Moldoff's Bob Kane, and arriving was next-generation artist Carmine Infantino. John Broome was the new writer. Batman's chest symbol suddenly had a yellow circle around it. The Batmobile overnight became a sports car. The Bat-Signal was ditched in favor of the Bat-Phone. Aunt Harriet arrived to live with Bruce Wayne and Dick Grayson. Batman held a GUN on a bad guy! What the—? And even the backup feature, "J'onn J'onzz, Manhunter from Mars," was given the boot from the book by the super-stretchy sleuth, the Elongated Man. (I have always wondered about those stretchy superheroes. If Elongated Man formed a group with Elastic Lad and Plastic Man, would they be called "the Rubber Band"? These are the heavy thoughts that keep us fanboys awake at night.)

12. **One Bullet Too Many** from 1969's *Batman* #217 by Frank Robbins and Irv Novick, in which Batman closes the Bat-Cave, ships Robin off to college, and moves into the heart of Gotham City above the Wayne Foundation. The times they are a-changin'!

13. *The Killing Joke* graphic novel from 1988 by Alan Moore and Brian Bolland had the largest impact on the Joker's portrayal in *The Dark Knight* movie.

14. **There Is No Hope in Crime Alley** from *Detective Comics* #457 in 1976 was another classic by the always reliable Denny O'Neil and Dick Giordano.

15. **A Death in the Family**, erupting in *Batman* #426 in 1988, was a story in which, once again, Robin dies at dawn. This time for real. At least I could've sworn! But … sigh … it's comic books …

16. **Challenge of the Man-Bat**, beginning in *Detective Comics* #400 in 1970 from Denny O'Neil and Neal Adams, was a truly chilling modern-day comic book version of Dr. Jekyll and Mr. Hyde.

17. **The Man Behind the Red Hood** from *Detective Comics* #168 in 1951 by Bill Finger, Lew Sayre Schwartz, and Charlie Paris. Just when you thought you knew all about the Joker …

18. Both **Batman** #253 and #259 in 1973 and '74, when he meets the mysterious figure who most directly influenced his own creation, the Shadow, as written by Denny O'Neil and rendered by Neal Adams.

19. **The Demon of Gothos Manor** from *Batman* #227 in 1970, which made our hero less the Caped Crusader and more the Dark Knight, compliments of Denny O'Neil, Irv Novick, and Dick Giordano.

20. **Secret of the Waiting Graves** from *Detective Comics* #395 in 1970 marked the first Batman collaboration between the Dynamic Duo of Denny O'Neil and Neal Adams.

The summer of 1974 saw Nancy and me back living with my parents in Deal Park, New Jersey, so I could commute to my DC Comics summer job, which I continued throughout law school. At the end of one long but fun day working at DC Comics, the clock was hitting 6 p.m. and I needed to commute back to the Jersey Shore. Just then, I heard yelling and screaming coming from an office across the hall from where I was kibitzing with assorted Junior Woodchucks and secretaries. The commotion was coming from the office of writer extraordinaire and new editor at DC Comics Denny O'Neil. I dashed in to check on him. I didn't know if he was being murdered or murdering somebody. It was far less dramatic. Denny was the writer and editor of the super-sensational comic book adventures of the Shadow, which had become one of my favorite comic books. I cautiously poked my head in first and said quietly, "Are you okay?" He wasn't. "Of course I'm NOT okay!" he bellowed . . . unusual for such a mellow guy. "Carmine canceled The Shadow a while ago, but the latest sales figures just came in and they spiked, so he just 'un-canceled' it!" his tirade continued. "So, if it's NOT canceled, isn't that a GOOD thing?" I asked, relatively lost. "It's NOT good, because it puts me back on the old production schedule and that means I need a script by tomorrow!" Denny panicked. "And you don't have a script around?" I asked as I walked in and sat down in the one chair across from his massively cluttered desk. "Not only don't I have a script, "he said hopelessly, "I don't even have an IDEA for a script!"

"I have an idea for a Shadow script, Denny!" I volunteered.

"You do?" he asked.

I didn't. But so what? This was a "moment"! One of those rare chances to stick my foot in a slightly open door and then follow it up with another step and another step, aiming all the way for my dreams. It was that old "drop back and punt" time again.

"Well, what's YOUR idea for a Shadow story?" Denny inquired.

I needed some quality bullshit to buy me just enough time to think up something.

"I'm SO glad you asked me, because my story is really pretty special. It's one of those stories you don't talk about every day, but would certainly be the basis for a GREAT Shadow story with your guidance and—"

"Mike . . . what's the story?" Denny demanded . . . but in a nice way.

I started thinking about the trip Nancy and I had just come back from. Niagara Falls. Niagara Falls . . .

"Okay . . . okay . . . so Nancy and I were just up at Niagara Falls. Now all the Shadow comic book stories are set in the 1930s, right? And during the '30s people were walking across the Falls on a tightrope. Uh . . . Picture a fight between the Shadow and a villain on that tightrope over Niagara Falls . . . at night . . . the roving searchlights catching a glimpse of him up in that sky!" I thought I pitched it pretty well.

"That would make a good cover! I like that image. But what's the STORY about?" he asked.

The first comic book I ever wrote is published by DC. *The Shadow* #9 with a cover by one of my favorite artists, the masterful Joe Kubert! I am back in Comic Book Heaven!

"I was just coming to that part, because it's a story I know you're going to like, because it's about . . . it's about . . . smuggling!" Whew! Pulled that outta my ass in the nick of time.

"Okay," mused Denny, "but what are they smuggling?"

"I'm so glad you asked me that question because I can't wait to tell you that what they're smuggling from Canada to the U.S. is . . . DRUGS! They're smuggling drugs!" I was so proud of myself. But now what?

"And what's so special about that?" asked Denny. "What's the angle that makes this different than any smuggling we've seen before?"

"Well . . . I've been saving this because it's the best part so I was hoping you'd ask me this question so I could tell you this best part because what they were doing was . . . Hey! You know how back in the '30s men were going over the Falls in barrels? Well, that's what the smugglers were doing! They were loading the false, hollow bottom of each barrel, which would then go over the Falls on the Canadian side and wash up onto the American side! That's how they smuggle the drugs!"

Denny didn't hesitate. He looked me in the eye. I was already on my feet from acting out the barrel going over the Falls. "Can you have a full script on my desk by 6 o'clock tomorrow night?" he asked as if the Lords of Order and Chaos were all banking on my next response.

"No problem," I pshawed.

"Go do it!" Denny commanded.

I shook his hand and thanked him profusely, before grabbing a spanking new yellow pad and two pens and racing for the E train back to Penn Station. I started writing on the subway. I wrote on the North Jersey Coast train home. That gave me plenty of time. Back then the train line was nothing like it is today. The cars' air-conditioning systems would shut down if the temperature hit eighty-five, and the heat was nonexistent under forty. The train cars were so old I used to swear I could spot arrow holes in them from when they used them out west. Then we had to sit and stew in South Amboy, because the tracks weren't electrified south of there and the engine needed to be uncoupled and switched with a different one. I finally got out in Elberon and zipped home. I yelled for my mom to put on a pot of coffee 'cause I was pulling an all-nighter. And I wrote through the night. I wrote the next morning on the train back to New York and on the subway back to DC. When I got into the offices, I sidled up to one of my secretary friends and cut a deal with her. She agreed to let me feed her my handwritten script pages all day long and corrections as we progressed. In return, I agreed to bring her her morning coffee and sticky buns for the rest of the summer . . . a negotiated settlement from her original demand, which was for the rest of her life.

At 6 P.M., I turned in my Shadow script to Denny. I was now a comic book writer for DC Comics!

When I was eight years old, I had begun dreaming of writing Batman comics someday. And here I was writing the Shadow . . . the closest character to the Dark Knight. My story would debut in *The Shadow* #9. I wondered which DC artist would wind up drawing my cover idea and which one would draw the interior story itself. Denny wouldn't tell me who would be drawing the cover. It was to be a surprise until the original art came in. I remember that moment. Great Scott and Great Guns, too! It was one of the immortals—Joe Kubert, an extraordinary artist, writer, and editor, who was there when comic books began and has remained vibrant, relevant, and important over a career spanning more than seventy years that included the drawing of such heroes as Tarzan, Sgt. Rock, and Hawkman. He is also one of the few people to embrace the concept of "pay it forward" by becoming a teacher and founding the first accredited school for cartoon and graphic arts to encourage and train new generations of young talent.

Now, would the interiors be by Denny's Shadow artist, Michael Kaluta? One of the new Filipino artists who were so good? Or a classic old-time artist? After all, the Shadow had to look scary, forceful, and mysterious. The art wound up looking like *MAD* magazine's "Spy vs. Spy," but it was received well enough. I realized that at that one moment in Denny's office, I had put my foot in the door and not in my mouth.

I quickly started grabbing assignments from anyone at DC who had a bone to toss . . . mystery stories for *House of Mystery* and *House of Secrets* and other books like *The Unexpected* ("The Curse of Donny and Mary" . . . my chance to melt the Osmonds), *Weird War Tales* ("Indian War in Space"), and the absolute sickest thing I ever wrote (and I'm told that at one time it was even the focus of special Web sites that all seemed to agree that it was, indeed, one of the sickest comic book horror stories of all time, ranking with the old EC story where they played a night game of horror baseball, using a player's head for a ball, a leg for a bat, his torso for a chest protector, and his intestines for the base lines). DC wanted holiday-themed stories for its mystery books. The other writers had already grabbed Christmas, Halloween, Valentine's Day, and all the easy ones. So I decided to take Easter. And no, it wouldn't be another Easter "dead come back to life" zombie story. I called it "Hopping Down the Bunny Trail." It was a sweet story, really. It was about a group of kids who loved to do what all kids enjoy on Easter . . . eat chocolate in the shape of an Easter Bunny. And all boys always do the same thing right away—they bite the head off the candy figure. So in my tale, these kids go to the supposedly haunted house on the outskirts of town where a huge Easter Bunny waves at

And now, the sickest comic book story I ever wrote, since nominated as one of the nine greatest horror comics of all time, from DC's *Unexpected* #202, "Hopping Down the Bunny Trail," a truly depraved little tale of children, chocolate, and the Easter Bunny!

them and welcomes them inside for candy. Once inside, the kids are tricked into sliding into a vat of chocolate. They're covered in it. Which is when they learn that this huge Easter Bunny is a vampire, and as he approaches their necks with incisors the size of a pair of full-blown scythes, we fade to black. Tastefully, no one sees him biting the heads off the chocolate-coated kids. My contribution to world culture. The clincher is that it has been named online as one of the nine best horror comic book stories of all time!

A few weeks later, just a day or so before it was time to head back to Bloomington, I was walking down the halls at DC when who should approach me but the god of comic book editors himself, Julie Schwartz, the editor of the "New Look" Batman, and the man who had ushered in the Silver Age of Comics with his versions of the Flash, Green Lantern, the Justice League of America, the Atom, Hawkman, the Spectre, Adam Strange, the new Superman, Captain "Shazam" Marvel, and hordes more! Julie was often gruff and intimidating, but once you got to know him, you realized he was a marshmallow underneath. His eternal slogan for all his writers was an incessant "B.O.!" "Be Original!" He called to me out of the side of his mouth, "Hey, kid!"

"Yes, Julie?" I responded, trying to remember how he liked his coffee.

"I read your Shadow script," he grunted.

"You did?" I gulped.

"Yeah," he said, "It didn't stink."

"REALLY?!?" I exclaimed. "WOW! Thank you!"

"How'd ya like to take a crack at writing Batman?" he asked.

I slowly opened my brain and my heart and let eight-year-old Michael out, and I watched, laughing and clapping, as he did cartwheels and tumbles down the halls at DC Comics.

Life-changing moments. Turning points. What do you do when they strike like lightning? Grab them and capture the lightning in a bottle! Don't let them slip through your fingers. The moment was here. I was going to make my dream come true.

I headed back to Indiana and got on the phone with Julie's assistant, my fellow Junior Woodchuck and friend, Bob Rozakis. Bob and I were going to write this Batman story together. How exciting! We wanted to create a super-villain with a pirate motif, something missing from Batman's rogues' gallery. I know I was influenced by my first-ever trips to Disneyland and Disney World and "Pirates of the Caribbean." I loved the DC Comics ads my favorite Silver Age artist, Murphy Anderson, drew for the plastic model kits based on that new Disney ride. Bob and I thought the name "Blackbeard" sounded dark and would work. While I was in school, Bob ran it by Julie, who hated it. It wasn't original enough. Bob said Julie suggested a name for our villain. He cleared his throat but good, which in Bob language I knew meant, "You're NOT gonna like this . . ." The name Julie suggested was "Captain Stingaree."

What the—?

With thanks to fellow DC Comics' Junior Woodchuck, Jack C. Harris, and to all the Woodchucks who produced the world's finest fan magazine, *The Amazing World of DC Comics* in the 1970s, an homage to one of the most important editors in the entire history of comics, Julius (B.O.) Schwartz! ("B.O." stands for "Be Original!" Julie's cry to all his writers!) TOP, LEFT: Julie's superheroes admire his carved head statue courtesy of artist legend Joe Kubert from the cover of *The Amazing World of DC Comics* #3; TOP, RIGHT: Super artist Murphy Anderson confers with Julie and acclaimed inker, Joe Giella; LOWER, LEFT: Julius Schwartz, author of his lively autobiography, *Man of Two Worlds* (Harper Entertainment, 2000); LOWER, RIGHT: Julie told me, "It didn't stink." But this writer wasn't as lucky.

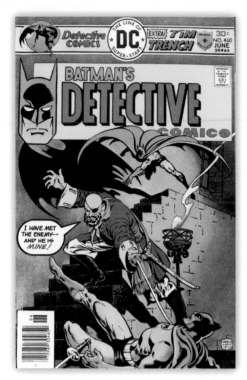

My first BATMAN comic book! *Detective Comics* #460 from 1976!

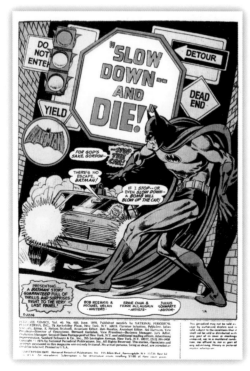

My name listed as writer of Batman! And thus, the dream I had since I was eight years old came true.

"He must've meant 'Captain Stingray'!" I said cocksure. "And if we lose the 'Captain' part, it won't sound so ... campy."

"Great idea," said Bob in that way that made you know it wasn't. "But Julie says 'Captain Stingaree.'"

"What the hell is a stingaree?" I asked.

Bob said it was the name of some old movie about a notorious highwayman played by Richard Dix or Fort Dix or some old actor. I hated the name Stingaree. Bob hated the name Stingaree. But Julie liked it, and so it came to pass.

Our one-part story had a simple premise. Bad guys analyzed every newspaper article and recording or bit of TV footage about Batman and for very logical reasons carefully set up in the script, came to the conclusion that no one human being could be so good at so many different physical and mental skill sets. They finally concluded that Batman was really three men operating under the cape and cowl. Julie liked the notion so much that he told us to make it a two-parter and that he'd run it in consecutive issues of DC's flagship title, *Detective Comics*. Bob and I were thrilled. We expanded our tale even more and laid it out for Julie. If we could slip in the Flash in a cameo, Julie was now prepared to make this a THREE-part story! There was one idea of ours he really, really loved. It was so far out that only in a comic book could we get away with it. A popular public service announcement campaign at the time was aimed at drivers, "Slow Down and Live!" So Bob and I figured we'd title our tale "Slow Down and Die!" Commissioner Gordon's police car has been tampered with. As he's driving down a highway, he learns there's a bomb attached to his car that will blow it to smithereens if he slows his car below fifty-five miles an hour. Years later, our comic was "honored" when someone thought of the exact same idea, made it a bus instead of a cop car, and made a movie called *Speed* out of it.

It turns out that Julie was the Mrs. Friedman of comic books. Before Bob and I could make our way through the rewriting and rewriting for Julie, I finished another Shadow script for Denny. He announced that he and I would now write alternate issues of *The Shadow*.

This made for rather unorthodox law school study habits. When the other law school students went home after classes, they studied. I went home (on the

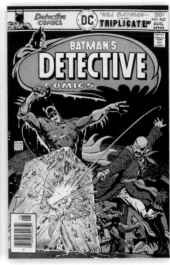

My second Batman story, *Detective Comics* #461 from 1976, co-authored with my Junior Woodchuck buddy, the all-seeing, all-knowing Bob Rozakis. He was the man who replaced me as driver of The Comicmobile.

Julie Schwartz liked our story so much that he told Bob and me to make it a THREE parter! *Detective Comics* #462 from 1976!

days I went to class) and wrote comic books. My pal John (Sully) Sullivan went home after Constitutional Law and read "Marbury vs. Madison." I went home and wrote "The Shadow vs. Shiwan Khan"! *The Shadow* #11 was to feature the first-ever crossover between the Shadow and his agents and the Avenger and his fighting group known as Justice, Inc. as together they fought the villainous Shiwan Khan. So while Sully was reading every Supreme Court decision of the early 1800s, I had decades of old Avenger and Shadow pulp novels to read.

I was further excited when my phone rang in Bloomington one day and a gentleman informed me he was organizing the first comic book convention in Indianapolis and wondered if I would be the keynote speaker, since I was an adopted Hoosier. I was flattered. The guy perceived me as a comic book pro. Wow! At this first Con, I talked about my collection, my I.U. course, and working at DC Comics and then went into detail about the Shadow and a new comic book project I was going to be writing for DC: a very loose, wild, and wacked-out version of the epic hero Beowulf in his battles with Grendel. It was inspired by John Gardner's book *Grendel*, which told the Beowulf saga from the point of view of the supposed monster. The audience had great energy. I especially liked the kid who came up to me when I finished. He was a huge, passion-

The first and thus far only meeting between The Shadow and The Avenger and I got to write it! Beautiful interior art by E. R. Cruz with a historic cover rendered by renowned Shadow artist, Michael Kaluta.

ate fan of DC's Shadow comics and he wanted to talk very specifically about them and had great, pointed questions. I told him about DC's secret plans to let Denny edit a black and white R-rated magazine version of the Shadow and that Denny and I had just started to plan the first one, which would at last delve into the unknown, mysterious origin of the Shadow. It was a glorious project that would never see the light of day, because DC decided at the last minute not to compete with Marvel's black and white magazine line, which was already light years ahead. It also didn't help that DC was still haunted by the utter failure in 1971 of two Jack Kirby black and white magazines for DC, *Spirit World* and *In the Days of the Mob*. This kid and I spoke for twenty minutes, and then he asked me if I would autograph my two issues for him. My first autograph signing! I couldn't wait to call my mom! I knew she'd *qvell*!

It seemed like an endless wait until Batman's *Detective Comics* #460, #461, and #462 went on sale. Their covers even featured the DC logo I had conceived. I think a tear fell when I saw #460 for the first time. Sol Harrison kindly sent me the original art for one of those covers. At that moment, I realized that the dream I had had since I was eight had actually come true! I was writing Batman comic books! Omigod! Then I became terrified. I no longer had a dream! What would come next? I needed clarity . . . a goal . . . a new mountain to climb. It took me ten minutes to figure it out.

"As if in answer, a huge bat flies through my open mind . . ."

"A bat! That's it! It's an omen!" I said to myself. "I shall become a Batman movie producer and bring a dark and serious Batman to the Silver Screen, just the way Bob Kane and Bill Finger created him in 1939 . . . a creature of the night stalking criminals in the shadows!" And then I recalled the vow I had made way back on that evening in January 1966. I renewed it that night. I would dedicate myself to bringing about the sort of Batman movies that once and for all would wipe three little words out of the collective consciousness of the world culture . . . "POW!" . . . "ZAP!" . . . and "WHAM!"

TOP, LEFT: The cover to my own wildly eccentric, fun comic book series, *Beowulf, Dragon Slayer*. This was the version drawn before that censorship board, the Comics Code Authority, rejected it. TOP, RIGHT: The cover of *Beowulf, Dragon Slayer* #1 from 1975 after the Comics Code had Nan-Zee's chest altered. Nan-Zee was, of course, named after my wife. BOTTOM, LEFT: First page of my script for *Beowulf* #1. BOTTOM, RIGHT: Here's how artist Ricardo Villamonte interpreted page one of my script.

Mrs. Nancy Ellen Uslan
requests the honor of your presents
at the graduation of her husband
Michael Elliot
Who,
after twenty years in school,
seven years in Bloomington,
and three years in Law School,
will be getting his ass
the hell out of there at last
on Sunday, the ninth of May,
nineteen hundred and seventy-six
at three o'clock
A drunken spree will follow.

# CHAPTER SIXTEEN

# GOING BACKWARD?
# ME, MR. MXYZPTLK,
# AND A TOYOTA!

As the years passed, feeling a need to improve my credentials to continue working on DC's Edu-Graphics Program, I took the summer off between my second and third years of law school at I.U. and, in an intensive eight-week period (with time off for a ten-day vacation), earned my Master's Degree in Education, specializing in Urban Education with a Master's thesis titled "The Comic Book Revolution," about the ways comic books can effectively be used in education. In actuality, this was a tailoring of my textbook *The Comic Book in America*, which I had written as an undergrad for Indiana University's Independent Study Division. Copyright law aside, picking up my Master's Degree in Education in that one summer was my favorite time while in law school. How many people can make a wild statement like that? But "unconventional" was the way I liked to play each phase of my life.

I graduated from law school without a job, but not for lack of trying! In December of my last year of law school, I took my first job-seeking trip to L.A. I still wanted a creative job writing for movies or TV, but I also realized that there was a good chance I would not get my foot in the door in a creative job in Hollywood. I banked on my law school education getting me in a rear window. I was sneaky. I printed up and sent out two completely different resumes—a total of 372. One listed the comic books I had written, the national creative-writing contests I had won, and the *Saturday Night Live*–type radio show I had written and DJed. It made NO mention of the fact that I was graduating from law school. I sent that resume to every production department, programming department, and producer I could find. Resume number two never ever mentioned the words comic books or anything that might remotely be considered "creative." It talked about law school and the award-winning paper I had written on copyright infringement and unfair competition in the comic book industry, and the college organizations of which I had been vice president. Before leaving for Los Angeles, I had lined up thirty interviews over the three weeks I would be there with Nancy, sleeping on the couch of my ol' college roommate Scotty Maybaum and his new wife Nancy (he always copied me) in beautiful downtown Torrance, California.

As it turned out, the most notable thing about three weeks spent living with another couple in a 200-square-foot apartment was their dog. Their big dog. Their big, big, BIG dog. How big was he? Well, one morning Nancy was stepping out of the shower in the bathroom and stepped into the dog's steamy new dump the size of the Great Pyramid of Khufu. It shot into the air through her toes like sliced sausage meat through a grinder, before she slid in it at 35 mph down the hallway, past the opening into the living room. All I saw was Nancy, naked, doing that same slide Tom Cruise would one day emulate in his underpants in the movie *Risky Business*. She wasn't quite a blur, but without knowing what had just happened, I could only assume she was roller-skating naked around the apartment.

Compared to that event, only three of the thirty interviews were worth remembering. I got positive responses to my resumes from two television networks . . . CBS and . . . CBS. Yup! I was granted an interview on Thursday at 3 P.M. with the head of Legal/Business Affairs at the network headquarters known as "Television City" on the corner of Fairfax and Beverly, just down the street from Cantor's Deli and not far from Golden Apple, the then principal comic book store in L.A., if not America. I would just barely have enough time to leave that 3 P.M. interview to make my Thursday at 4 P.M. interview, which was for a Programming position also at CBS. My plan worked! Each department had received a completely different resume, and they were both now granting me interviews! That afternoon, I drove up to the intimidating checkpoint gate at Television City. The guard actually had my name on a list! Me! He tattooed a permit to the inside of my rented windshield which came with the rented car, and had me park in my own studio parking space! I wondered if my name would be stenciled on it like I saw in movies about Hollywood. Nope. "Visitor" was stenciled on it. But for the next two hours, that parking space was MINE! I got out and, like anyone else from Jersey, locked my car door. I proceeded up the stairs in my perfect three-piece lawyerly suit, carrying the official lawyerly attaché case I had borrowed from my dad and which he used the year he was president of the Ocean Township Lion's Club. It was an American Tourister, so from the commercials, I knew even a gorilla could throw it around and jump on it and it wouldn't dent. I wondered how it would do with sharks.

Thank goodness this wasn't my first interview for a legal job, because after having been through a couple, I had learned better how to mask my utter disinterest in being a lawyer . . . even as just a means to an end. By this interview, I was getting much better at it. If they'd stick to a discussion about copyright, I'd be fine. If they started asking me about "Marbury vs. Madison," I'd have to ask to call a friend and refer them to Sully. It went pretty well. Then on my way out, the exec said, "I'll get back to you." UH OH! I was just then in my third year on Georgetown University Law School's waiting list, and was still waiting for them to get back to me. I knew what that line meant. But there was no time to dwell on it. It was now 3:46 P.M. and my interview with the head of Programming for a creative job would begin in just fourteen minutes. I hopped on the Television City elevator, tore down the Television City hall, raced down the Television City stairs, and then walked to my car so as not to arouse anyone's attention. I had the old Eatontown Drive-In's intermission announcer's voice in my head—"Eleven minutes 'til showtime!" I opened my rented Ford Pinto, which featured an interior about the size of a walnut, and smunched my way into the backseat. I changed into jeans and a T-shirt and a very cool open sweatshirt, topped with a Steven Spielberg/George Lucas "Hey! I'm a Filmmaker!"–type baseball cap. I had done my research and found out that the person interviewing me was originally from New York . . . the City not the Island . . . so I purposefully chose a Yankees cap over a Mets. I left behind my dad's attaché case, to give me that "free spirited" creative look. "Five minutes 'til showtime!" I exited that mustard-colored vehicular deathtrap, and headed back up those Television City stairs and went over to the same receptionist and reintroduced myself for my Programming interview. She stared. Announced me. Absorbed the situation. And then she said to me, "I thought I'd seen everything in Hollywood. But THIS is a NEW one! Good luck, son. You got balls." Of course, she turned out to be from New York, too. A long time later, I learned that that job had gone to the exec's wife's dentist's son. It was an early lesson in Hollywood nepotism, cronyism, and the importance of networking, because no matter what I wanted to believe, I learned that it too often comes down to who you know.

Getting into this business, and then staying in this business, requires first and foremost a high tolerance for frustration. Why? Because if you're not born into it like some Prince or Princess or Wife's Dentist's Son, you have no guarantees that you will make it or sustain once you're in it.

Case in point: In 1975, the start of my final year of law school, I finally just sat down and surveyed my favorite shows on television. I loved everything Norman Lear touched as an Executive Producer, especially his huge hit TV series, *All in the Family*, which single-handedly broke down more television barriers and taboos than Soupy Sales and Groucho Marx combined. My other favorite was from the diseased mind of funnyman genius Mel Brooks, and was a TV parody of Robin Hood called *When Things Were Rotten*. By endless attempts at networking, I got to an agent with a personal "in" to Norman Lear. I had just sat down and written two "spec" TV scripts to try to prove I had some sort of "powers and abilities far beyond those of mortal" . . . writers. I wrote an episode of *All in the Family* and an episode of *When Things Were Rotten*. This agent actually agreed to read my two scripts because someone I had met at CBS agreed to nudge him. When he called me back, he raved. He said he wasn't into slapstick and puns and the Mel Brooks humor, so had no interest in that script. But he absolutely loved my *All in the Family* script and was willing to put his head on the chopping block and get it to Norman Lear. "Sit tight," he told me. I sat as tight as humanly possible. I clenched my butt cheeks hard for two weeks. And then the answer came. It was from the executive producer and head writer of the show, the famous Hal Kanter. He called my script, ". . . obviously the work of a talented professional. . . ." I was to come see him on my next trip to L.A. from Indiana about a job as a staff writer on *All in the Family* and possibly other Norman Lear shows.

"YYYYYYYYYYYEEEEEEEEEESSSSSSSSSS!!!!!!!!!!!!" I screamed, and jumped and jigged and spun and cried and laughed! And then I explained to this wonderful agent that I was still in my last year of law school and wouldn't be available to move to L.A. until the next June, but that I could get there over Christmas break to meet with Mr. Kanter and close the deal. He grimaced over the phone. I could hear it. He explained that this isn't a business like any other business. People don't recruit and line up employees six to nine months in advance. But . . . he would call Kanter and make what arrangements he could. The result was a set appointment for just two months from that day in L.A. with Hal Kanter! I built my whole three weeks in L.A. around that one meeting.

I didn't know about show business. Not a clue how it operated. No idea it was unique. I had no hint the "rules" that applied to every other industry didn't apply here. So not knowing about confirming a meeting set two months before when the time drew near, I just showed up at Sunset-Gower Studios in a nice tie and jacket at the prescribed time and had a hard time getting through their security gate. I explained three times that I had an appointment with Hal Kanter and, finally, I was told I could park in a guest space and see the secretary. My parking space said "Guest." I was moving up in Hollywood! My parking space at CBS had merely said "Visitor," not "Guest."

Then my world crashed down on my head. The secretary informed me that Mr. Kanter no longer worked there. (In fact, on my second interviewing trip to L.A. the following September, I found that twenty-seven of the thirty people I had interviewed with back in December were no longer in the same positions. Welcome to Hollywood, Michael!)

The secretary must have felt abject pity looking at the pathetic figure I made while I was mumbling in shock . . . "But I have an appointment . . . and he said I was a talented professional . . . and there would be a job . . . and . . . and we had an appointment. . . ." She brought me one of those black coffees I forced myself to start drinking in law school when I realized I really needed to study for hours and hours. Then she told me to wait on the lobby couch as she walked off. A pretty long time later, she returned and said that the man who had taken Mr. Kanter's place would see me. WHEW! What a relief! Saved! Thank God! I got my act together, and she led me to his office. We passed by the actress who played Mother Jefferson on *The Jeffersons* and past *All in the Family*'s Sally Struthers (when she was young and bright-eyed and not doing late-night TV commercials advertising African babies). The secretary ushered me into my very first interview with a real-life Executive Producer in L.A.

The man was about my dad's age I guessed, and looked like any other older Jewish uncle from New York. By now I was convinced that nobody was actually born in L.A., but that everyone just moved there from New York. He didn't smile. He wasn't talkative. This was not Indiana. So I explained about my spec script and Mr. Kanter's gratifying response and appointment to see him for a staff writing job. He responded quickly and clearly, yet none of it made any sense to me. "There is no job," were the exact words. So I reiterated what Mr. Kanter had said. And then he let me have it.

"Do you expect me to make this easy for you?" he shouted. My brain was telling me he was joking. My heart was telling me this was no joke. "But I wrote this script that Mr. Kanter really liked and—" "I read your script. So what if it was any good? I started writing on radio for Jack Benny and *Duffy's Tavern*. I wrote for Lucy and Milton and Bob Hope, and now at this age, I'm writing this hit show," he stated as if he were a defense attorney in the court battle of the century. I was about to say "Wow!" and compliment him for that awesome track record . . . truly the best in comedy . . . but couldn't get a word in edgewise. "So you think I like seeing you here? You think I'm happy to see some kid come marching in here who could steal my job?" he asked. I must've been red if not purple with shock and awe. "Sir, I don't want your job. All I want to do is write," I squeaked out. "Then move to L.A. and see if there's a spot for you here then," he concluded. "But my agent had explained my situation to Mr. Kanter," I pleaded. "My wife and I have no money to just move across country with no job lined up, but if you can tell me I'll have a job, we'll find the funds to—" "Like I said," he said, "I'm not about to make this easy for you. Move here and see what happens. Good-bye." And that was the end of my job interview.

Many years later, when I was in L.A. for the premiere of *Batman Begins*, I took some flowers to Forest Lawn Cemetery to visit the graves of my Aunt Hana and Uncle Abe Zemser. It took me awhile to find their graves. They all have plaques rather than headstones up there. As I spotted them and walked over, I caught a glimpse of the grave next to theirs that I was stepping by. It belonged to that very same man from *All in the Family* so many years before. I took one of the flowers out of my handful and placed it on his grave. As I did, I said in a whisper, "I really DIDN'T want your job."

My next interviews would all be in New York City . . . finally back to a "normal" place

*Culver City, California 90230*
*10202 West Washington Boulevard   (213) 559-3450*
*Cable Address: UNARTISCO, CULVER CITY*

An Entertainment Service of
Transamerica Corporation

# United Artists Corporation

December 30, 1975

Mr. Michael E. Uslan
3209 East 10th Street - Apt. 7A
Bloomington, Indiana 47401

Dear Mr. Uslan:

I am sorry that it has taken so long to get back to you regarding your inquiry about employment with United Artists, however, we were in the midst of settling into new quarters and you initial letter was placed in our files.

Since our office staff is a small one and we have very little turnover in either of the areas of your interest, there really would be no reason to set up an interview. However, if you are interested in locating in New York perhaps you could inquire of Mr. Robert Schwartz as to the opportunities with that office.

Please accept our apology for not getting back to you.

Sincerely,

*Rose Palumbo*

Rose Palumbo
Office Manager

/rp

My sorta rejection letter from United Artists, the only major movie studio based in New York circa 1976. I learned during my seven years getting my three degrees at Indiana University to never simply accept "No" for an answer. Thus, I soon got that UA job!

where there seemed to be a whole lot less of what I call the "baby-cookie-sweetie" thing you often get laid on you in Hollywood. It's the stuff Woody Allen movies are made of! I had an interview with a *macher* at International Creative Management, one of the top two talent agencies at the time. He told me up front that while he had no immediate job opening, there was something about my creative resume and about the enthusiasm he heard over the phone that made him want to meet me. We just started TALKING to each other. I felt a connection and just kind of poured out my hopes and dreams and need to get my foot in the door, and he told me I was hyperventilating and to just relax, sit back, and take a deep breath. He canceled his next appointment and kept me in his office for an hour and a half. Then he introduced me to key people at ICM and started right there making calls to his friends at other companies to see if anyone was looking for a great young man to hire. Irwin Moss became my mentor and friend, a human life preserver in a sea of sharks. He encouraged me when I needed it, calmed me when I needed it, steered me, and counseled me. He was the one who told me to send a resume to United Artists, the only major studio back then based primarily in New York, not Hollywood. So I did.

Meanwhile, I had to bring in some money. I was a married man who was now, with my wife, living back at home with my parents in the bedroom I had shared with Paul growing up. Now the two beds were pushed together. As a married couple's master bedroom, it was filled with stacks of comic books and drawers jammed with baseball, basketball, Beatles, Elvis, and Zorro trading cards. But who would temporarily hire a guy who might suddenly need to take the day off to go on last-minute interviews in New York City, and then overpay him for work he wasn't qualified to be doing? My dad would . . . and did . . . probably at my mom's insistence. Five months after law school graduation, while I was tarring a foundation for Pop (the worst job, requiring a burning washdown in turpentine afterward), it hit me that I had no job, no prospects, and would be working on my dad's crew for years to come and that my dreams of movies and animation and TV and making *Batman* were only dreams. As I was tarring, I started tearing up. Unable to wipe my nose for fear of tarring it, I just stood there and dripped on the foundation of someone's ritzy new house. No one was around to see, but the hopelessness of the moment was just completely overwhelming. That night, Nancy and I had a long talk. While not telling me to give up, she urged me to start sending my creative resume to the major Madison Avenue advertising agencies, because she knew I would be great at creating ad campaigns and commercials and advertisements. So I found out the names of the ten biggest such companies in New York and sent out my resume begrudgingly but acceptingly. Two days later, a vice president of one of the biggest ad agencies, Foote, Cone & Belding, called me to come in for an interview for an account exec position that he told me over the phone would, indeed, be a creative job. Well, I wasn't thrilled about it, but I went. Jesus! Am I glad I did!

Racing to make the 6:25 A.M. train from Elberon, I tried getting dressed in the dark, half asleep. No matter what I did, I could not get my tie to tie right. The back kept coming out way too long. In utter frustration, but with my normal sense of humor, I looked at Nancy. She wanted to help, but there was nothing she could do. Finally, I just ripped it off and tossed it to her. "You want to help, Nan? Fine! This tie doesn't fit me. It's the wrong size! Take it to some tailor and have it shortened!" I yelled. In total frustration, I grabbed another tie and headed out to make the train in the nick of time. Not getting that I was kidding, that morning Nancy drove my tie to Jacques, the tailor in Asbury Park, and told him she had inadvertently bought me the wrong size tie and needed to have it shortened. Jacques, who was Chinese, looked at her like she was crazy. He had to bring out four ties to compare the lengths to prove to her that ties don't come in large, medium, and small sizes for men. But she HAD SEEN that this tie didn't fit me. "Maybe this one's defective!" Nancy offered. With a look of total incredulity, Jacques picked up my tie, put it on, tied it, and, like magic, it fit fine. Nancy's mystification was slowly replaced by her desire to get back at me when I got home.

At the midtown office of Foote, Cone & Belding, the man in the dark gray suit welcomed me in. He told me that four things caught his attention in my resume. He liked that I had won some national creative-writing contests; had been published; that, like him, I had been a Sammy in college; and mostly that I was the first person he ever met who wrote comic books! It was an interesting interview, as he laid out for me how the advertising business worked. He told me that a big part of the business was taking clients or their products that might lend themselves naturally to creative ad campaigns and then working up new and catchy approaches to keep the advertising fresh. As examples, he asked me to imagine having to come up with something fresh for an airline or car that had been around a long time. I replied that would be fun and that I'd love to take a crack at Toyota. He gave a little laugh. "You like cars?" he asked. "What do you think you could do for Toyota?"

I said, "My ad or billboard would just have in big block letters the words, 'A TOYOTA.' Underneath that in smaller letters, I'd have it say, 'Spell it forward. Spell it backward. It still spells 'Quality.'"

He paused, thinking. "Why, 'A TOYOTA' spelled backward spells, 'A TOYOTA'!" he blurted out. "Gee, that's very creative, Michael," he said, and I felt really good. He didn't realize that since the age of five, I'd been reading stories about Superman's funny villain from the fifth dimension, Mr. Mxyzptlk. The only way Superman could get rid of this annoying pest was to trick him into saying his own name backward. Ever since that time, I had been looking at words and often reading them frontward and backward as a silly game. My favorite was my brother Paul's friend, Clifford Lipson (who wound up starring in the original Broadway production of *Hair*). Spelled backward, his last name was "Nospil." I loved the concept of a "Nose Pill." This advertising job interview was fun! But apparently, the gentleman was saving the hard part for last.

"But, Michael," he said, sounding like he was writing me off as he spoke, "what separates the men from the boys creatively around here is something like THIS!" He challenged me as he pointed to a corkboard behind his desk that had a big picture tacked to it of a package of Kent cigarettes. "Kent Cigarettes is our oldest and biggest client. After all these years, what can you say differently about Kent Cigarettes?" he asked, or dared, I wasn't sure which.

"I have an idea," I replied without the slightest pause.

"YOU have an idea?" he asked with an incredulous grin. "So what's YOUR idea?"

I didn't think it registered for him the extent to which I was a comic book fan. The mention by someone of the word Kent does NOT conjure up an image of a cigarette to me at all. I thought my answer was pretty obvious. "The center of the ad is a picture of a telephone booth," I described. "Rushing out of the phone booth is Clark Kent, tearing open his shirt to reveal Superman's big "S" symbol. The copy underneath reads, 'Inside every KENT, You'll find something SUPER!'"

He stared at me. No expression. Then he got up from his desk, telling me only, "Wait here," as he walked out of his office. I had no idea what had just happened. I wasn't sure what the heck was going on, but I sat there for some five minutes. He came back in with three more guys in gray suits like his. He looked at me and said, "Tell them what you just told me."

I did. And he offered me a job.

I told him I'd like to think about it and would get back to him before the end of the week. I was flattered. It was really good for my steamrolled ego. Nancy was as happy as could be. A job! Money! New York and not L.A.! And I would be where she was convinced I should be . . . Madison Avenue, NOT Hollywood and Vine. The next morning, I got a call from the secretary for the head of the Legal Department at United Artists in New York asking if I could come in at 4 P.M. that day for a job interview. They had one opening for a motion picture production attorney. Ugh! A legal job? Be a lawyer? I stuck my fingers down my throat in a fake vomit reflex as I told the pleasant young lady on the phone I couldn't make it. She put me on hold to relay my disinterest to her boss. She came back on. "How about tomorrow at 12:30? He'd really like to see you." I didn't want to waste the time or expense of yet another trip to New York, but with the advertising business now staring me in the eye, and this being one of the major movie studios, I figured I might as well at least just go and listen. I made the appointment.

The next day, I showed up at the address on the north end of Times Square. This was an era when Times Square was more famous for its squalor, peep shows, porn, drugs, dealers, hookers, and squeegee guys than for anything remotely tourist-friendly beyond the safety of the inside of the Broadway theaters. Yuch! Like I would work here? I took the elevator at 729 Seventh Avenue up to the eighth floor. The place was a dump. Much of the furniture looked like it came from Charlie Chaplin and Mary Pickford's era. I sat and waited and waited, bored and disinterested and not wanting to be there interviewing for some legal job. I was finally ushered into the large office. I know my attitude must have come off as "give-a-shit." The exec directed the conversation to copyright and trademark. We discussed the Lanham Act and several key cases. This was clearly a very, very bright man and top-notch entertainment attorney. I really had no desire to waste too much of his time. Suddenly, he got up and started to walk out of his office. (Was it ME? Why did I have this effect on job interviewers?) He stopped at the doorway, turned around, and said, "C'mon. I'll take you to lunch." So I said, "No thanks, I already ate." He was stunned. I suspected that I might have been the first job applicant ever to turn down a request to go to lunch. "Uh, well, will you go with me and have coffee or some dessert?" he asked, uncertain if I was pulling his leg. Unenthusiastically, I agreed I'd have a cup of coffee. Over coffee, he told me he was amazed that I had taken seven hours of copyright in law school (actually two hours for the one and only course I.U. had back then, plus five hours of credit for researching and writing my thesis), whereas none of the other two hundred applicants for the job—even the Ivy League guys and the students out of Georgetown University Law School (Ha! So there!)—had more than three hours' credit. That impressed him. And he offered me the job. I would be a noble new experiment. They had always hired experienced entertainment lawyers in the past, but now they had room and wanted to try hiring a kid right out of school who could be trained from day one in the UA way of doing business. I was to be the guinea pig. I told him I had to think about it and still had a number of interviews lined up. He asked me not to accept another job without coming back to him first. I thought that was fair and agreed. I never so not wanted a job in my life. And it was probably exactly that attitude that made him want me more.

Thus came the moment of truth. The next turning point. That Robert Frost moment of two roads diverging in a yellow wood. Choices. It's always about choices and, ultimately, the consequences of those choices. This time, there would be no "omen" . . . no bat flying through an open window. I needed the counsel of the wisest people in my inner circle and the input of anyone they could steer me to who might have insight into how good or bad, important or inconsequential, a legal and business affairs job with United Artists might be.

Nancy was advocating the advertising job, but was aware of my dream of making my Batman movie one day and my primary desire to work in the movie industry. My Jewish mom saw the chance to have a son, the lawyer, and even if I eventually became a writer, it would give me something to fall back on beyond a Serta Perfect Sleeper. My dad told me to follow my heart. Paul wanted to know if I could get him into movies for free if I worked there, and whether, if I went into the advertising business and made up Toyota's ads, they would give him a free Toyota. I think he was pulling my leg. Irwin Moss said grab the UA job! Nancy's dad, the wisest of the wise, drew no conclusion, but wanted me to speak with his nephew, the son of the brother of Nancy's mom. He was a big-time entertainment lawyer in L.A. who had a lot of hot young clients like George Lucas, Sylvester Stallone, and many others. It turned out that he also represented the producers of the Superman movie. Tom Pollock said that there was no choice. Absolutely, I should take that United Artists job. It was a fantastic opportunity for me to learn the business, learn how to finance and produce motion pictures, meet the power brokers, and network throughout New York and L.A. My head was in the process of doing the same thing that little girl's did in the movie *The Exorcist*, spinning around 360 degrees atop my neck. It was becoming clear, despite every bone in my body crying out against it, that I was going to have to take the job as a lawyer as the means to a specific end. But there would be a plan here with a clear and definite exit strategy. I would do this, and learn everything I could. . . for four years . . . as if this were graduate school. But by the end of four years, no matter what, I would quit to pursue my dream to be on the creative side of filmmaking and make my Batman movie happen. I would quit and either be writing and producing movies and TV and cartoons OR I would be delivering pizzas for Domino's, but what I would NOT be is trapped into becoming a lawyer for the rest of my life, putting out a shingle and handling someone's divorce or drafting someone's will. I had shoved my foot in a new door, and it was time to walk in, straight ahead.

# CHAPTER SEVENTEEN

# RAGING BULLSHIT on a "ROCKY" ROAD!

My first day working in the motion picture industry—I started on Monday, October 10, 1976—was unforgettable for the explicit reason that it was totally forgettable. I set my clock alarm extra early. I made the earlier choice of trains from Elberon. I walked on that bright, clear, crisp October day from Penn Station to Seventh Avenue and 49th Street. It was my favorite time of the year in New York. Everything went like clockwork, except one thing. The building was closed. It was Columbus Day. A holiday. Nobody had told me United Artists was closed. They had told me to report on Monday. Oh well, it was a great run-through . . . one of life's little dress rehearsals, an important part of the movie biz.

The next day was different. WAY different. I was told I'd be doing virtually nothing but reading for the first few weeks, getting acquainted with the documents used to put together deals for movies, as well as with the terminology and the technical aspects. My favorite part was being sent to the corporate medical department downstairs for my introductory physical. As I poked my head in the door, a pretty, young blonde smiled and greeted me as if I were her long-lost friend. "Wow!" I thought, "is this who the movie business hires to check for hernias?" I never so looked forward to coughing. But alas and alack, she was from the Midwest. That explained it. She was just FRIENDLY. Her name was Geri Brahney, and brainy is what she was. She and her husband, Tim, would become part of the UA family we all formed out of the core of the Legal Department. UA truly exuded a family atmosphere. So many people were just happy and smart and great at their jobs and willing to go the extra mile and explain everything from the financial side of making movies to how tax-shelter deals worked, the tax issues in financing films, and how the business of music works in motion pictures. Everyone in the Legal and Business Affairs department became my mentors and teachers. I knew I would be out of there once I had learned all I could and networked like mad, but these guys and lady were in for the long career haul and each one of them went on to important positions in the industry and are still out there in the thick of it and have my undying respect and admiration for all they've achieved and continue to accomplish.

We all worked our asses off under lots of pressure, but we also had our fun. We had a volleyball team, which I named "The Net Prophets" (and our opponents I dubbed "The Gross Participants" . . . both just industry lingo in-jokes that kept everybody minimally amused), which played weekly after work in Central Park. Nancy and I were building our first house in New Jersey (well, actually, my dad and Uncle Irv and cousins Sammy and Arthur Uslan were). We all partied together in New York in the mid '70s and early '80s, when the studio sent us to so many premieres, industry functions, opening nights, and special events that they bought all the guys tuxedos. Then there were those nights the president of UA had us pile into the limo with his wife and him and whisked us all off to the hottest discos in the City, namely the now-legendary Studio 54 and Xenon at their peaks. (Okay, so I went to discos then and actually danced The Hustle, which my secretary had to teach me, and, yes, I admit I wore those embarrassingly stupid clothes and those stupider glasses back then that were four times bigger than my face and made me look exactly like Atom Ant. There's nothing anyone can say or do to me about it that is worse than the existence of some pictures from that era that my son and daughter pull out when they feel like laughing until they throw up.) Barr Potter in our Legal Department threw himself a thirtieth birthday blast at one of the hottest discos in the City, where naked trapeze artists were swinging over our heads as we all danced amid smoke and mirrors and special effects and a state-of-the-art sound system, culminating with I forget how many disco dazzlers popping out of Barr's gigantic birthday cake to kiss him happy birthday. We were in the middle of it all! We went to listen to the studio's pride and joy, Woody Allen, play with his jazz band Monday nights at Michael's Pub before heading to Elaine's on the East Side for a late dinner. In those days, the Russian Tea Room was the center of Hollywood East, Sardi's was a factor, but the Stage Deli, Carnegie Deli, Gaiety Deli, and Edison Coffee Shop stole our hearts.

As the newest guy in the department, I was assigned the scut assignments none of the other lawyers wanted. One of those was the industry labor contract negotiations with various Locals of the International Alliance of Theatrical Stage Employees (IATSE)— the cameramen, makeup and hair technicians, and the like. Each studio had to send one representative, and the ringleader on our side was the brilliant, canny, and very entertaining lawyer for Warner Bros., Norman Samnick. At my first-ever bargaining session facing Mike Proscia, the IATSE powerhouse, and his minions, all we studio lawyers were told to walk in behind Norman, who was carrying a big gym bag, and not to crack a smile. We filed into the room where the IATSE boys were already seated at the table and took our seats opposite them. Then, our fearless leader removed his suit jacket and draped it around his chair. The rest of us from UA, Columbia, Paramount, Universal, MGM, 20th Century-Fox, and Disney followed suit by removing our suit jackets, too. He slowly rolled up the sleeves of his white dress shirt, sat down in the middle of us all at the table, reached down into his gym bag and brought out a vintage U.S. Army World War II general's helmet and strapped it on his head. Then he bent down and yanked from his bag a vintage army ordnance machine gun and laid it on the table in front of him as he looked Mike Proscia in the eye and said, "Let's negotiate!" The entire room collapsed in laughter. All the tension was shattered, and the negotiations went smoothly. He was brilliant! What a lesson in my first weeks of working in the "real" world! Be forearmed so that you can disarm your opponent. (By the way, the illustrious Mike Proscia became chairman of the New Jersey Motion Picture and Television Commission and yours truly served under him as vice chairman. The Sopranos, therefore, technically reported to us.)

The first movies I worked on, learning how to negotiate and draft producer contracts, actor, screenwriter, director, and other employment agreements, plus the critical financing and distribution contracts, included *Rocky*, *Black Stallion*, *Raging Bull*, and *Apocalypse Now*. Every day my learning curve was 100 percent, and I was meeting more and more attorneys, agents, managers, production execs, producers, guild and union officials, and talent.

There was to be a pre-Thanksgiving 1976 UA company screening of *Rocky* at the Criterion Theatre in Times Square. The execs who had seen the final cut of the picture were raving that not only would this become the movie of the year, but it would make an action star out of an actor named Sylvester Stallone. I thought that sounded preposterous. How could you ever have an action hero movie star named Sylvester? Next thing they'll be telling me is they have an action hero star named Arnold. Ridiculous! The film ran less than two hours. Half an hour into it, Nancy turned to me and said, "You told me this would be a super-exciting movie. Well, there's only about an hour or so to go, and I don't think so." What sort of movie magic could possibly transpire in the next sixty-five minutes? It was time to dash to the concession stand for the free nonpareils.

As I opened the rear door of the theater, I nearly bumped into a guy pacing in the lobby, peeking in. It took me a second to realize it was Sylvester Stallone. After all, the guy I had just seen on screen had to be six foot two, but this guy was my height, and I was five foot ten standing real straight and tall in shoes. He looked really nervous. Not as nervous as he'd be in a month when his $1,240,000 film ($240,000 over budget!) was a rip-roaring sensation and a little old porn film suddenly surfaced and was being booked into movie theaters, not under its original title, *A Party at Kitty and Stud's* but rather under a new title, *The Italian Stallion*. The next thing that happened was that the Legal Department was ordered to stop it if we could. We didn't know legally how we could. But first, we had to know exactly what we were dealing with. One of my bosses gave me a hundred dollars to venture into the porn palaces of sleazy Times Square and purchase a Betamax videotape version of the offending film. I found a copy in a dive at the north end of Times Square. By the time I brought the tape back to the office, I found that not only had my secretary Amy ordered the big TV and tape player, but she had moved my desk and office furniture off to the side and set up sixteen chairs for all the attorneys and secretaries, and had bought enough Jiffy Pop to make a bag of popcorn for each person, cooking them on one of the secretary's illegal hot plates. Amy also gave each person a handmade "Review" card and pencil for movie reviews. Those were interesting reviews, and they varied from one extreme to the other. One secretary wrote that it was too long, while another wrote that it wasn't long enough. Someone else anticipated that audiences would give it a standing ovation or, at least, a hand. In the end, UA couldn't stop its release.

They were fun, though challenging, days learning every aspect of the movie biz. I often used my copyright background. I learned to do deals and contracts for novelizations, music, records, toys, and other assorted merchandising.

The arrangement I had made with UA prior to taking this job was that I would be free to write books or comic books on the side on my own time. That's what kept me sane during the years I worked as a lawyer. I wrote a bunch of books with either my cousin Brucie or my friend from grade school with the treasure trove of old comic books in his closet, Jeff Mendel. They included *The Comic Book Trivia Quiz Book* (which, when it was released, had been changed to *The Pow! Zap! Wham! Comic Book Trivia Quiz Book*. GAAA!), *The TV Commercials Trivia Book*, *The Gossip Trivia Book*, *The Rock 'n' Roll Trivia Quiz Book*, and a book on TV trivia. In comics, I worked again for Sol Harrison at DC Comics, putting together a series of comic book compilations: the best of DC war comics (*America at War*), the best of DC science fiction comics (*Mysteries in Space*), and the best of DC romance comics (*Heart Throbs*). (The rare hardcover edition of *Heart Throbs* now sells for as much as $1,000.)

For G.P. Putnam's Sons, Jeff Mendel and I did the first-ever hardcover and trade paperback collection and history of Archie comics. For *The Best of Archie*, Jeff and I went to their offices and, as I had at DC years before during my lunch hours, sat for days and days in their vault and read every single Archie comic book story ever produced.

Then we selected the ones that we felt qualified as the best. Little did I know then the impact Archie and his friends would have on my life in the years to come!

During my years at United Artists, my book and comic book writing saved my creative sanity. DC back then had been planning a new round of backup features to add to their comic books and they okayed me going forward with my two favorites. One was to be called *Tales from Earth 2* and would feature looks at whatever happened to the superheroes from that earth who weren't getting much play anymore in the pages of the latest comic books. My first scripts dealt with a third-banana member of the Justice Society of America whose name was Mr. Terrific, although, to be frank, in the 1940s, he wasn't. Unfortunately for him, some TV producer lifted his name and made a TV series at the height of the *Batman* TV show's popularity when camp was in, and we were abused by this silliness. In my script, the faded hero knew when to throw in the towel. A few post-forty-year-old baseball players and football players could've taken a lesson from him. The second script was for Hour-Man, a Golden Age hero who popped a Miraclo Pill and gained super-strength for one hour. In my '70s version, being older than his fellow JSA superheroes, his physical condition was really waning and he became addicted to his pills and spiraled downward. The Sandman followed with a fearsome network of agents reporting to him a la the Shadow. Also part of that series were: Johnny Thunder, who would combine with his magic thunderbolt into one legitimate superhero; Earth 2's Robin, who would try to win the respect of the team as Batman's successor, but who wouldn't be accepted easily; the New Seven Soldiers of Victory, comprised of the second-banana heroes of Earth 2, such as the Crimson Avenger, the original Robotman, Congorilla, Sargona (daughter of Sargon), the original Green Arrow and Speedy, and the original Aquaman; and Starman, who would become involved in space fantasy adventures more befitting his name. Then DC's backup plans were snuffed, and my completed scripts never saw the light of day. But some years later, DC went forward with that Hour-Man addiction theme. My other backup opus had been one of my favorite DC heroes when I was little, Congorilla. The premise there was that a great white hunter named Congo Bill encountered a Witch Doctor. And with one "Ooo eee ooo ah ah, ting tang walla walla bing bang," he gave Bill a magic ring that, when rubbed, caused a magical transference of Bill's mind into the body of a great golden gorilla . . . and, sadly, vice versa. My version would switch the story's focus from following the adventures of the gorilla's body possessing Bill's consciousness to Bill's body possessing the mind of an ape, as he/it gets into all sorts of embarrassing predicaments while on the loose. The Congorilla title logo was made out of bananas. I still have the original art to his splash page. Too bad it never saw print; it was a lark to write!

The comic book I was most proud of writing in that era was one I had the good luck to work on with one of the greatest artists of the Golden and Silver Ages, Alex Toth. As a teen, Toth began by drawing *Green Lantern*, and later gave us fanboys the definitive comic book version of Zorro. Toth drew the best western comics in history and a stunning Black Canary, before venturing onto the Hollywood animation field, where he

Oh! The cosmic weirdness of the circle of life! Some ten years after I bought *Fantastic Four* #1, *Incredible Hulk* #1, and *Fantastic Four* #12, from Marc D. Nadel of Brooklyn, NY, for the sum total of $2.50, he would turn out to be the artist drawing my new "Congorilla" story for DC, which was aborted at the last minute due to the infamous "DC Implosion" when it canceled many of its comic book titles and eliminated all backup features. Sigh.

designed everything from *Jonny Quest* and *Space Ghost* to *Super Friends*. It was Alex's and my job to take the Question, one of the greatest creations of the godlike artist Steve Ditko (Yep! The co-creator of Spider-Man and Dr. Strange and Captain Atom and the new Blue Beetle), and bring that character back to comics after a lengthy absence. Ditko's Question was a right-wing newscaster/investigative reporter, and though my politics were formulated in the late '60s and early '70s and tilt left, I had to write the kind of political gobbledygook found today on Fox TV. I loved writing as if I were Ronald Reagan! It was like being in the Twilight Zone again! On that project, Alex Toth taught me more about visual storytelling and comic book writing than anyone else in my career. I absorbed it all like (you're expecting me to say "a sponge" but you're totally forgetting who I am) . . . the Absorbing Man! One of the greatest compliments I ever received came years later from Alex. He had been doing a series of recollections about his life, his career, and his work. In his later years, he created for himself a persona of a real curmudgeon and was pretty merciless in his opinions, not only of other people and their work, but also of his own work over the years. But he cited my script for the Question as being a good one. Who could ask for anything more? (If you've ever read one of the greatest graphic novels of all time, Alan Moore and Dave Gibbon's *Watchmen*, you may know that their odd character Rorschach was originally going to be the Question. For assorted reasons we need not delve into here, the decision was made not to use Ditko's original version and just call him something different.)

Meanwhile back at UA, every day was different and I kept learning. Some days were grinding and tough, some were fun and wacky, and some were spent just dealing with Hollywood's raging bullshit. There are many stories of these L.A.–specific kinds of experiences, but two of the strangest tales revolve around horses and piranhas. . . .

There was the day I got a call from the horse in *The Black Stallion*. (Okay, so maybe it was his attorney who called me. Remember, we're not going to let the facts get in the way of a good story here.) He was complaining that he didn't have in his contract any merchandising rights, and he wanted a merchandising royalty. I offered him five bags of carrots and extra oats, but the horse said, "Nay!" (Sorry). I checked with one of my bosses and was instructed to offer him the same merchandising deal Sly Stallone had in *Rocky*. If the horse's likeness was merchandised as "The Black Stallion," the horse wouldn't get a royalty because that would be considered to be the image of the Black Stallion. But if UA merchandised any images of the horse as himself, he would get a royalty. And the only way to tell when he was the horse as himself was by the white diamond on his head. When that was colored in black, he was, instead, the Black Stallion. Done deal.

UA was happy. The horse was happy and awaited the day the studio would pony up. Like movie studios do, it never did.

Raging bullshit.

My love for movies was never more evident than when I was put in charge of a project that Roger Corman, King of B pictures, was putting together. Roger loved cultivating young (and therefore cheap) talent, and some of the biggest names in the business came out of his stable. This film was going to be his cheap version of *Jaws*, but be about piranha. It would be the first project I handled from start to finish at the studio, and I plunged into it with energy and enthusiasm. Many of us working on it were getting our first major experience in the moviemaking process. The producer was Jeff Schectman, a really smart entrepreneur. The line producer was Jon Davison, who seemed to have the answers for every production problem that cropped up. John Sayles was the screenwriter, and it may well have been his first film and helped him pay for his first pet independent project, *Return of the Secaucus Seven*. Joe Dante was the first-time director. He'd show up in my life again for about three minutes as a potential director of our first Batman movie, before *Gremlins* and *Explorers* appeared in theaters. The very, very young Gale Ann Hurd was a production assistant on that project for Roger. Paul Bartel was the mad creative genius behind it all, and our association led to us working again in what was then the not-too-distant future. And then there was Roger's special effects guy, Jim, who had been given a budget of about nine hundred bucks to work with. I clearly remember everyone else who worked on this picture, but what the hell was Jim's last name again? Oh, yeah! "Cameron." I wonder whatever happened to him?

Fun and wacky.

Every day at United Artists certainly was different, but often, so were the nights! The NYC blackout of July 1977 happened while I was working at UA. That night, we were all up in the fourteenth-floor screening room watching *New York, New York* when the projector died. We were in pitch blackness waiting for either the movie or the lights to come on. Neither did. We had to feel our way in a procession, holding the person in front of us by the waist down the fourteen flights, and we found ourselves in the thick humidity and heat of an utterly dark and inhospitable Times Square. Taking our lives into our hands (this was not the Disneyesque Times Square of today), we ran over to Sardi's, where there were candles on every table. They were giving away all their ice cream before it melted. The uniformed doorman there had made a deal with a cab driver. He would drive each patron home safely in Manhattan and then come back for the next patron. So we sat in the upstairs window looking out over history in the making and the dark silhouettes of skyscrapers, eating enough ice cream to last us till the '80s.

Our car was parked at the Port Authority on Eighth Avenue at 41st Street, perhaps the last place in midtown you'd want to find yourself (if you even COULD find yourself) in the blackout. It was dangerous. Finally, our turn came. I gave the cab driver all my cash on hand to go to the parking lot's exit ramp and drive up it in the wrong direction in order to drive us right to the space our car was parked in. As we rode down the ramp toward the Lincoln Tunnel, we looked back. There was no doubt. This was a real-life version of one of those 1950s end-of-the-world movies. It was a real Twilight Zone moment. As we crossed the magic tunnel line separating New Jersey from New York, I nervously glanced in my rearview mirror, just to be absolutely sure there were no giant ants following me to the safety of the Garden State.

Before I knew it, I was creeping past the three-year mark at UA. I reminded myself about my promise . . . my plan. I would spend no more than four years as a lawyer . . . to learn all I could about financing and producing movies and to meet as many people in the industry as possible. And then I would quit and not allow myself to be trapped being a lawyer for the rest of my life. It was time to make my move. I discussed it with Nancy. We decided it would be a calculated risk. I tried to project myself far into the future and understood the risk of one day becoming one of those pathetic guys who tells everyone, including his children and even himself, "Hey! I COULD HAVE been. . . . I COULD HAVE done. . . ." It was time to roll the dice. I called Sol Harrison and said, "Sol, I have the credentials now. I did everything I said I would. I want to buy the rights to Batman." He was aghast! He knew that Batman had peaked and flamed out with the rise and fall of the mid-'60s television series and took down all the merchandising with it. He knew that the execs at Warner Bros. to whom he reported considered Superman to be the one and only comic book property sufficiently well known worldwide to be capable of being made into a big live-action movie. If he even mentioned Batman to them, he said, they'd laugh him out of the room. Sol asked me if there was any way he could convince me not to waste my money and time and talk me out of it. I said emphatically there wasn't. Sol sighed and said, "Okay, Schmoozle . . . come on in!"

# PART IV:

# AT LONG LAST,
# THE DARK KNIGHT RETURNS!

# CHAPTER EIGHTEEN

# Ben and Me, the WORLD'S FINEST PRODUCER TEAM!

"Michael, Michael, Michael," moaned Sol Harrison, the vice president of DC Comics, "I would say this same thing to my own son. Don't waste your money! Find something else to do with it! Since he went off the air on TV, Batman is as dead as a dodo! Nobody's interested in Batman!"

"But I still want to, Sol!" I protested. "If I can do it in a dark and serious way, it'll be a chance to make a feature film like no one's ever seen before . . . a new kind of hero for the '80s and beyond!"

He warned me I'd have to negotiate the deal with an exec of Warner Publishing who was not a comic book guy. He for sure would want the same contract or one similar to the one he had with the Salkinds for the rights for Superman, although the conventional wisdom was that Superman was in a class by himself. So, he thought the powers that be might well admit that at least to some extent that Batman was worth only some percentage of the Superman deal.

In that moment, on the phone with Sol, I realized that I was so emotionally attached to Batman and to my dream of making this movie that I would probably just agree to anything and everything. What was that old adage I had heard around the eighth floor of the UA Building? "A lawyer who represents himself has a fool for a client"? I needed to find someone who could negotiate this deal on my behalf . . . and someone who actually knew how to mount a production, which was something I had not yet attempted. I spoke to my United Artists lawyer compadres for their brain-trust input on this issue and possible candidates to explore. The answer came from Charles Melniker, the new kid on the floor. He had started a year after I had in the department, and we had quickly become friends. Little did I know that a chunk of a lifetime later, we would be more like brothers than friends. Charles asked me if I'd like to meet his dad to talk about Batman. Was he kiddin'?

Benjamin Melniker was already a legend way back then. There was reverence for his name within the Legal Department at UA, as well as at the other studios. The things I had heard about him over the years were the equivalent of hearing the story of the movie industry itself. He began his career at MGM in 1940 and worked his way up from lawyer to the head of its antitrust division in its negotiations with the U.S. government, which back then was trying to break up the studios' monopoly on production/distribution with exhibition. In short, the major studios were being forced to divest themselves of

The legendary Benjamin Melniker, executive vice president of MGM and known as "The MGM Lion" in his deal-negotiating heyday during MGM's "Tiffany" days, with his elegant wife, Shirley, at the premiere of Ben-Hur.

their theaters. Most concerned parties were seduced by the sexier production side of MGM in the split, but Ben said the smartest people were the Tisch brothers, who recognized the value of the real estate on the theater ownership side and, thus, gravitated to Loews Theatres. Ben worked with world-famous attorney Louis Nizer on the divestiture and a number of other high-profile legal matters, and documentation of his participation can be found in Nizer's best seller, *My Life in Court*. Ben started commuting to Washington, D.C., once a day from his office atop the Loews Building in Times Square, across from the Astor Hotel, so he could personally negotiate with the Attorney General what came to be called the Paramount Consent Decree of 1947, whereby all the studios divested themselves of their theaters.

In connection with that case, Ben appeared before the Supreme Court. Before long, he ascended at MGM when it was the Tiffany of motion picture studios. He became its only executive vice president, a member of the parent board of the company, and chairman of its Film Selection Committee. Ben negotiated the deals for *Ben-Hur, Dr. Zhivago, 2001: A Space Odyssey, Gigi*, and all the MGM musicals of that era. He brokered the deal with Colonel Tom Parker for Elvis Presley to make movies for MGM and negotiated with Grace Kelly's father to place her under contract at the studio. So yes, I wanted to meet with him!

Ben became my partner, my friend, my mentor, my idol, and my second father. He revealed to me so much behind-the-curtains/behind-the-screen movie history that no one else alive today knows. He was there and he lived it. He was privy to lots of secrets. At a dinner we had in Charleston, South Carolina, with Louis Jourdan, I heard the fascinating story of how the Oscar-winning film *Gigi* came to be made, even with the studio fearing World War II backlash about one of its stars, who might have been a collaborator with the Vichy regime in France. Years later, at a dinner in Atlanta with David O. Selznick's son, Jeffrey, I not only heard about *Gone With the Wind* and *King Kong*, but witnessed a revelation. Our first Batman movie had come out to a box-office bonanza. And shortly thereafter, we were at Turner discussing a new project. When Ben was at MGM, he was in charge of David O. Selznick's pictures, Selznick being the son-in-law of studio chief Louis B. Mayer. So at this dinner, Jeffrey asked Ben why MGM had been so tough on his father, refusing to put so many of his projects into production. Ben explained to Jeffrey that that had not been the real situation at all. He said MGM was dying for Selznick to make many more films for them, but increasingly Selznick himself refused to push that final button for the film to be shot. Jeffrey was baffled by that statement. Ben laid out his perspective on it all. He said, "Jeffrey, your father was one of the best producers of all time. Yet he came to live in fear. He became fearful of going forward with pictures that might not live up to *Gone With the Wind* and his other hits. He became fearful of tarnishing his own reputation." Jeffrey was clearly stunned by what he was hearing and quietly processed it for awhile. That's when he turned to me and said, "Michael, don't make the same mistake my father did. Don't feel you have to top *Batman* every time. Just enjoy the fact that you're doing what you enjoy doing. Not many people are lucky enough to be able to do that." I've never forgotten that discussion or Jeffrey's words to me.

Charles Melniker agreed to set up a meeting for me with his dad at his office in New York's MGM Building at 1350 Avenue of the Americas. Ben had a longstanding reputation in Hollywood of being rough and tough, but fair. His nickname, bestowed on him by the producers, agents, and entertainment lawyers who dealt with him, was "The MGM Lion."

In my world of comic books, superhero team-ups were always special, especially when they involved Batman. He was teamed up with Superman in every issue of *World's Finest Comics* when I was growing up, and with all the other superheroes in a comic book called

*Brave & Bold*. So to me, working with Ben was like having my World's Finest adventures in Hollywood or being Brave & Bold in our New York movie meetings. One of my favorite days in L.A. on the producing trail took place in the Valley when we were scheduled to have an important late-morning meeting at Universal Television and an early afternoon meeting at the Hanna-Barbera animation studio, home to *The Flintstones, The Jetsons, Tom & Jerry, Super Friends, Jonny Quest,* and *Space Ghost.* (Loved him! Hated the two kids he hung around with! Thought his monkey was annoying!) We were at Universal to close the deal for a Swamp Thing live-action TV series. Ben was amazing in his dealings. He granted the companies that wanted to finance Swamp Thing films one-picture licenses only and reserved all other rights to us, including merchandising. In this case, as we closed the live-action TV deal with Universal, we simultaneously closed an animated TV series deal with Fox Kids and a master toy license deal with Kenner, then makers of the best boys' toys in the business. Our exec at Universal TV was a bright and personable man in his mid-thirties who offered to take us to the Universal Executive Dining Room to celebrate the deal. While there, he pointed to the tall, silver-haired man with the giant-sized '80s glasses who walked in and sat down by himself at the first table to have lunch and read his trades (*Daily Variety* and *Hollywood Reporter*). "You see that man over there?" he whispered. "That's Lew Wasserman, the King of Universal Pictures! On our way out, when we pass by his table, if he's not busy, I'll introduce you to him," he generously offered. I was excited at the prospect of meeting one of the real giants in the history of the motion picture and television industry. Ben said nothing. Not a word. At the end of lunch, we headed on out. Our exec worked up the nerve and approached the King. "Mr. Wasserman, sir? I wonder if I might introduce—" He got no further. Wasserman had glanced up from his reading, his face erupted into a wide grin of genuine excitement, and he cried out, "BEN!" He stood up and gripped Ben in the kind of bear hug you've seen in old movies when guys who were comrades in battle together in World War II meet each other again years later.

As we turned to leave, Wasserman gave the MGM Lion one last bear hug. "Ben," he said, "do you realize we're the last two of our whole group who are still standing and active in the business?"

Ben outlived Lew Wasserman, becoming "the last one standing" from the Golden Age of Hollywood.

Our next meeting was with one of the heads of Hanna-Barbera to close our deal to produce an animated TV series. As the deal was signed, the exec said to us, "You boys are in luck! Joe Barbera is in the office today. How'd you like to meet Joe Barbera himself?" I was so excited to have the chance to meet the co-founder of this great animation studio that created many of the cartoon shows my childhood was built upon, beginning with *Ruff and Reddy*! Ben said nothing. Not a word. We were ushered into the Big Man's office, and as we entered, the exec said, "Joe, I'd like to introduce you to two producers we're going to be working with on a great new prime-time television show—" He got no further. Joe glanced up from his desk, his face bursting into a stunned, wide grin as he yelled, "BEN!" He rushed over and hugged him like he had just been reunited with his long-lost brother. The president of Hanna-Barbera was dumbstruck. I was getting used to this. Another chapter in the history of the Biz unfolded before me. Joe said, "Ben, if it wasn't for you, there would have been no Hanna-Barbera, no Flintstones, no Jetsons!" He then explained to us that Ben had been instrumental in getting the head of MGM Animation, Fred Quimby, to hire him and Bill Hanna, since that division reported to Ben. And then years later, when the powers that be were shuttering MGM's animation studio, and Joe and Bill told Ben about them forming their own new animation studio, it was Ben who gave them Tom & Jerry for a pittance to help them get on their feet. This was the incredible man who had become my producing partner.

The first time I ran over to Ben's office on the eleventh floor of the MGM Building during my lunch break from UA, I pitched my little heart out as to the history of Batman, why I felt it was commercial, why it had to be dark and serious and called THE Batman and not just Batman, and the potential for sequels, animation, toys and games, and all forms of merchandising. I felt awe just being in the presence of the man I had heard about ever since I joined the movie biz. But Ben knew nothing about comic books and had never read one in his life. Like most adults from my parents' generation and like virtually every studio executive and agent at that time, he didn't realize the difference between comic strips and comic books. His primary exposure to Superman was the George Reeves TV series and the radio show starring Bud Collyer; his knowledge of Batman was limited to the 1960s television show; and his general attitude toward comic books themselves was a holdover from the Dr. Wertham generation. I quickly surmised that my pitch would of necessity have to begin with educating each and every pitchee as to the history of comic books in America and the role played by THE Batman.

Once I started rolling, there was no stopping me. I spoke at a quick clip as I do whenever I'm pitching about something that excites me from my heart to my brain, God help Ben. . . .

"The comic book industry was officially born in 1933 when M.C. ('Max') Gaines, working with Harry Wildenberg of Eastern Color, folded a section of a newspaper a few times and realized it could be cut, stapled, and sold as a book of comic strips. When sold for 10 cents in chain stores and newsstands, America had the comic book," I explained. I was just getting warmed up.

"In 1938, the industry would enter its Golden Age with the advent of the superhero in the form of Superman, who debuted in June 1938's *Action Comics* #1. The moment it became clear that the superhero was a successful concept, the powers that were at DC Comics asked teenage cartoonist Bob Kane if he could come up with DC's second one. Kane, along with his collaborator Bill Finger, reasoned that if the first superhero had amazing superpowers, they should take the exact opposite approach for the second superhero and, thus, The Bat-Man would have no such superpowers. His greatest superpower is his humanity!" I proclaimed.

And then I powered into the gut-wrenching origin of The Batman for Ben so that he would understand not only what drove young Bruce Wayne to wear a cape and mask, but why this primal story makes a dark and serious approach to the character the only valid way to bring him to life in the movies.

"When Bruce Wayne was a boy of around twelve, he watched his parents murdered on the streets of Gotham City. On their graves, he swore he'd get the guy who did this and all the bad guys, sacrificing his childhood from that moment on and committing himself to a lifelong mission that would require him to walk through hell in order to get to the other side . . . if ever he could.

"Bruce Wayne then perfected his mind and body, representing the best level a human being can reach. Millions and millions of children, teens, and soldiers of the World War II era could relate to this character and bought up every issue of the comic books The Batman appeared in. One of the three top-selling superheroes of the Golden Age, The Batman appeared back then in such comic book titles as *Batman Comics*, *Detective Comics*, *World's Finest Comics*, and select issues of *All-Star Comics* with his super-pals in the Justice Society of America. Robin even had his own feature in the pages of *Star-Spangled Comics*," I poured out.

Already more than five minutes into my pitch, I knew I had to swiftly get to the TV show or risk losing the attention span of my pitchee.

"By the 1960s, following two Batman Columbia movie serials in the '40s and ongoing guest appearances on the Superman radio show, Batman made his debut on TV and made ratings history. The country . . . the whole world . . . went Bat-Crazy! There was tons of merchandising, hit cartoon shows, and a movie version in 1967 of the TV series. It seemed as if every major star in Hollywood was clamoring to play a super-villain on that show, as the Joker, the Penguin, the Riddler, and Catwoman became as famous as Batman himself. Batman's comic books were out-selling Superman's now, and he was soon starring in such new comic book titles as *Brave & Bold*, *Batman and the Outsiders*, *The Joker*, *The Justice League of America*, and more!

"But the world outside true comic book fans has never really seen The Batman as created by Bob Kane and Bill Finger in 1939 . . . the creature of the night . . . the darkknight detective . . . stalking criminals from the shadows. Every true comic book fan understands that inserting the word 'The' in front of the name Batman indicates the version that is dark," I explained.

And with that, I showed comic books from my extensive collection and articles showing early art from *Detective Comics* and *Batman Comics* that could dramatically point out the difference. A 1939 pre-Robin drawing of The Batman as compared to a 1967 pop version of Batman was illuminating. I showed comics from the '70s by Denny O'Neil and Neal Adams reverting Batman to The Batman, and stylish issues of *Detective Comics* by Steve Engelhart and Marshall Rogers. The point was clearly made.

But while my pitchee could now wrap his head around the visuals, he still could not grasp what a story of The Batman would feel like as compared to a story of Batman. And that's when I pulled out a full-blown screenplay titled "Return of The Batman." I had written one draft and co-wrote another with my Indiana University pal, Michael Bourne (today an internationally famous jazz critic and DJ). I handed it over to Ben so that he could read it and have his questions answered. I did not write it expecting that it would be the movie we would make, but rather to have a document that would shake up anyone used to seeing the campy TV Batman. In this 1975 script, there were no super-villains. I wanted to show that The Batman did not need over-the-top super-villains in order to be a great story. It was grounded much more in reality and in everyone being human. It showed off the darkknight detective's ability to be just that . . . a DETECTIVE. It showed The Batman without Robin, but with Alfred being his closest confidante. But it also showed something unparalleled. It featured The Batman in his fifties, forced to come out of retirement to deal with the first appearance of terrorism on America's shores. Years later, the president of DC Comics would frame it this way, "You wrote a sort of *The Dark Knight Returns* ten years before *The Dark Knight Returns.*" I think I wrote simply one vision for what a serious Batman might look like. This is in no way intended to distract from the great Frank Miller's seminal work in the deconstruction of the superhero and the growth of the graphic novel. Miller's 1986 work would actually prove helpful in getting the 1989 Batman movie made, as execs, agents, and talent saw that a dark and serious Batman could be colossally successful. But my 1975 script, submitted with all the pitch material, helped open people's eyes to a very different version of Batman from the one they had previously known. (As evidence that my script worked as I intended, the first screenwriter we submitted the project to, one of my two favorite screenwriters of the James Bond films, Richard Maibaum, said the script provided him with clarity as to what we wanted to do with this movie and the difference between Batman and THE Batman. When my other favorite screenwriter of the James Bond movies, Tom Mankiewicz, came aboard to write the first drafts, his reaction was similar.)

Leaving my pitchee with what I hoped was a memorable oral pitch along with carefully selected comic books and "Return of The Batman" to peruse, I moved on to the part of the producing business I hate the most—waiting.

Ben said he wanted a day or two to consider everything I had laid out for him and that he would call me. He did so the very next day. We came to a quick understanding. Dark and serious or nothing. No one, no company, could come aboard without subscribing to that philosophy. Better to let it die than do it any other way. I told Ben this was my life's dream. He said, "Then let's start making your dream come true, Michael." How could anyone say "No" to this?

Our negotiations with DC Comics to buy the rights to Batman took six months. It was just as well, because in 1979 dollars, a huge amount of money was needed upon execution, so much so that we could only afford to get a six-month exclusive option, with a six-month renewal for the same price, before having to put up the big, big money at the end of a year to exercise the full option. DC Comics, under orders from above, was told that despite its lack of faith in Batman as a movie, it would not dilute the deal it got on Superman and that either we paid for Batman the same amount of money paid for Superman or there would be no deal, and Batman would continue to gather dust in their library. We were under the gun and the pressure was mounting. On October 3, 1979, Ben and I formed BatFilm Productions, Inc., and paid the option price with money we had raised from friends and family. Contractually, Warner Bros. had the right of first negotiation. Not only did they have no interest whatsoever in making a non-Superman comic book character into a feature film, they so hated the idea that they declined to even listen to my pitch. It was just thanks for the right of first negotiation, but no thanks, goodbye,

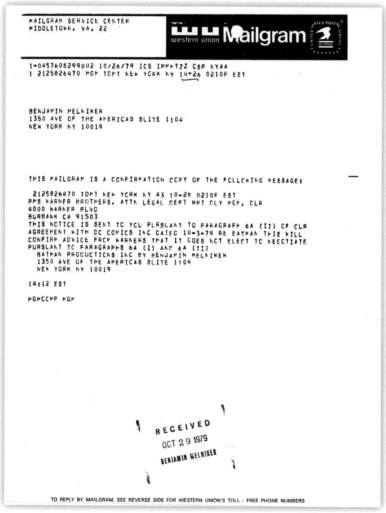

Every single studio passed on my dark and serious vision for a Batman movie. Some didn't even wish to hear my pitch at the time!

and good luck. I still have their mailgram passing on Batman as part of my favorite rejection slips collection.

I was stunned by the stone-cold rejection we got without even a chance to pitch the idea. Ben always knew how to take bad news and turn it around. Whenever something bad or devastating happened in business, he would tell me to complete the following sentence: "This is the GREATEST thing that could have happened because . . ." We always found a way to complete that sentence, no matter how bleak things became. Now, it was the fact that, in the end, Warner's passing opened the door for other studios to make a deal with us for Batman. I really wanted to go back to my alma mater United Artists first, so this was my big chance! I went in to pitch to a Production VP, who was an interesting guy with a habit of using a classic expletive after almost every other word, so I'll present every OTHER word of his rejection following my heartfelt pitch. "Michael, you're _____ insane! Batman and Robin will _____ never be successful because the movie _____ *Robin and Marian* didn't do well!" (*Robin and Marian* was a '70s movie starring Sean Connery and Audrey Hepburn as an aging Robin Hood and Maid Marian.)

I give up. YOU tell ME.

I stared at him in silence for a few long moments, and then scooped up the Batman comics I had brought in to illustrate my pitch, stood up, turned around, and walked out of his office. But at various times over the following ten years, I would climb to the top of a mountain and sit in a lotus position and ponder what he had said to me. After all this time and thought, I can only conclude that he said what he said because the movie title "Robin and Marian" and the comic book characters Batman and Robin share the common word Robin. There's simply no other nexus. So much for my alma mater.

I thought every studio would line up at my doorstep for my vision of Batman. But everywhere we went, the results were the same. "Michael, you're out of your mind! You can't make a movie out of some old television series! That's never been done!" "Michael, you're nuts! You can't make a comic book superhero 'dark and serious'!" "Michael, you're crazy! The world will only remember and love the potbellied, funny, Pow! Zap! Wham! Batman. We'll consider that, but only that." At several times, we had development funding but distribution deals fell through. As a result, one day we found ourselves pitching at Columbia. The head of Production then was a dapper, silver-haired gentleman who, like just about everyone I had been pitching to, was of that Dr. Wertham generation. When I concluded my pitch, he shook his head and gave me a real old-fashioned "tsk-tsk" and said, "Michael, you're wrong (at least for the first time I wasn't "crazy"). Batman will never work as a movie, because our movie *Annie* didn't do well."

"Wait a second," I said, caught somewhere in between the Twilight Zone and the Bizarro World, "are you talking about the little redheaded girl who sings 'Tomorrow'?"

"Yes, of course," he smiled.

"But what does SHE have to do with Batman?" I begged, pleading for sanity.

"Oh, come ON, Michael!" he said dismissively. "They're BOTH out of the FUNNY pages."

And THAT was my rejection from Columbia Pictures.

Rejected! Rejected! Rejected! Rejected! Rejected!

"We're going to 'pass.'" "We're 'passing' on Batman." "It's a 'pass' for us." "While we're 'passing' on Batman, our door is open if you want to come back and discuss the campy TV version." "Thanks, but it's a 'pass.'"

Every single studio turned me down. What I thought would be a quick sale with studio after studio competing for the rights was quickly becoming one dead end after another for Ben and me.

I wound up doing three things along the way to try to make the concept of The Batman stalking criminals from the shadows into a concept Hollywood execs might find easier to grasp. In addition to that "Return of The Batman" script I wrote with Michael Bourne, I wrote a seventeen-page, single-spaced creative blueprint memo specifically explaining the difference between the campy Batman these people knew from TV and the original Bob Kane–Bill Finger concept of Batman as a creature of the night. The third piece of the puzzle fell into place for me in late May of 1980. Memorial Day weekend was upon us, and I hopped on the NJ Transit bus in New York City, headed for home. At the Port Authority Bus Terminal, I bought the *New York Post* and opened it to the weekend movie section. And there it was! Staring back at me was that famous Jack Nicholson "Here's Johnny" publicity still from the horror film *The Shining*, which was opening that weekend along with the higher profile *The Empire Strikes Back*. I immediately realized what I was looking at. I tore it out of the newspaper. I could barely contain myself until I could get off that bus, race home to my desk, and get to work on that picture. I used White-Out to whiten Jack Nicholson's face. I used a red pen to do his lips. Then I used a Magic Marker on his hair. Voila! He was the only actor then who could play the Joker! No, he WAS the Joker!

So with the clock ticking loudly in our ears, Ben and I found ourselves with a pile of rejections from all the major studios and what were then called mini-majors like the Ladd Company and Lorimar Pictures. "Rejections" is not the correct term. They were more along the line of "This is the worst idea I've ever heard!" But Ben had a Plan B. He explained that when he had been running MGM, he had attempted to hire three talented young guys to run the studio's production as a "troika." They were Barry Beckerman, Jerry Takovsky, and Peter Guber. Guber had gone on to become a vice president at Columbia Pictures. But now, he and Beckerman were working together at Casablanca Records with Guber's partner, Neil Bogart. Casablanca was a record label mainstay of the disco era. Ben had heard they were about to be funded by PolyGram of Europe to do a slate of feature films. Ben felt that Peter and Barry were younger and

There it was, staring me in the face aboard a bus back to New Jersey in 1980, Jack Nicholson in his "Here's Johnny!" publicity photo for the film *The Shining*. But it wasn't Jack I saw! Racing home, I whited out his face, colored in his lips red, re-did the hair, and "Voila!" To me he was the ONLY actor who could play the Joker in our first *Batman* movie!

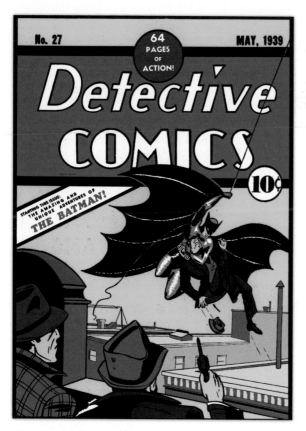

The comic book that introduced The Bat-Man to the world: *Detective Comics* #27 from May 1939, which in 2010 sold at auction for $1,100,000!

more hip than the production execs I'd been pitching to thus far. With one call, he got Peter on the line and put me on the phone to provide the short version of the pitch. Peter thought it sounded great and wanted all the details and the full pitch. He asked if we could come in to see him the very next day at his office on Sunset Boulevard near Laurel Canyon. I explained that we were in New York but could be there in two days. And we were.

At Casablanca, we met Peter, Neil, Barry, and their biz affairs lawyer, David Saunders, whom I had dealt with lawyer-to-lawyer at United Artists. My pitch would be to Peter and Barry. Exactly the way I had pitched to Ben, I launched into my passion-filled pitch for Batman . . . "The" Batman . . . to be brought to the silver screen. I took them through the comic book history of Batman, using comic books from my personal collection to usher them into the world of this creature of the night. I showed them the first Batman story from *Detective Comics #27* and the first Joker story and Catwoman tale from *Batman #1*. I showed them "Night of the Stalker," my favorite ever Batman story, and "Night of the Reaper." I gave them the overview of the Denny O'Neil/Neal Adams and the Steve Engelhart/Marshall Rogers runs on Batman and Detective. I guided them through the script I had written . . . just enough to give them the feel for a dark Batman. I reintroduced them to Batman's villains . . . NOT the way they were portrayed on the TV series, but the way they were originally conceived. And I introduced them to the greatest Batman villains created after the TV show, Ra's al Ghul and Man-Bat. I told them the story of the origin of Batman and the origin of the Joker, and when I was done, both Peter and Barry were enthusiastic. We discussed possible writers and directors. A picture of this size and packed with action and SFX led us all quickly to the James Bond films, and everyone was in agreement that the two best Bond writers were Richard Maibaum and Tom Mankiewicz. (Tom had also been the lifesaving script doctor on the Superman movie.) Guy Hamilton's name was the first mentioned for director. (He had directed *Goldfinger* among other films.) Peter, who was pacing while I was pitching, was totally caught up in it and on board. "Let's do it!" he proclaimed, and instructed us to lock ourselves in a room with David and not emerge until a deal was made. Barry would be the day-to-day production exec working on this with us. And Universal would be the distributor because Casablanca had an overall deal with them. And we were then locked away for three days and nights until a deal was reached.

This was it! We were on our way! What I did not know was that we were on our way to a ten-year odyssey that would test my mettle, test my ability to withstand inhuman levels of frustration, challenge my belief in myself and my work, and force me to pull my belt to its last notch with my back financially against the wall. Where was my own superhero now? Where was Batman when I really needed him? Maybe I had to look within.

# CHAPTER NINETEEN

# BLACKEST NIGHT: The TEN-YEAR HUMAN ENDURANCE CONTEST!

New York ComiCon 1980 was my seventeenth annual comic book convention, and we were about to do something that had never been done before. I told the good marketing/public relations folks at Casablanca how important my fellow comic book fans were to our getting a great positive send-off. I asked them to let us announce the film there. But no movie project had ever been announced at a comic convention. It was preposterous to them. They had never heard of such a thing, but they ultimately agreed. We made an arrangement with the new president of DC Comics, the talented and creative Jenette Kahn, who had taken over from Sol Harrison, not only to make the announcement together, but also to share the cost of the collector's item buttons we would distribute at the press conference with the bat symbol and the words "1980—The Year of The Batman." Casablanca put us in funds to host

# BATFILM
## PRODUCTIONS INC.

**BENJAMIN MELNIKER & MICHAEL USLAN, PRODUCERS**

1350 AVENUE OF THE AMERICAS, SUITE 1104   NEW YORK, NEW YORK 10019 □ (212) 582-6470

BatFilm Productions, Inc. requests the honor
of your presence at our first public announcement
of a major theatrical motion picture based on a
world renowned super-hero who has become a legend
over the past forty years.

The announcement will be made Friday July 4,
1980 at 7 p.m. in the Georgian Ballroom of the
Statler Hotel, Seventh Avenue at Thirty-Third
Street, New York City.

A cocktail party will precede the announcement
at 5 p.m. in the Petite Terrace of the Statler Hotel.

THIS INVITATION IS NOT TRANSFERABLE

*INDICATES TRADEMARK

The first time a movie company ever showed up at a ComiCon to announce a feature film was in 1980 in New York . . . and it was us announcing the *Batman* movie with DC Comics and Bob Kane! Here's BatFilm Productions' invitation to the press and the fans.

DC Comics' coordinated announcement for the 1980 Comicon unveiling of a dark and serious Batman feature film.

---

DC COMICS INC.
75 Rockefeller Plaza
New York. N.Y. 10019
(212) 484-8512

### For Immediate Release

### NEW YORK CITY CONVENTION TO SPOTLIGHT DC COMICS SUPER-HEROES

DC Comics Inc. today reveals its participation in announcing the production of a <u>multi-million dollar theatrical film by a Hollywood studio, based on a world-renowned DC Super-hero.</u>

The announcement will be made at the <u>13th Annual New York Comic Art Convention</u> at the <u>Statler Hotel</u> in New York City on <u>Friday, July 4th,</u> at <u>7 PM.</u>

The New York Comic Art Convention, which runs from July 4th - 6th, is the biggest and best established convention of its kind in the world. Thousands of comic book fans, young and old alike, attend the event each year, making it a fitting site for an announcement that will thrill both the comic book world and the film industry.

The announcement will be made on the convention floor of the Statler Hotel on 33rd Street.

The theme of this year's comic convention will be the <u>40th anniversary of The Batman</u>'s appearance in his own monthly comic book. <u>DC Comics Inc.</u> plans a number of events to celebrate the occasion, including a panel discussion featuring the current creative staff of the Batman comic.

One of the highlights of <u>The Batman</u> celebration will be a giant-sized exhibit featuring photo boards which allow fans to appear as The Batman, Robin, or their favorite super-villain; a scale model of the <u>Bat-Cave</u>, The Batman's mysterious headquarters; a Batman villain make-up demonstration; and a <u>slide presentation of all 330 Batman comic covers</u>, a sequence which stretches from 1940 to the present.

To top off this July 4th Batman weekend, the world-famous <u>Bat-Signal will be projected onto the west side of the Empire State Building</u> from 8 - 10 PM on July 4th, 5th and 6th !

############

FOR MORE INFO CONTACT:

Jack C. Harris
212-484-8512

A Warner Communications Company

an elaborate pre-announcement cocktail party for comic book industry professionals, the press, and, for the first time ever, the comic book fan press, which had never before been treated with respect outside the cloistered world of comic book publishing. For me, this was a fanboy's dream come true. And we could not proceed without a strong vote of confidence from Bob Kane himself.

The room was jam-packed on that hot July day in the Statler-Hilton Hotel in midtown New York. Jenette welcomed the press and fans, and then I made the first official announcement, pointing out that the days of Pow! Zap! and Wham! were over and that this movie would NOT be about a superhero named "Batman," but rather about a superhero known as "THE Batman." And the place went wild with cheers and a standing ovation that went on and on. Ben had heard from me ad nauseam that to the real fans, the difference between the TV Batman and what I wanted to do could be summed up for them just by adding "The" before his name. Now, he finally saw the amazing impact of what that little word signaled to my fellow hard-core comic book fans. I then turned the podium over to Bob Kane, who described the original intent in the creation of The Batman as being what he called a "mysterioso" tone and characterization and spoke about how much it meant to him to have filmmakers return his character to those true roots. That Christmas, Bob mailed me an original drawing of that "mysterioso" Batman as a

token of his thanks for my passion and commitment to the dark Batman. It's artwork that has remained since then on my office wall under glass.

We were off to a magical start! But then . . .

The production chief at Universal who was so close to Peter left and moved to Filmways. Ben and I were informed that Universal would no longer be distributing Batman, but that Filmways would do so once a long negotiation was completed. "Long" proved accurate. And then, Orion bought Filmways, and the management changed. That deal stopped, and we were told to prepare for many months of negotiations between Casablanca and Twentieth Century-Fox. That deal ultimately did not come together, and we were told to fasten our seat belts for Casablanca's negotiation with Warner Bros. Meanwhile, Casablanca Records had become Casablanca Records and Filmworks, with a splinter company called Boardwalk, and still later the company became PolyGram Pictures, with lauded industry vet and friend of Ben's Gordon Stulberg at the helm. Time passed. More time passed. Even more

The treasured Batman sketch Bob Kane sent me in 1980 in honor of our going forward with what Bob always referred to as a "mysterioso" movie version of The Batman.

time passed. On the directing side, things drifted from consideration of Guy Hamilton to Richard Rush, and Casablanca hurried to have us screen a final cut of his new film, *The Stuntman*. But the speed of action with Rush slowed . . . and then stopped. Joe Dante, my old friend from *Piranha*, had done a marvelous job on his feature film *Gremlins*, and was attached briefly before he left to direct *Explorers* for Paramount. Ivan Reitman was then attached for a long time that included downtime waiting for him to shoot *Ghostbusters* first. And then Reitman was no longer attached. Time passed. More time passed. Even more time passed. Guber's efforts were relentless. He was determined not to let our Batman project succumb to what is known as development hell in Hollywood. Casablanca/PolyGram had hired Tom Mankiewicz to write the first screenplay. He was a consummate pro, major talent, and genuine nice guy. Barry Beckerman was great to work with day-to-day as our initial exec, and he was followed by the brilliant Michael Besman. The long movie development process that would stretch into years involved many, many top-notch execs who all contributed to that first revolutionary Batman film. Among the many execs who deserve credit for the film's ultimate success are Peter and Barry, of course, and hardworking and dedicated pros like industry leader Mark Canton, the extraordinary Roger Birnbaum, the talented and creative Lisa Henson, Bonnie Lee, and Tom Lassally, among many others.*

Ben and I had nabbed the rights to Batman on October 3, 1979. *Batman* was released on June 23, 1989. How do you survive for ten years pursuing a dream? What do you do to support a family and make ends meet? Where do you turn when you have no money and no immediate prospects? Between October 3, 1979, and June 23, 1989, life was not put on hold waiting for *Batman* to be made and made "right." In that time, Nancy and I had a son, lost a baby daughter, had a daughter, had both our moms diagnosed with cancer, and faced financial disaster. These are the aspects of life that have defined me. I wished I could have been my daughter's Batman and saved her. I wished I could have been my mom's and Nancy's mom's superhero and protected them from disease. But I wasn't Batman. All I really ever was was another Bruce Wayne . . . a kid who made a vow to himself about what he wanted to do with his life . . . Here and there, it was my own personal hell. Yet as Dorothy told Aunt Em upon her return from Oz, ". . . but some parts were beautiful!"

*Whenever the success of a comic book movie franchise is discussed, it's easy to forget all the people on the DC comic book side, from the presidents like the legendary Carmine Infantino, Sol Harrison, Jenette Kahn, Paul Levitz, and Diane Nelson to those Batman execs, editors, writers, and artists, inkers, colorists, and letterers who, since 1939, have had to keep the fans coming back every week and find new ways to hold their interest and entertain them. When I stop to consider the dozens and dozens of Batman-related comic book titles over the years and the thousands of stories that have been produced, the very first tip of my cowl goes to them. There could be no *Batman* or *The Dark Knight* without them and their work. When the story is told that Bruce Wayne is an orphan, don't believe it. Batman, from comic books to movies, has so many wonderful fathers and mothers from Bob Kane, Bill Finger, and Jerry Robinson to Tim Burton and Christopher Nolan. And every one of them truly cares.

At my farewell luncheon at United Artists, Batman showed up to carry me off into the world of producing and writing!

Our son, David Miles, was born in 1980, just at the moment I was prepared to quit my job at United Artists, turn in my lawyer's hat for that of a producer and writer, and venture forth into the creative side of Hollywood. Initially, I didn't really intend to produce anything besides the Batman films. I expected to spend the rest of my career as a creative writer doing screenplays, books, comic books, and those new-fangled things Will Eisner was calling "graphic novels." But I soon learned that too often writers were stuck waiting for their phones to ring and their literary babies were being kidnapped or put up for adoption. I wanted more control, but knew full well that the movie studios were really just like Harvey Civins when we used to play football as kids. Harvey owned the only football in the neighborhood, and when his mom whistled for him to come home for dinner, Harvey left and took the ball with him, and the game was over. In the meantime, you just try your hardest to play the best game you can before the ball gets yanked away. Nancy was 9.1 months pregnant when I went in to my boss at United Artists to resign to go produce *Batman*. My boss was a wonderful and caring man, as well as a legal-business whiz, and was concerned that I'd be giving up UA's medical insurance at an inopportune time for Nancy and me. And he was so right. There have been many times over the years as an independent producer when I roamed the halls of my house late at night offering my kingdom for a dental plan! He also didn't want to lose me, as by that time I think I was overseeing some thirty UA film projects in the department. He offered me a large bonus and a significant raise if I would agree to stay just one more year. He pointed out that *Batman* would take two to three years to happen anyway. If I had known at that moment that it would take TEN years, I'm not sure what I would have done. But the allure of that much additional money and the security of the medical plan were tempting, and I told him I'd discuss it with Nancy and would sleep on it. The next morning, I woke up and knew exactly what I needed to do. I quit. Why? I got scared. It terrified me just how easy it suddenly was for me to say, "Just one more year . . ." And then I projected out to a year later when the house we were building would be finished and we'd be paying a sizable monthly mortgage, and when we would have a year-old baby en route to becoming a toddler. I wondered what I might say a year from then when my boss offered me another bonus and raise to stay "just one more year . . ." I could see myself becoming trapped into being a lawyer for the rest of my life and becoming one of those pitiful "I COULD have been . . ." guys. So I quit. It was time to roll the dice.

With special thanks to Nancy, my best co-productions of all time, my children, David and Sarah!

Two years after David was born, we lost a daughter who was stillborn after six months for no determinable reason. We were devastated. It took Nancy a full year to recover, but helping us make the journey back was a fine group of people in a life-enhancing support group in New Jersey called MIDS. Then, Sarah Rose came along. Because we had no idea what had happened to our stillborn child or why, Nancy's pregnancy with Sarah was nine months of paranoia and fear as we tried to do everything "different" from last time. Sarah was so active and feisty during the last trimester that we nicknamed her "Spike," figuring we had a strong little guy en route, kind of giving up all hope for a girl. But it was definitely a girl who popped out that night with me once again playing Nancy's "Coach Mike" in the delivery room. With David, Nancy chose natural childbirth. With Sarah, she was hoping they'd start her on intravenous drugs immediately after conception. Sarah slept for the first week she was home from the hospital, to the point that we became concerned. No need. She was one of those kids who just slept through the entire night starting on day one . . . as opposed to David, who slept through the night for the first time when he was three! Nancy and I survived for three years on *Mary Tyler Moore Show* reruns from 3 A.M. to 4 A.M.

With the arrival of our babies, I decided to prepare my own special welcoming gifts. I bought a bound blank book for each of them. And every single day for a year, I kept a diary describing what happened that day—special moments in their development, who came to visit, their first movie, toy, cartoon, or book. I figured that our lives on earth are short enough and nobody remembers any of his or her first year here. So I preserved it in writing for David and for Sarah and gifted them with their first year of life.

Now Nancy and I were faced with a decision that would impact the rest of our lives. If I wanted to be a producer and writer in movies or animation and TV, I really needed to live in L.A. so that I could network and develop relationships with everyone in the Biz. Otherwise, no matter how often I went to L.A., once I returned east it would be "out of sight, out of mind." On the other hand, we wanted to bring up our kids around my parents and our family and within a proverbial stone's throw of Nancy's family in Ohio. We believed that life was tough enough for kids and weren't very interested in raising them in the midst of the movie business in the heart of Beverly Hills. I did not want my kids judging people based on the cars they were driving and, not knowing much about the L.A. culture, felt much safer with them growing up under the same wings I had. Right or wrong, all I know for sure is that after my mom and my dad were gone, I could look in a mirror and be happy with the person staring back at me. But this choice certainly took a toll on the career opportunities emanating from the nerve center of the entertainment industry. I hung my hat on the theory that if I stayed in New York and continued to cultivate my relationships with the comic book companies and creators, I would have my own niche that couldn't be duplicated by anyone in L.A. And in that era, it was a strategy that worked.

But there were serious challenges ahead to my goal of bringing comic book heroes to life in movies, animation, and television. Every day for decades, I battled in the trenches with studio execs who didn't get it. They had no respect for comic books, comic book characters, or comic book writers and artists. I argued and fought continually against the warped thinking that comic books were a genre that could be hot one summer at the box office, and then cold the next summer. WRONG! Comic books are NOT a faddish genre, but a wonderful ongoing source of great stories and colorful characters in the same way novels and plays are. I had to argue and fight against the erroneous thinking that comic books and superheroes are synonymous. They are NOT! Any type of book those execs could find in Barnes & Noble, I could find in comic books: high adventure, fantasy, horror, science fiction, romance, humor, western, war, mystery, you name it! I argued and fought continually against the mistaken beliefs that the only comic books that could be turned into successful branded movie franchises were the biggest selling, oldest few titles like Superman, Batman, and Spider-Man. NOT TRUE! For ten plus years after our Batman movie franchise ignited in 1989, it was comic books that never sold more than 5,000 copies of an issue that generated some of the biggest movie successes—*Men in Black*, *The Mask*, and *Teenage Mutant Ninja Turtles*.

Staying in the New York area in order to court the comic book companies and creators did require monthly trips to L.A. I decided up front that my family would always come first. Thus, while I may have missed some big Hollywood events and some meetings, I never missed even one of my children's plays, recitals, parent-teacher conferences, Halloween trick-or-treat outings, birthdays, or games. Did it make a difference? Are they even aware of it? It made a difference to me, and if they're not aware of it yet, by the time they have their own kids, it will dawn on them. A tougher adjustment for me was when my parents would drive the hour and ten minutes to us from the Shore and walk in the house and all but bulldoze past me to get to their darling grandchildren. I had spent my lifetime being co-number-one in their lives and I suddenly felt like the Invisible Kid. It took me a little time to figure out the so very obvious. I looked at my children. Now, it was their turn. I had had my turn, and it was glorious. It was time to grow up and "get" how life works. Once I did, it all made perfect sense.

David was my clone. To this day, we have exactly the same voice, and neither of us can identify whose voice is whose on old voice-mail messages, much to the consternation of Nancy, who never has any idea who she's talking to during any phone conversation, especially when I'm in L.A. on business and David and I keep switching off the phone between us. There is some magic to this genetics business. As I insidiously planned it, David is a comic book fan (with Valiant Comics being his very favorite), is a Yankees fan (passed down from my grandpa to my dad to Paul and me to David), feels most at home and happiest at Disney World (we're investigating opening a branch office on the Dumbo the Flying Elephant ride if they can install a phone line and wi-fi on the blue one), and is a music buff (he minored in music at Indiana University and is a walking encyclopedia of jazz, blues, classical, rock 'n' roll, and rap). When he was growing up, we had a deal about rock 'n' roll. If he asked me to buy him a Metallica or Poison album or whatever, I would get him the one he wanted, but would also give him one classic album to become familiar with (*Sgt. Pepper* by the Beatles, *The BeeGees First*, *Mixed Bag* by Richie Havens, *Cheap Thrills* by Janis Joplin with Big Brother & the Holding Company, *Strange Days* by the Doors, *Child Is Father to the Man* by Blood, Sweat & Tears, *Orpheus*, *The Monkees*—yes, their first two albums are great—*Tommy* by the Who . . . you get the idea!). That's how he learned the history of rock.

Sarah is "My Special Angel" (the song by the Vogues that I had NY's CBS-FM Oldies DJ, Harry Harrison, dedicate to her the night she was born), who was a photo-double for Shirley Temple when she was little, with the curliest long locks I had ever seen, until one day she woke up and they had all straightened out. I was in mourning. From the beginning, Sarah showed a stubborn streak and devolved into crying/screaming fits that were absolutely uncontrollable. On one airplane trip when she was three, she "Hulked-Out" on us and tore off all her clothes. On a family trip to Mt. Vernon when she was four, we told her we were going to see George Washington's house and that George Washington was in a crypt in the backyard. Once there, Sarah demanded to see George Washington. We took her around to where his crypt was, but this proved to be grossly insufficient. She wanted to SEE George Washington! When no one would open his crypt for her so she could do that, she "Hulked-Out" at Mt. Vernon. Nancy and I were amazed Washington didn't stir.

Starting at about age three, Sarah began painting. Her brushstrokes of colors and patterns were astounding. Nancy took her works to a local upscale gallery to frame for us. While Sarah's paintings were waiting there for pickup, a few of the gallery's well-heeled clients noticed them. They were chagrined to hear the paintings were not for sale and inquired about the artist. The gallery owner revealed that she was new on the art scene. Just shy of her third birthday, we thought that was a fair description. She was also a gymnast, a dancer, a champion basketball player, a little dress designer, and a star competitive equestrian whose specialty was jumping and who sported a bedroom overflowing with blue ribbons. When Sarah turned eight, we bought her a pony (which Nancy had to explain to me was NOT a young horse, though I claimed that eight out of ten people in New Jersey would also believe a pony was a young horse). Mia, who is now probably the oldest pony in history, is well into her fifties and turning gray.

I closed my eyes tight one day, and then opened them, and the kids had grown up. Life is fleeting. The years were passing, and I kept up my monthly trips to L.A., attending Batman meetings and pressing wherever and whenever possible to get traction. It was 1986 when I heard from Roger Birnbaum about Tim Burton. This was the budding young genius behind the wonderfully demented short *Frankenweenie*. Warner Bros. wanted Ben and me to see what Tim was doing, and they set up a screening of the fine cut of *Pee-Wee's Big Adventure* for us. I had never before seen such a wild marriage of direction and art direction. Tim was a purely inventive new director, and the thought of Batman winding up in his hands was exciting. But as everyone at the Studio and Guber's company felt, it was critical that Tim be exposed only to the early Batman comic books and be kept away from any other versions, tones, and comic book interpretations. A series of three lunches was arranged for me and Tim. And I carefully assembled the comics I wanted him to see as I made my Batman pitch. Of course, I started with my favorite, "Night of the Stalker," which would find its way into the opening of our eventual movie, the origin of the Joker, the origin of Batman, and so many other classic edgy Batman tales. By the end of our third lunch, I had no doubt this was the director who could make an incredible film true to the integrity of The Batman.

Something else happened on that trip I made to L.A. to see *Pee-Wee's Big Adventure* and meet Tim Burton for the first time. A young lady (let's call her "Elaine") who had been a film student at the Tisch School at NYU had been an intern for Ben and me. I had trained her for a year, and then she had wanted to pursue a career in L.A. I had introduced her to as many people as I could there and was thrilled when she wound up involved in a couple of small movies that I thought were creative and a really good start for her. I hadn't seen her in about two years when I made the trip, and she was already deeply ensconced in the young Hollywood scene. We met for lunch at one of those West Coast outdoor cafés that Woody Allen has immortalized in his motion picture dissections of L.A. We quickly got caught up. She asked me what brought me to L.A. this time, and I told her I was there for Batman meetings with a possible director who—. But Elaine cut me off. "Oh, Michael, you have to stop." "Stop what?" I asked blankly. "You have to stop telling people you're still working on Batman and that you're still having meetings about Batman. I know you've been telling everyone that movie's going to happen but it's been what—seven years?" she asked. "Yeah, but this director will—." There was no way I was getting a word in edgewise in this one-way conversation. "No, you just need to stop talking about Batman to people, because to everyone out here, the Batman movie is a joke and everyone knows it's never going to happen. And when you talk about it as if it's really going to happen, then it's kind of like you're the joke," she informed me for what she claimed was my own good. I felt like I had just been lanced in the gut and then had the knife twisted. I wanted to reply with something brilliant and cute and ironic, but the only three words that kept coming to mind were, "Et tu, Brute?" And here we have the concept of "negative reinforcement."

As Paul told me, I needed to teach myself to take negative, hurtful, debilitating actions and comments and not let them hurt or debilitate, but rather motivate. With "positive reinforcement," I'm thinking, "I want to make my mom proud of me . . . my teacher proud of me . . . my dad proud of me . . . my wife proud of me, my children proud of me. . . . " With "negative reinforcement," I'm thinking, "I'll show her! I will accomplish this somehow . . . someway!" If I didn't learn to master the technique of "negative reinforcement," I'd be taken down by the bad people who are hoping I'll fail, and then the bad guys will win. I will not give them that satisfaction. The bad guys will not win!

As I was battling through seemingly endless years pursuing my vision of a Batman movie, I was able to remember what I had learned the hard way . . . better to take all the bad juju being thrown my way and turn it into the ultimate motivator. All I hoped and prayed for now was that the bad guys would just not win in the end. And I knew in my heart they wouldn't . . . not as long as I continued to find ways to stand tall . . . and stand year after year for these ten years, holding on by my fingertips until my dream finally would come to fruition. But how could I keep hanging on? How?

# INFINITE CRISIS!
# THE HUMAN ENDURANCE CONTEST CONTINUES!

Many projects kept me afloat (and busy) while I inched forward in my Batman saga. About half of those came to fruition, among them *Three Sovereigns for Sarah*, the American Playhouse PBS miniseries about the Salem Witch Trials of 1692 that starred Vanessa Redgrave and Patrick McGoohan. As a history major and buff and with my production office located on the second floor of the real House of Seven Gables in Salem, Massachusetts, I was utterly pleased with the movie's 100 percent historical accuracy. Also a hit was *Where on Earth Is Carmen Sandiego?*, which brought education to kids in a way so entertaining they didn't even realize they were being educated. We had a long run with this show and won an Emmy Award for it. About half the projects frustratingly never came to fruition despite being unique, with wonderful stories, like "Monopoly: The Movie,"

SCIENCE TRANSFORMED HIM INTO A MONSTER. LOVE CHANGED HIM EVEN MORE!

SWAMP THING
THE COMIC BOOK LEGEND LIVES!

"SWAMP THING" A MELNIKER-ISLAN Production of a WES CRAVEN Film
LOUIS JOURDAN  ADRIENNE BARBEAU
Based upon characters appearing in magazines published by DC Comics, Inc.
Produced by BENJAMIN MELNIKER and MICHAEL E. ISLAN  Written and Directed by WES CRAVEN

*Swamp Thing*, America's favorite walking, talking spinach soufflé and a nostalgic favorite of boys who were little in the early '80s.

a real story with real characters based on the world's most popular board game in a Wizard of Oz–style Monopoly world; "Kidd," the search for Captain Kidd's buried treasure under modern-day New York City in an adventure like a contemporary, urban Indiana Jones; a *Star Wars* Broadway musical stage play; a reality TV series before there were any reality TV series, based on actual files and in complete cooperation with the Secret Service; "Mr. Potato Head," no—NOT animated for kids but live action in prime-time TV; "Hero-for-Hire," a live-action film with Motown based on Marvel Comics' *Luke Cage, Hero-for-Hire*; "Dr. Strange," also based on a Marvel Comics series; a fantastic "Lone Ranger" TV series actually sold to syndication just before its holding company went bankrupt; and "Roll Call at the Alamo," a CBS-Lorimar historically accurate miniseries portrayal of the defenders and the battle.

But it was, of all things, *Swamp Thing* that became the answer . . . making a small film to keep things bubbling while our Batman film was mired in Development Hell. It would bring in some needed money and be an excellent opportunity for me to learn how to line produce a movie filled with the seven enemies of filmmakers: terrible, uncontrollable logistics/locations replete with poisonous snakes and alligators; lots of stunts; lots of special effects (SFX); lots of SFX makeup; insufficient budget and schedule; child actors; and animal actors. "Oy!" as Gram would say.

Just after we acquired the rights to Batman, I told Ben that the time was ripe for a little 1950s throwback monster movie featuring a monster in a rubber suit where kids could "boo" for the bad guy and cheer for the good guy and run to get popcorn during the romantic scene. The object of our affection would be the canceled DC comic book that I used to love called *Swamp Thing*, a tale of America's favorite walking, talking spinach soufflé. We went in to talk about it with an exec at Warner Communications, the huge corporation that owned DC Comics, and he could NOT believe DC published a comic book with "such a ridiculous title." Then he found out that DC didn't even publish it anymore. I explained, "Exactly, but if we can turn it into a movie and build it up as a brand, DC can bring it back again and it won't just gather dust in its library." "We will NEVER publish this again!" he bellowed. "It's defunct. It's WORTHLESS!" And without the slightest hesitation, Ben jumped in, "You're right! It IS worthless! So give it to us for free and we'll spend our own money and make all the effort to breathe new life into it. Not only that, we promise within the next ninety days to spend not less than $15,000 to do so."

We were given the rights for free...ALL rights, except comic book publishing and a split of merchandising. We had just become the literary property owners of Swamp Thing. And in the negotiated language of the contract, Ben noted that we had all rights to any characters, stories, or elements HERETOFORE OR HEREAFTER appearing in the pages of the *Swamp Thing* comic books. As a result of this language, we wound up owning the rights to some eleven different DC characters, including one John Constantine, Hellblazer.

We quickly moved to make a movie happen. I went back to United Artists and spoke to one of the heads of International. I laid out my vision for the film and asked him for half the budget in exchange for foreign distribution rights. He made me an offer. The trouble for him was that until just weeks before, I had been negotiating all his deals for him and so I knew his bottom line position. He grimaced and said that was unfair and that I should pretend not to know that stuff. I told him I was awful at pretending and wanted UA's best deal. He told me I could have it IF I got Wes Craven to write and direct because UA had made a ton of money on the foreign rights to Wes's movie *The Hills Have Eyes*. I agreed. Meanwhile, Ben had the doppelganger meeting at Avco-Embassy Pictures with Bob Rehme concerning the domestic distribution rights. We now had our full financing and world distribution PROVIDED we could get Wes Craven. Wes's agent at the time was one of the grand agents of old Hollywood, the one-of-a-kind Marvin Moss, with whom I had had amicable dealings when he represented director John Avildsen on *Rocky*. Ben and Marvin went back together to the year zero. A classic old Hollywood lunch meeting was set up at Musso and Frank's, a landmark on Hollywood Boulevard dating back to the nineteen teens and one of the few surviving pieces of early Hollywood. I think every time I ever went there, Mickey Rooney was holding court in the back room the way Milton Berle and the old comedians held court daily at the Friars Club.

Wes and I hit it off great right from the start. This master of violent horror was a former English professor and was shockingly mild-mannered while as smart a person as you'd ever want to meet. Creatively, we were in sync. Now we turned the matter over to the lawyers, Melniker and Moss, who were two masters of the movie deal. They parried and thrust with each other, occasionally resorting to speaking Yiddish. They then took a napkin and wrote up the deal in pen. Wes and I LOVED what we were seeing. I think we both felt at that moment that we had become part of Hollywood, and we reveled in the knowledge that no other business operates like this. Bitten by the bug, we knew we would never be able to do anything else in life. This was our nirvana. And yes, I still do have that napkin somewhere.

I was in my twenties and had never before produced a movie, so how was I to know that what we were planning to do for just under $1,900,000 in hard cash would have required about $19,000,000 to do the best possible way. The whole rubber suit and appliance special effects makeup sounded fairly state of the art way back then, but there were a few things we didn't know. We decided to shoot in the actual wildest, woolliest swamps we could find if they didn't seem to pose a significant, immediate chance of death by being eaten by giant snakes or alligators. We found the perfect spot on the outskirts of Charleston, South Carolina. Unfortunately, as a result of the centuries of leaves falling into the swamp, the water was contaminated with tannic acid, and the moment our actors and stuntmen in all these great rubber suits and appliance makeup plunged into it, the liquid dissolved the glue holding everything together. Too late to change locations, the brain trust came up with one stopgap measure: the actors in their suits were to be scrubbed down in a bath of liquefied antacids. That's right. They had to be coated in a bizarre combination of Tums and Rolaids (I was now spelling "Rolaids"—"R-E-L-I-E-F"!). And through it all, poor Dick Durock, our never-complaining star and stuntman, almost passed out daily from heat prostration in the suit that took three hours to put on. We had to blow up a little kid's plastic swimming pool for him to lie in between takes just to try to cool down his body temperature.

The big creative decision to be made in approaching the film dealt with the backstory that Swamp Thing had been a scientist, Alec Holland, who transformed into this muck-encrusted mockery of a man. So when he became Swamp Thing, would he still be able to speak? Some at the studio thought the creature should not talk, but that the "Beauty" to his "Beast" should do all the talking for the both of them. But the other camp firmly believed

Sarah and David on the set with their strict babysitter, Uncle Swamp Thing!

that Swamp Thing had to speak. At that precise moment, I leaped up from the studio conference table and yelled that one line I had memorized from law school, "Res ipsa loquitur! The Thing speaks for itself!" Who said you can't use a legal education in the creative side of Hollywood?

Dick Durock was heroic. An actor and an amazing stuntman, he wanted to make personal and TV appearances in his Swamp Thing makeup to encourage kids to protect the environment and keep it green. As a stuntman, Dick had an unusual way of looking at life and risk-taking and valuing his own life. He came to me one day on the set and said, "Hey, Michael! You know in tomorrow's stunt sequence, I'm gonna be out there in the swamp with all those snakes, and in water over my head, in this suit that will absorb water and weigh me down, as two airboats come at me and turn at the last second. I could be drowned or crushed or chopped by those big fans on the back of the boats." We had a strict policy of safety first, so without hesitation I told Dick that if he didn't think the stunt team had planned this right and felt it was in any way unsafe for him, I would scrub it and we'd come up with something else. "Oh, no, no, no!" cried Dick. "No, these are all my guys and are professionals and we all know exactly what we're doing." He then explained that he thought that due to the complexity and risk, he should be entitled to a "stunt adjustment," which was a union bonus payment the stuntmen could negotiate if they felt it was appropriate back in those days. I gulped a big comic book word balloon "GULP!" Visions of our budget were flying out the window. My God! What price would Dick place on his life in this stunt scenario that involved possible long-shot exposure to drowning, being crushed, or being cut to ribbons. "Uh, what do you have in mind, Dick?" I asked. "$125," replied the super-stuntman. "Uh, would you take $75?" I asked without a hint of embarrassment. "Yeah. That's okay," answered Dick in a way only a stuntman could.

The female lead was tougher to cast because United Artists' list of actresses who meant something for foreign box office wasn't the same list Embassy Pictures had for domestic purposes. Eventually, we boiled down the possibilities to two ladies, Adrienne Barbeau and a newcomer out of the TV soaps named Kathleen Turner. Her agent got us a rough cut of her first feature still in editing. It was called *Body Heat*. I told Ben that this woman was the new Lauren Bacall. Neither UA nor Embassy would approve her because she wasn't yet a "name." So Adrienne was the only actress they could agree on. And that was sheer joy, because she was professional and a gem to work with. We asked her to do the toughest stuff in and out of the swamp amid the snakes, and she did everything we asked and took what Wes dished out in a very physically challenging role. As fate would have it, years later, Adrienne voiced the character of Catwoman on the Batman cartoons.

The two most challenging roles to cast in that film were the young boy and the villain's pretty handmaiden. I remember the day Wes flew into Charleston from L.A. on a Delta flight and came rushing up to me on the set. The most beautiful flight attendant on earth had been on this flight (they may still have been called stewardesses back then). Wes had boasted to her who he was. She wasn't particularly impressed. So he told her (God help us . . . it's a Hollywood cliché!) he would make her a star and that she could play a small role in our movie. While she did NOT believe him, didn't buy any of it for a second, she decided he was both cute and not an ax murderer, and so gave him her phone number. Now Wes was pleading with me to call her and tell her that I was the producer and that he was really a director and that this was a real, legit movie and not a white-slavery ring or porno film. Her name was Mimi Myers, and my phone call with her was memorable. It turned out that she had also attended Indiana University and had been a freshman when I was in law school there. We compared notes and realized we had been at many of the same places and events at the same times, though we had never met. I actually convinced her to come to the set and that Wes would guide her through the part. She and Wes fell in love and eventually married, and Mimi and I bonded and became lifelong friends. I watched her grow into a superb actress and a super-talented photographer.

At this point, the movie was about to roll, and we had no kid to play Adrienne's sidekick. Desperate, we opened a casting call to boys ages ten to twelve in the Charleston area. Wes and I must have auditioned a hundred kids, but we couldn't find our boy. At the very end of our casting session, in trudged a sixth-grade boy who plodded down the aisle and plopped down in the chair in front of me and Wes, holding his head as he lowered it as if in pain or embarrassment. The kid had giant-sized Lew Wasserman 1980s glasses on. I said hi and asked him his name. It was Reggie. "Uh . . . are you all right, Reggie?" asked a bewildered and concerned Wes. "Nope," responded the boy with a real sense of hopelessness. "What's your problem, Reggie?," I inquired. "Girls!" he responded with some fervor. "You don't have a girlfriend?" asked Wes. "That ain't it," Reggie retorted. "Got too many! There's Debbie, Susi, Loreda, Sandy . . . ." I looked at Wes. He looked at me. We had found our final star.

What incredible adventures we had with Swampy! On the set of my first movie, still just in my twenties, I realized that two things I had learned in law school were essential and one was worthless. The self-discipline I learned was now necessary as I worked twenty-hour days, seven days a week with only half a day off between January and July of 1981. Line producing a film was all-consuming. Also, the job proved to be one of continual crisis management. There was a budget and a schedule and the balancing of artistic demands and personalities and egos. My first time working with actors and crew made me realize that I needed to toss away everything I had learned in law school about the classic "Reasonable Man." But the point of view law school bequeathed me, from which I did not see multiple "problems," but rather multiple "solutions," was an absolute lifesaver now. The key was to take a problem and hold it up to the light and move it all around like a prism, looking every which way for creative solutions. That was invaluable, and without this skill I could not have succeeded, because I had no experience, yet had to keep making good decisions. Sometimes I was lucky enough to have Ben nearby to counsel me. But sometimes I was there on my own, scared, but careful not to reveal it.

There is definitely an absurd side to what I do for a living. Case in point: we had a key scene coming up to be shot that required a trained opossum. Our Animal Wrangler was a pro from L.A. and had his team back there ship us the opossum so he would arrive on location in Charleston, two days before the shoot day. They put him in his travel cage and sent him by plane. We drove over to Charleston's airport and, after a delay during which the crew tried to locate the cage, they brought him out. Unfortunately, the opossum had expired en route. Sad and chagrined, the Animal Wrangler called his L.A. team. They had one trained opossum left. But how could we be sure this one would survive the flight? The cargo holds were supposed to be okay for pets, but could we take that chance again? It was time for a Michael producer-decision. After talking to the airline supervisors, I bought the opossum a ticket, and they kept him on a seat in the cabin. To this day, I don't know who sat next to him on that trip. I tried to get him an exit row aisle seat, but I was told he'd be in a middle seat. If he had my luck, he'd have the two largest people in America sitting next to him. We returned to the Charleston Airport the next evening to welcome opossum number two to South Carolina. The flight arrived and . . . no opossum. They searched their cabin and their cargo hold again and again, but nothing. Then the airline finally confessed . . . the opossum had had to change planes in Atlanta and had not made the Charleston flight. They had lost our opossum like he was someone's luggage.

Desperate, we raised bloody hell with the airline. They probably had every employee in Atlanta searching for our boy. Eventually, the call came in to us in the Baggage Office in Charleston. They found him . . . in his cage . . . endlessly circling around on a luggage carrousel in Atlanta . . . looking very dizzy and particularly weak. And we needed him for the shoot that next day. The airline was prepared to put him on its next flight to Charleston and in an aisle seat . . . but suggested that from their laymen's point of view, they couldn't be sure he would survive another flight. After getting as many facts as possible and considering whatever the alternatives were, and appreciating the consequences of not being ready to shoot the scene the next day, I hired a limousine and had our opossum driven in the limo from Atlanta to Charleston. The little fellow arrived safely, though a bit spoiled. The next day, the scene was shot, his performance was award-winning, and they all lived happily ever after.

Tony Cecere was renowned in Hollywood as the best fire gag stuntman in the business. He and a partner had developed a gel that, for a short period of time, allowed Tony to do fire burns without the need of a protective suit. He would coat himself in the gel and then have a certain number of seconds in which to execute his fire stunt before the flames would burn through that gel. The origin of Swamp Thing required Dr. Alec Holland to catch fire in his laboratory. Tony would therefore have to ignite in our lab set, run blindly for the door, burst through the doors onto a wooden porch, crash through the railing and fall to the ground, then race to the dock, run to the end, and leap into the swamp, which would then douse the flames. But not only would he be racing the clock before the fire burned through the gel and consumed him, he'd also be running totally blind because he had to close his eyes and cake his lids in the gel. In the process of filming this sequence, we were going to blow up and burn the big laboratory set we had built in the middle of the Georgia swamp. So we had only one take to get all this and get it right and safely. We had two fire departments out in the swamp with us this night, along with paramedics and the Red Cross. Tony spent the whole day pacing off his blind run. He knew he had two critical danger points. When he lunged through the railing on the upper porch and dropped to the ground, if he didn't get up facing the perfect direction, he would not make it to the swamp in time. Second, the dock was narrow, and he had to get to the end of it successfully and know exactly when to leap, or he would fail to douse the flames in time. The stunt team was lined up off camera to the sides of his projected path, clutching thick blankets in case they needed to tackle him and attempt to smother the flames if the stunt went awry. The tension that night in the swamp was as intense as anything I had ever experienced.

Tony was convinced that everything would go right. One thing, however, did not. The SFX (special effects) team controlled the stuff used to light Tony. It would be coated over his gel and ignited, and it would then burst into flames over his entire face and body. But someone laid on too much of the stuff. So with everyone in their places and the stunt team ready, director Wes Craven called for action. They lit Tony inside the lab and screamed "GO! GO!" and Tony began to flame and shuffled his way through the lab on fire, up the stairs, down the corridor. But as he broke through the wooden laboratory doors and into the night air, rather than bursting into flames, he nova'd! It was an explosion of fire several times what anyone was expecting. I was terrified, but the calls to terminate the stunt were to be made by the stunt coordinator and he kept the cameras rolling as the fireball known as Tony Cecere lunged through the railing and fell several feet to the ground below... then stood up and ran across the yard and onto that narrow wooden dock. Staggering forward, he managed to stay on the narrow path and leaped into the swamp at exactly the end of the dock. And he sank. The stunt coordinator counted to five, and then the entire team leaped, ran, dove into the swamp to retrieve Tony. Everyone held their breath as the paramedics rushed in amid the now furiously burning lab set. It felt like an eternity, but the shout came—"He's okay!" And the hundred assembled people burst into spontaneous applause of marvel and relief at what we had all just been privileged to witness. You don't believe in superheroes? Take a look at the stuntmen and stuntwomen in the movies. They're the closest to men and women of steel you'll find in real life!

But me? I'm a Jewish boy from New Jersey. The last day of the shoot, I was talking to Wes Craven by the edge of the swamp. Most of the coral snakes and cottonmouths and copperheads were gone by June 1 when all the alligators started emerging, chasing them off. Except this day when, as we were talking, a rattlesnake dropped out of a tree and landed a few feet away from us. That was it for me. I was cool wearing my snake boots and watching carefully where I was walking through the swamps. But when they started raining from the trees, I was outta there. It was time to head back to the safety of north Jersey, where all I had to worry about was what was in the trunk of some guy's car.

*Swamp Thing* met with quite a bit of success and became a beloved part of the childhood of a generation of boys who are just now in the process of becoming fathers themselves. Another "Swampy" film followed, backed by a company looking to reposition the character for a future in toys and animation.

Our 1981 production office in the MGM Building in New York where I watch with awe as my producing partner, Benjamin Melniker, presents the head of Swamp Thing on a silver platter!

But *Batman* was not yet in sight, and the years after *Swamp Thing* were passing. Eventually, I had no money left and a family to take care of. My back was as far against the wall as is humanly possible. And that's when the wisest man I ever met flew from Cincinnati to New Jersey to sit and talk to me . . . my father-in-law, Dr. Morris Osher. He did not say anything I really wanted to hear. What he reminded me was that first and foremost I had a responsibility to my family . . . my wife and children. Under the circumstances, he thought it was clear that what I needed to do was go back to being a lawyer, a profession I studied and learned in case I ever needed to fall back on something. Well, this was "fall-back" time. He assured me I wasn't a failure. I had tried my best and, in fact, actually produced some projects in Hollywood, and that alone was a significant accomplishment. But now it was time to do what I needed to do . . . be a lawyer.

I agreed that I would do whatever was necessary, but vented my frustration at being so close with several major projects including *Batman*. I think he was tuned to both my frustration and sincere, if ridiculous, belief in myself and my work. That's when he popped the question. "Mike, how close are you really, with no exaggeration, not to having a signed contract or a promise, but having in your hand a check for six figures?" he asked me with all the directness and candor that was his trademark. I thought hard. "Five months," I replied. Then it was Daddy O's turn to think hard. He made me a proposition. "Mike, I will pay all your bills for the next five months PROVIDED that five months from today, at 6 P.M., you either have in your hand a check in the amount of six figures from *Batman* or any other of these projects you believe you can make happen, or if at that time on that day you don't have it, you give me your word you'll put all this behind you and get a job immediately as a lawyer." My father-in-law gave me the gift of time ... five months ... in an industry where time drags on ad infinitum. But not this time. It was all or nothing. I thanked him profusely and began working seven days a week around the clock to make everything and anything materialize. If I didn't, like Moses, I would never step into the Promised Land of Gotham City.

My son, David, was my clone all right. Just as I had when I was little, he loved anything having to do with outer space or with dinosaurs. Before he could say the word spaghetti, he could say the words Tyrannosaurus and Styracosaurus. He knew the distance between the Moon and Uranus. I was thirsting to create my own cartoon show and, realizing that these two subjects were loved by virtually every boy of every generation, I began to ponder just how I could create something that would combine dinosaurs with outer space. Like many of my best ideas, it came to me while I was shaving one morning. Dinosaurs ... outer space ... dinosaurs ... outer space ... *"DINOSAUCERS"*!

I'll spare you the details, but suffice it to say that eventually this harebrained idea became a reality and helped me across my do-or-die finish line. Lightyear Entertainment and Columbia Pictures' syndicated TV division, Coca-Cola Telecommunications, brought it home and made it happen, thanks directly to nine supermen, Tom Kuhn, Chuck Mitchell, Andy Heyward, Mike Maliani, Robby London, Arnie Holland, Herman Rush, Bob King (of the King Brothers), and the "never-give-up" Rick Rosen, whose friendship as well as professionalism helped me cross that finish line. Shortly before 3 P.M. on the very last day of the five-month period I had agreed to, a FedEx truck pulled up to our family condo in Florida. The driver handed me an envelope with two items in it: a fully executed contract for sixty-five half-hour episodes of *Dinosaucers* and a check for six figures to go along with it.

That money, combined with the fees Ben and I eventually secured in deals for live-action and animated *Swamp Thing* TV shows, was enough to both reimburse my father-in-law and get me to the commencement of principal photography of *Batman*.

It was time to celebrate! My grade school/high school friend Steve Huntington was now a DJ and program director of a major Orlando radio station. I called him to see if he'd do some celebrating with me in Orlando while we were there at Universal Studios filming seventy-two episodes of the new *Swamp Thing* live-action television series. Steve informed me that my childhood friend from Raymere Avenue in Wanamassa, Timmy Hauser, and his singing group, Manhattan Transfer, were headlining the twentieth anniversary of Disney World at a private party being held that night in the Magic Kingdom, not far from Universal Studios. But, he cautioned me that it was the hottest ticket in town, strictly VIP, tie and jacket or even more formal, and that the president of the United States would be there, the first President Bush. Thus, there were no spare tickets around and, for the first time ever, there was no way that Steve knew how to cop one. The radio station had received only one ticket, and Steve had it. He had interviewed Manhattan Transfer for his station, so he let me know what hotel Tim was staying at and suggested I try him. If anyone could possibly find a ticket, the headlining act should be able to do it. And so, I tracked down Tim Hauser, who was thrilled to hear from me, but confessed that for the first time, the group was not permitted any comps and there wasn't even a "list" that someone could

My guardian angels—and in-laws—Dr. Morris S. Osher and the ever wonderful Mrs. Anne Osher.

be added to. The Secret Service was apparently running the show, and getting in was an impossibility. I asked Tim what time the group was performing. He said 8 P.M. in the outdoor theater in Tomorrowland. I told him I'd meet him backstage before he went on. "If anyone can figure out a way in, it's you, Michael! I'm sure I'll see you then," laughed Tim. I then called Steve back and told him I'd meet him at the outdoor theater in Tomorrowland at 8 P.M. He said that he knew I didn't have a ticket, and that he didn't know I had a tux or a suit with me. "Actually, Steve, we're just wrapping up filming for the day here. I'm in jeans, sneakers, a Swamp Thing t-shirt, a windbreaker, and a Batman baseball cap." "If anyone can get into a formal party dressed like that, it's you, Useless!" laughed Steve. And so, I walked from the set, heading to my car, reminiscing about my nighttime foray inside the Capitol back when Senator McGovern was giving his nationwide address.

"Are you interested in some dinner tonight?" asked Ben as he saw me leaving. I quickly explained I was a man on a Mission: Impossible and was going to try to crash the Disney-World twentieth anniversary party. Ben had on slacks and a windbreaker. He asked if he could join me. I reiterated that the chance of my getting in was close to nil and that I didn't want him to waste his evening. "If anyone can get us into this thing, I know you can do it, Michael," Ben replied and slipped into the front passenger seat of my car. As I started to pull out of my parking space, who was getting into the next car but Bonnie Hammer and another top USA Network Executive. "Where are you boys headed?" asked Bonnie. I told the story one more time. "Can we go with you?" she asked enthusiastically. I now spoke slowly and clearly, so the futility of my mission would be comprehended. Bonnie was not dissuaded. "If anyone can get all of us, dressed like this, into a formal party secured by the Secret Service, it's you, Michael!" she said. I took a deep breath and said, "Come on in! Let's do this!"

How can I combine Dinosaurs and Outer Space? *Dinosaucers!* And thus was born my first television cartoon series!

We drove to the entrance to the monorail at the Magic Kingdom. It was 7 P.M. and a long, long, long line of fancy-schmancy people in suits and tuxes and cocktail dresses and evening gowns were waiting to board the transport that would take them to this once-in-a-lifetime extravaganza. I sauntered up to a young man at the equivalent of a ticket window.

"Hello. My name's Michael Uslan. I'm a friend of the Manhattan Transfer and I'm supposed to meet them backstage in Tomorrowland before they go on tonight at 8 P.M. It's Uslan plus three, thank you," I didn't lie.

"Uh, sir, I don't have any names here. Do you have your tickets?" he asked politely.

"No, I thought my name would be on a list like usual. It's Uslan. I'm sure it's on there."

"Actually, tonight, because the president of the United States will be here, there is no list," he stood his ground.

"Then there's been some miscommunication. If it's been on my side, I apologize for that, but it's now 7:20 P.M. and Manhattan Transfer is going on at 8 P.M. and we arranged to meet backstage before then, so please just get on the phone and call whomever you need to and they'll straighten all this out to your satisfaction," I countered.

"Well, give me a few minutes, and let me see what I can do," he offered.

I reported back to my minions. "Well?" taunted Ben. "He's checking. Let's give him a few minutes," I responded, refusing to let any of them see me doubt myself.

I re-approached the booth when the young man gave me a little, meek wave. "I assume everything's settled now," I preempted.

"Uh . . . well, I don't know what's happened, but they tell me there just is no list," he apologized.

"Do you see how old I am?" I asked him. "Do you see that elderly man over there who's with me? He ran MGM for thirty years and put together the deals for *Dr. Zhivago*, *Ben-Hur*, *2001*, and most recently *Batman*. Do you think he's some kid just trying to sneak in to a party tonight?"

"No! No, sir. Of course not!" he responded.

"Therefore," I moved in for the kill, "don't you think someone just made some mistake or oversight that you now need to correct? It's now 7:40 P.M. and we need to be in Tomorrowland before 8 P.M.!"

He asked me to give him just a few minutes and he'd resolve this. This time, I did not retire to my weary entourage. I stood my ground at the booth. That's when the young man said, "We apologize, sir. You and your party please go right up and board the monorail," he beamed.

"That won't work now," I said with a straight face. "There's a very long line and we have only ten minutes left to meet the group backstage."

He assured me he'd resolve this and got back on the phone. Smiling triumphantly, he gave me the news that I then took over to my colleagues, but only after offering the young man a sizable tip for his efforts, which he firmly and politely declined.

"Well?" asked Ben.

"Are we in?" asked Bonnie.

"We are in," I revealed.

In a moment, a limousine pulled up. The four of us piled in, and the Disney driver drove us through the park's service roads into Tomorrowland and pulled up behind the stage. We got out, and at 7:55 P.M., I greeted Timmy Hauser minutes before his performance began. He said he had had no doubt I'd show up, but was surprised at what a close call it was. They had a big backstage spread of food, and Ben was a happy Disney camper. I walked out onto the stage and into the still-empty amphitheater, selecting my front row center seat and one next to it. Suddenly, the flood-gates opened and the fancy-schmancy crowd of hundreds poured in. Way in the back, I spotted Steve Huntington and stood on my chair to wave him up front. The concert was awesome! The party was amazing! Everything was free . . . stands featuring every imaginable type of food were everywhere. A 360-degree fireworks show began, far more magnificent than any fireworks I had ever experienced. It was the party of the decade, and I was there with my next-door neighbor, Timmy; my grade-school/high-school buddy, Steve; my partner/mentor and second father, Ben; and my favorite industry exec, Bonnie. It's a small world, after all!

PROCTOR & GAMBLE
9200 SUNSET BLVD NO. 525
LOS ANGELES, CA 90069 27PM

Western Union Mailgram
UNITED STATES POSTAL SERVICE
U.S.MAIL

1-086795U058 02/27/90 ICS WA16614        NYAC
  00265 MLTN VA 02/27/90 JN07764

MR. MICHAEL USLAN
123 WEST 44TH STREET #10K
NEW YORK NY 10036

DEAR MR. USLAN:

WE ARE PLEASED TO INFORM YOU THAT IN THE SPECIAL POLL GALLUP
CONDUCTED FOR "THE SIXTEENTH ANNUAL PEOPLE'S CHOICE AWARDS,"
BATMAN WAS DECLARED THE WINNER IN THE FAVORITE MOTION PICTURE
CATEGORY.

THIS RESEARCH WAS CONDUCTED UTILIZING THE MOST MODERN SCIENTIFIC
POLLING TECHNIQUES AND STATISTICALLY REPRESENTS THE OPINIONS
OF MORE THAN 197 MILLION INDIVIDUALS 12 YEARS OF AGE AND OLDER IN
THE UNITED STATES.

THE GALLUP ORGANIZATION CERTIFIES THAT THE RESULTS OF THIS STUDY
ARE ACCURATE AS REPORTED.

WE ARE PLEASED TO BE A PART OF THIS STUDY OF THE PUBLIC'S FAVORITES
IN THE ENTERTAINMENT FIELD. PLEASE ACCEPT OUR HEARTIEST
CONGRATULATIONS ON THIS AWARD.

WE HAVE BEEN ASKED TO REQUEST THAT YOU KEEP THIS IN TOTAL
CONFIDENCE UNTIL YOU ARE CONTACTED BY "THE PEOPLE'S CHOICE
AWARD'S" PROGRAM.

                              VERY TRULY YOURS,

                              GEORGE GALLUP, JR.
                              CO-CHAIRMAN
                              THE GALLUP ORGANIZATION

CC: PEOPLE'S CHOICE AWARDS

08819

23:34 EST

MGMCOMP

5241 (R 7/82)

Congrats to all! *Batman* wins "Best Picture" in The People's Choice Awards!

# CHAPTER TWENTY-ONE

# It's the Stuff Dreams Are Made Of!

The best my still-stunned brain can recall was that the call came from Michael Besman at Guber's company. He knew how much this one meant to me when he confirmed that the one and only actor I believed could play the Joker in our Batman movie, Jack Nicholson, had been hired! I was on the highest natural high possible! I let all the little kid and teenage Michaels living inside me out for a frolic to celebrate in a phantasmagorical phalanx of cartwheels, pinwheels, and human wheelies! This was a miracle! We got Nicholson! Omigod!

Ten days later, I was ready to slice my wrists. It was another call from Michael Besman. This time, knowing me, he was hesitant and was wearing an extra extra large pair of kid gloves as he spoke. "So, Michael . . . what . . . uh . . . do you think . . . of Tim's idea . . . to cast Michael Keaton as Batman?"

"Hahahahahahahahahahahaha!" I laughed heartily. "Gee, Michael, what a GREAT idea! Let's have a comedian . . . No! Let's have 'Mr. Mom' play the dark, serious Batman!" What a kidder! That Michael would do anything for a laugh.

It took him twenty minutes to convince me he wasn't joking . . . and neither was Tim Burton. Nine years since we acquired the rights to The Batman . . . down the drain. How many additional years since the dream, itself, had begun? Four? My heart and soul were suddenly and unexpectedly being beaten down by the damned Pow! Zap! and Wham! I went nuts. I yelled. I screamed. I carried on like a baby. I argued. I protested. I fought. I reasoned. I swore. I begged. I pleaded. I countered. I discussed. I debated. I called in allies from DC Comics. But missing from my gut fanboy reaction was accounting for the genius that is Tim Burton. Of course, there was method to the madness. His responses to my problems were a revelation:

- **PROBLEM:** "But Michael Keaton is a comedian. He's not a serious actor capable of being a serious Batman!" **RESPONSE:** Michael Keaton is, absolutely, a wonderful serious actor. **RESOLUTION:** They set up a screening of the fine cut of the upcoming movie *Clean and Sober* so Ben and I could see for ourselves. Tim was right. Michael Keaton was an excellent actor.

- **PROBLEM:** "But Michael Keaton is, like, my height! He's not a tall, imposing superhero figure!" **RESPONSE:** Tim knew how to cheat the height when filming.

- **PROBLEM:** "But Michael Keaton isn't muscular like The Batman is!" **RESPONSE:** The apparent musculature will be carved into the costume.

- **BIG PROBLEM:** "But Michael Keaton doesn't have a square jaw like Batman does!" **RESPONSE:** Ah! Here was the sheer genius of it all . . . Tim's vision embodied in a few short sentences . . . "Michael, a square jaw does NOT a Batman make." Tim had the revolutionary job ahead of making the first truly dark and serious feature film based on a comic book superhero. The movie audience MUST be made to suspend its disbelief and BELIEVE that a man could dress up like a bat and fight crime. The only way Tim saw to accomplish that feat was to make them believe in BRUCE WAYNE. The key was Bruce Wayne, not Batman. They had to believe that Bruce Wayne was a man obsessed to the point of being almost psychotic, who would get dressed up as a bat to get the guys who murdered his parents . . . to get ALL the bad guys. We had talked about our list of "serious actors" of the late '80s who might play the role . . . or the possibility of getting an unknown to play Batman the way Chris Reeve played Superman. Tim knew that once Jack Nicholson had been hired, there was no way an unknown actor could play Batman without Jack wiping the screen with him. As to that "serious actor" list with names like Harrison Ford, Dennis Quaid, and Kevin Costner, Tim indicated he didn't know how to show any of them getting into a Bat-Suit without getting unintended laughs from the audience. But he knew that with Michael Keaton, he could paint a picture of a Bruce Wayne so driven to the breaking point that audiences would say, "THAT'S a guy who would put on a Bat-Suit to fight crime!" And that alone sums up the genius of Tim Burton. He also knew that Gotham City needed to be the third most important character in the movie from the opening frames, for if audiences didn't believe in Gotham City, they would never believe there could be a guy like Batman running around there fighting the Joker.

Since Gotham City held an important key to the success of this groundbreaking movie, thank the stars that there was a second genius working on this picture. His name was Anton Furst, my good friend and our production designer. When Sam Hamm's marvelous script came in, there was only one line describing Gotham. And it was the screenplay's first line: "Gotham City—as if Hell has erupted from under the earth." I remember Anton recounting how puzzled he was, asking Tim what he thought this meant. Tim told him he thought it meant New York City . . . had there never been any planning and zoning. That was just what Anton needed to hear! He went off and researched conflicting styles of architecture, especially Japanese influences, and eventually came back with the drawings of a brave new world unlike anything ever seen before in cinema. It was its own universe. It was a place where a Batman was a natural fit and made sense. It was a place where a zany force of evil had a believable place. It was a dark, gritty, violent, and timeless place. Tim and Anton wanted it to be a mixture of past, present, and future so that nobody could really pinpoint when the movie was taking place. As a result of that remarkable creative choice, the film holds up great to this day and doesn't look like just another '80s film. Like Gotham City, the movie itself is timeless.

A while later, when I saw the first frames of footage, I knew it had been silly of me to doubt Tim. On screen was The Batman! It was Bob Kane's and Bill Finger's Batman before Robin. It was Neal Adams's and Denny O'Neil's Batman returned to his roots. It was Marshall Rogers's and Steve Engelhart's stylized, romanticized Batman. It was "Night of the Stalker." It was the first of four Bat-Dreams come true for me.

We had David and Sarah with us on the set at Pinewood Studios. The first day we were there, the stunt driver took David and Sarah for a ride in the Batmobile through four square city blocks of Gotham City built on the back lot. Though we later took the kids all over London from the Tower to Big Ben and all over England, it's the ride in the Batmobile that they remember best. And, of course, eight-year-old David was terrorizing his four-year-old sister on the ride, claiming he was going to press the button on her ejector seat and send her flying across Gotham City. She remembers that best.

In the studio executive dining room for lunch on the second day, Sarah was in a foul mood. Nothing we could do would snap her out of it. And just then, Batman walked by. It was Michael Keaton in his costume, but without the cape and cowl. He spied the sad-looking little girl and bent down and asked Sarah what was wrong. She wasn't even

Premieres! Special screenings! Parties! Interviews! *Batman* is a blockbuster! After the hoopla dies down, we pack up the kids and spend two weeks driving through the west from national park to national park!

ready to be cooperative for Batman. So he sat her down in his lap and started flicking the green peas from her plate onto her forehead, one by one. Sarah started smiling and reached out and threw a small handful of peas at Batman. Soon, a full-blown food fight erupted. When Batman finally had to go, Sarah was as happy as could be, her curly hair dotted with green peas. David and Sarah didn't stop laughing for hours.

At one point, Nancy and I had them up on the rooftop set so they could stand right behind Batman when he grabbed a terrified bad guy and told him, "I'm Batman!" before leaping off the roof and into a net. Every time I see that scene in the '89 film, I keep looking down and to the left to see if I can spot Sarah's curls or the top of little David's head. They do the same for me in one of the *Swamp Things* we did when I appeared in an uncredited cameo. But they know just how to freeze-frame me and then get to laugh their heads off seeing their dad made up and dressed like the stupidest bad-guy commando the world has ever seen.

I recall talking with another Jersey boy on the set of *Batman*. Robert Wuhl is not only a top-notch comedian and star of the classic HBO series *Arliss*, but also a fine actor and great guy. He played reporter Alexander Knox in the 1989 film. Robert mentioned that he was very much looking forward to working with Jack Nicholson because Jack was "the coolest man on earth." One night, he got to go with Nicholson and some others to a club in London. Robert reported that while Jack was just standing there in his shades looking cool, a beautiful young lady in the world's shortest miniskirt came up to him and asked Jack, "You want to dance?" Nicholson's reply was, "Wrong verb." Robert said that was the COOLEST thing he ever heard anyone say in his life!

When Tim Burton finished the final cut of the film, a screening was set up. We had to pass through a thick black curtain to get to our seats. Just before Ben and I walked in, Ben said to me, "Michael, you're going to walk through this curtain, and then two hours from now, you're going to walk back out, and your life will be different." Ben was right. Instead of me knocking on everybody's doors until my knuckles bled, they started calling me . . . knocking on my door. New opportunities would arise. Companies would have enough trust in me to give me movie rights to their crown jewels . . . properties that were the lifeblood of these companies or creators.

*Batman* opened in June of 1989 and broke box-office record after box-office record.

College students lined up to get into the first showings for two and three days in advance, with many people in Batman T-shirts and caps if not in full-blown costumes. People were playing guitars . . . grilling as if a part of some movie version of a tailgating party. And in many cases, those lines stretched entirely around theaters and sometimes even around blocks. Bus stops were smashed and the glass was broken so people could grab the movie posters. The teaser posters didn't even have the name of the film on them . . . just that iconic black bat within a gold oval (except, we were told by someone in Warner's Advertising Department that a study showed that nearly 20 percent of people did NOT see a black bat in a gold oval, but rather saw gold teeth and tonsils in a mouth— 97 percent of these people were dentists). At Comic-Cons and on the black market, pirated versions of our first three-minute trailer for the movie were being sold on boot-leg tapes for $25 each. Better yet, theater owners were reporting that patrons were calling to find out what movies were showing the trailer for *Batman* and were then buy-ing tickets to those movies, staying for the trailer, then just leaving before the main feature started. In New York that month, it was impossible to walk fifty steps in or around Times Square without seeing someone wearing a Batman T-shirt or hat.

The impact of *Batman* was not measured simply by what the movie grossed at the worldwide box office, but by the huge effect it had on world culture. A friend of mine was writing at the time for *Parade* magazine and was on assignment in South America. He had been on a trek all night through the jungle and a rain forest, finally arriving at the remote hut he would be staying at for some time. It was dark when they arrived, and he collapsed, exhausted from his adventurous trip. When he awoke the next morn-ing and walked out of his tent, the first thing he saw was a local boy . . . wearing a Batman cap. More telling, later that summer when the Berlin Wall fell and masses of humanity were pouring through from East Berlin to freedom in West Berlin, I was transfixed, con-tinuing to watch history unfold on CNN into the wee hours of the morning. And that's when I spied him . . . an East German boy, climbing through the toppled Berlin Wall . . . wearing a Batman cap. That was my favorite moment in achieving my dream of bring-ing a dark, serious Batman to the movie screen. The almost incomprehensible thought crossed my mind that this had become more than just a movie. It was, indeed, revolu-tionary. It successfully crossed borders, cultures, and demographics. The darkknight version of the former Caped Crusader was becoming ingrained globally. Over the next twenty years, *Batman*, *Batman Returns*, *Batman Begins*, and *The Dark Knight* accom-plished my dream and erased from the collective consciousness of the world culture the words "Pow!" "Zap!" and "Wham!" Tim Burton's vision and tone took hold, along with Anton Furst's designs and look, and Danny Elfman's haunting, inspiring music, which gives me the chills to this day when I hear it. To me, they deserve all the credit. Their work was as astounding as it was groundbreaking.

To celebrate this lifelong dream-come-true, I had a top jeweler make up three specially designed necklaces. Each was a gold oval with a large, polished mother-of-pearl center, on which was mounted a bat made out of black onyx. I presented one to each of the three most important women in my life: my mom, Nancy, and Nancy's mom. Today, Sarah has my mom's bat necklace.

Two weeks after the picture opened and broke all those records, I got a call. I was sitting in the office with Ben when the phone rang. It was the production exec from United Artists I had spoken with ten years before . . . that *Robin and Marian* guy. He said he was calling to congratulate me on the success of *Batman* because he always said I was a visionary.

As I hung up the phone and recounted to Ben what had just happened, the next epiphany in my life occurred, and it was a revelation—if you don't believe them when they tell you how bad you are and how terrible your ideas are . . . and then, if you don't believe them when they tell you how great you are and how wonderful your ideas are . . . but rather just believe in yourself and in your own work . . . you'll do just fine in life. If this were Oz, and if Glinda the Good Witch of the North were here, she'd be telling me, "That's all there is!"

My collection of Batman buttons from the past thirty years includes the rare "1980: The Year of The Batman" pin and two pins with the Bob Kane-attributed illustration of Batman, which was used to promote the 1989 film. The button commemorating the Tricentennial of Gotham City was meant to be a prop in the 1989 movie worn by citizens in the celebration in the opening scenes and later at the parade. It was later changed to Gotham's Bicentennial and this button is now an extreme rarity.

PART V:
# "BATS" OF LUCK

# CHAPTER TWENTY-TWO

# After THE DARK KNIGHT, the BRIGHTEST DAY!

A spooky business this producing is sometimes. But it can be so much fun! It's the only job I could find where I get to be six for half a day and sixteen for the other half no matter how gray I get. Every day is different. When I wake up in the morning, I truly don't know what I'll be doing—or where I'll be doing it, for that matter—by nightfall. What do I actually do? Simply put, every day, I report to a sandbox and play with my favorite toys. All in all, it's a helluva sandbox.

From *Batman* in 1989 to *The Dark Knight* in 2008, life was insane! Great opportunities arose, and I could seize maybe only half of them. There are eight million stories in Hollywood's Naked City, and I was in my fair share of them. . . .

Ben and I continue the Bat-Celebration at the premiere of *Batman Begins*.

Great projects were produced, yet half the time, there were painful ones that got away and never came to pass. When people in the Biz hear that, they smile and pat me on the back and say how amazing it is to bat .500 in this crazy industry. That's nice, but doesn't lessen the pain of losing your dream project or spending years in the trenches striving hard to make people and companies understand why it's so important to respect not only the integrity of comic book characters but also the integrity of the fans, and then fail to be able to get them to do so. There were actually two movies that Ben and I were tied to that we did everything we could to convince powers that be NOT to go forward with . . . at least not in the direction they were insisting on going. It was against our own financial interest to try to stop them from progressing, but if I could have just magically wished them away, I would have. Those two films were the apex of pain to this comic book geek-at-heart. But as I've learned the hard way, it can all be much more complex than simply a case of pleas falling on deaf ears. Generally in the industry, what were once just movie studios are now often worldwide media conglomerates that own many businesses and have their fingers in many pies, from theme parks and video companies to toy companies and T-shirt companies. Many corporate wheels need to be greased. Sometimes, the tail starts to wag the dog, and priority is given to merchandising, toys, and "Happy Meals" over great scripts and great filmmaking. If filmmakers are told that a movie must have multiple heroes and multiple villains with two costumes and two vehicles each, then the danger becomes making two-hour infomercials for toys rather than great films.

If an inspired filmmaker has a respectful vision for a particular comic book character and knows how to execute that vision, then there is the chance for something special . . . something amazing . . . to occur. Too often, though, for reasons that may be limited to ego, people want to put their own stamp on a comic book movie and make wholesale changes in the character and premise just for the sake of change. To ignore ten years, or twenty-five years, or fifty years of history and mythology to create something out of whole new cloth can be akin to peeing on the heads of every fan who ever was. In this day and age, one has to be careful to make the translation from one visual medium to another work successfully and be embraced by the fans and public alike on a global basis.

When a genius like Christopher Nolan has a vision and can execute it, he succeeds in raising the bar for all comic book–based movies. When people walk out of *The Dark*

*Knight* or *Batman Begins*, they don't just say, "That was a great comic book movie!" but rather, "That was a great film!" And Christopher Nolan deserves all the credit in the world for that.* He is probably the first director of the twenty-first century to be studied in film schools. And for him to be the director and visionary for a historic trilogy of Batman movies culminating in the July 2012 release of *The Dark Knight Rises* has proven to be a godsend for hard-core fanboys as well as mainstream audiences around the world. It was no

Me and Nancy with Mr. and Mrs. Jerry Robinson at the premiere of *The Dark Knight*. Jerry is the co-creator of the Joker, not to mention Two-Face, Alfred, and Robin!

simple thing to reignite the Batman franchise. In his brilliance, he realized the way to make Batman work again would be to make him real. The audience had to believe that Bruce Wayne could be a real person in a real city in a real world. Thus, from the early minutes of *Batman Begins*, the audience does not feel as if it is in another comic book movie. Instead, the audience seems to feel like it does in *Lost Horizon*, following a desperate man on his search for truth and his search for himself. In order to believe in Bruce Wayne and that in our world today a Batman could exist, Gotham City now had to feel real, too. Thus, Chicago was used for Gotham City. With just a couple of iconic landmarks removed from the skyline, most people around the world did not recognize the city. Had it been filmed in New York, however, the second the audience saw Central Park or Times Square or the Statue of Liberty, it would have been jarred right out of its suspension of disbelief and the whole thing might have failed. The third element that Christopher Nolan had to convince the audience was real was the Joker. Jack Nicholson's Joker in *Batman* was the perfect Clown Prince of Crime as portrayed in the age-old comic book world of black versus white, good versus evil. But in our tumultuous planet today, the world is gray. It's no longer so much good versus evil as it is order versus chaos. The Joker is a homicidal maniac, a terrorist, an agent of chaos, who places no value whatsoever on human life—not man's, woman's, child's, or even his own. Together, the incredible Heath Ledger and Christopher Nolan crafted a performance for the ages and made the audience believe the Joker could exist . . . could possibly be real in our too often nightmarish world. That was an achievement of a lifetime. The final element that the audience had to believe in was all the technology and gadgetry. If the people sitting in the theaters didn't believe in it all, the picture might not work. So how did Christopher Nolan convince them it was real? In his genius, he hired Morgan

*Beyond Christopher Nolan, the kudos must go to his talented brother, Jonah; his wonderful wife, Emma; former comic book writer David Goyer; the master producer Chuck Roven; as well as Alan Horn, Barry Meyer, Steve Spira, Jeff Rabinov, Greg Silverman, and all the Warner Bros. execs who so "get it" when it comes to Batman, the Dark Knight. That passion and integrity and ability has led to the bar being raised for all comic book movies.

Freeman to TELL everyone it was real! Well, if Morgan Freeman says it's real, it MUST be! Hell, I believed him! I believe anything Morgan Freeman says!

The night of the world premiere of *The Dark Knight* in New York City was beyond special…another of those fantasy moments…dreams…come true. We were at a special Tavern on the Green dinner given by then-president of DC Comics and, more importantly, former fellow Junior Woodchuck, Paul Levitz. Paul always made sure credit was given where credit was due and tried to be as inclusive as possible when it came to the talented people who contributed to the success of Batman along the way, and the impact of whose work was felt in each film. At the dinner, Nancy, David, Sarah, and I were privileged to be seated next to my old buddy Jerry Robinson, who had been Bob Kane's first assistant and first ghost artist (to be followed by George Roussous, Shelly Moldoff, Lew Sayre Schwartz, Dick Sprang, Charlie Paris, Winslow Mortimer, Curt Swan, Jack Burnley, Fred Ray, Irwin Hasen, Jim Mooney, and so many others). Let me repeat that Jerry co-created The Joker, as well as Robin, Alfred, the Penguin, Two-Face, and a number of villains, but never received his due until *The Dark Knight*. Jerry Robinson's name, like Bill Finger's, never appeared in a *Batman* or *Detective* comic book he drew. Bob Kane's contract with DC provided that Bob's name be the only one to appear in print. Finally, in 2008, DC Comics acknowledged the valuable contributions of Jerry Robinson and made him a creative consultant and its goodwill ambassador to worldwide comic book fandom. And now…this night…there was another chance to make sure Jerry received his due.

At DC Comics' premiere dinner party, when I asked Jerry how he and his lovely wife were going to the premiere following this wonderful dinner in Central Park, he told me he was going to hail a cab. I said, "No way!" and brought him into the stretch limo with my family and Ben Melniker and his most elegant wife, Shirley. We all piled in, and along the way to the theater, just as at our very first *Batman* movie premiere in 1989, the crowds grew thicker and wilder as we drew nearer and nearer. I never saw so many people in Joker makeup…including at San Diego Comic-Con, where about one in every six people were dressed like the Joker that summer of *The Dark Knight*.

As we disembarked at the curb, Jerry whispered to me that he would walk around the red carpet and would meet me inside. Once again I said, "No way! You're coming with me!" I put my arm around him and as we faced what seemed to be a few hundred TV cameras, photographers, and reporters, I cupped my hands to my mouth and yelled to them as loudly as I could, "Ladies and Gentlemen! This is Jerry Robinson, co-creator of the Joker!" And with that, the cameras all turned toward Jerry, the flashes went off in his face, and reporters rushed him to get interviews. It took him half an hour to walk the red carpet, and I never felt happier in my life! At last! A comic book creator and artist extraordinaire from the Golden Age of Comics…who contributed to our art, our American folklore, our contemporary mythology, was getting recognition with no one else jumping in front of him to grab any credit. Once we got to the big party after the film, I was introduced by Paul Levitz to Athena Finger, the granddaughter of Bill

Finger. Leave it to Paul to have the heart and compassion to invite her. I took Athena and Jerry by the hand and brought them over to meet some people. I introduced them first to Michael Caine and said, "Michael, Jerry and Athena's grandfather, Bill Finger, were two of the co-creators of your character, Alfred." Michael embraced them physically and emotionally, with gratitude and appreciation. I then repeated the introduction with Aaron Eckhart, who played Two-Face, and Danny DeVito (my old Asbury Park compadre, and, yes, we immediately started again debating which restaurant has the best pizza on the Jersey Shore!), who played the Penguin. I then explained Jerry's contribution to the Batman mythos and Bill Finger's up-front essential creation work on "The Batman" to Christian Bale, who was wonderful to both Jerry and Athena. My son David took pictures of each encounter to preserve this evening that Jerry called "one of the greatest evenings of my life." I was just so pleased.

There's an important lesson to be learned from *The Dark Knight*. Unfortunately, not everyone in Hollywood gets it . . . sigh. . . . The movie's stunning success does NOT mean that all comic book superhero films must be dark, gritty, and violent and set in contemporary times. But that's exactly what some industry people are claiming. If that's the case, duck and cover, because it just may spawn movies like "Casper the Unfriendly Ghost!" But *Iron Man*, a huge success, which I saw three times in the first week, is just plain FUN! Aha! There's room for many tones in our superheroes. Even so, whenever my nemeses "Pow!" "Zap!" and "Wham!" rear their heads, I've been known to toss scripts across rooms and out windows. I do understand that sometimes a studio and producer invest themselves in the vision of a filmmaker and in the course of things that vision takes unanticipated twists and turns. I know all about that. These are some of the vagaries and frustrations of filmmaking that lead to batting averages of .500 or .300 rather than 1.000.

When a comic book character that has been around for decades is intrinsically tied to a specific period in time or at least to a "timeless" time as opposed to the modern day, the lesson from *The Dark Knight* is not to violate that by making it modern day, but rather to honor the essence of the character and be true to it. Many young production execs live by the Hollywood "Rules" (which seem to change faster than a speeding bullet), which dictate such corollaries as "period pieces don't sell." I guess they don't . . . until you look at the Indiana Jones films . . . or *Titanic*. This sort of thinking makes bright and creative people spend too much time looking over their shoulders at whoever may be sneaking up behind them looking for their jobs or to put their heads on studio chopping blocks, instead of feeling confident enough to look forward and be daring and take creative risks. It's what I've fought for my thirty-five plus years in the trenches of Hollywood, often failing in the process. My mom used to tell me it was okay to fail because that's not only the way we learn, it's the way we learn about ourselves. Why is all this so important to me? Maybe it's because I'm only a fanboy . . . a comic geek at heart. And, yes, it just does matter.

# THE ROAD TAKEN,
## *THE ROAD NOT TAKEN*

Comic books are often about journeys. The adventures of superheroes often take on epic proportions rooted in the quests of warriors and gods from classical mythology. Everyone from Hercules to Wonder Woman has undertaken his or her own variation of the twelve labors. Everyone from Odysseus to Captain Marvel has experienced his own challenging odyssey.

Comic book philosopher-king and writer Stan Lee might have guided you from mundane Midgard (our earth) across Bifrost, Thor's magical Rainbow Bridge, to the lofty heights of Asgard, glorious home to the Norse gods. Writer Jerry Siegel might have taken you along on baby Kal-El's journey through cold, dark outer space from the dying planet Krypton to the strange new land of earth. Writer Bill Finger might have ushered you in with Bruce Wayne as he entered the secret passageway behind his grandfather clock and descended into the Bat-Cave where he would transform into The Batman. (If right about now, you're one of those people thinking, "Hey! Don't you mean the Bat-Poles—that larger one labeled "Bruce" and that skinnier one labeled "Dick"? I'd very much like to "Wham!" you upside your campy head!) Poet Robert Frost, however, would simply have urged you to choose "the road not taken."

Life itself is a journey . . . a journey comprised of an unending stream of choices and their consequences. Often, I've made good choices on my own personal journey. Occasionally, I've made great choices. Sometimes, I've made bad choices. As a result, over my career I've won some and lost some. In the Biz, the highs can be astronomically high, but the lows can be debilitatingly low. It's often described as a "feast or famine" business, where your luck and success tend to run in streaks. Same for your bad luck and lack of success. I found that these extremes create an impossible up and down atmosphere in which to live. The secret for me is to find ways to absorb enough energy from those high highs to get me through those low lows, so that each day will feel like a smoother, wavier line rather than resemble a jagged, peaks-and-valleys seismograph line during a 9.0 earthquake and its ongoing aftershocks.

As a boy, I always loved the comic book adventures of Batman when he needed to play Darkknight Detective and investigate some eerie mystery rooted in the past. My favorite was the time he needed to uncover the secret origin of the Bat-Cave. To accomplish this, Bruce Wayne and his ward, Dick Grayson, paid a visit to Bruce's genius inventor friend, Professor Nichols, who invented a standard comic book "time machine" that would take the boys to a time and place in the past where they would solve such important mysteries as how and why Emperor Julius Caesar invented his pleasant-tasting salad.

Sometimes, Batman would also wind up propelled into the future, most often in his '50s and early '60s stories, where he'd coincidentally run into one or another Batman of the future. (Hey! There's a great idea! Let's call him "Batman Beyond!" Someone could even make a live-action movie out of it and have Clint Eastwood play eighty-year-old Bruce Wayne, who serves as the new, young Batman's very own Obi-Wan Kenobi!)

Why did I so love time travel stories? I think I did so because I was a lover of history. As any history major worth his salt will assure you, if we fail to learn from history, we will be doomed to repeat it . . . mistakes and all.

But also, I've been inextricably tied to my own past during my forward journey through life. I can clearly remember now what I was thinking and feeling back when I was five or eight or twelve or sixteen or twenty-one and up. I still feel like I'm in touch with "me" at all those ages.

After *The Dark Knight* opened to rave reviews, historic box-office receipts, awards, and accolades, Nancy sat me down and asked me, "So now, what do you want to be when you grow up?" The answer to that was as clear as Phantom Girl to me. I wanted to write more and speak to more young people. I wanted to go back in time and take college students along with me so that I could share my story with them. The fact that my journey to bring a dark and serious Batman to the silver screen did, in fact, turn into a ten-year human endurance contest has become an integral part of my life's personal history. The best way I could conceive of to validate that journey would be not simply to preserve it, but to impart it to students everywhere, letting them know, with no bullshit, that if I was able to make my dreams come true, there's no reason they can't make their own dreams come true. After all, I was that blue-collar kid from Jersey, later sitting in classrooms in the middle of Indiana, with no money to buy my way into Hollywood, no relatives I knew in Hollywood, no friends in Hollywood. So the answer to that burning question regarding my or anyone's goal in life, "How do you get there from here?" was something I had to learn for myself. And I did. Now I had an opportunity to give back and impart what I had learned. When I was in school, no one gave his time to come back and share his pilgrimage . . . to tell me that it was possible . . . that I could make my dreams come true. So what's the magic? It's the fact that there is no magic.

First and foremost, my dad was so right. When you are forced to choose between your work and your family, put your family first. Always. Find out what you love in life and make that passion part of your work, even though that means you sometimes have to take calculated risks and roll the dice. And that passion doesn't have to be about something glitzy and glamorous like making Batman movies. It can simply be about "bricks and stones."

My mom was right about everything. Specifically in terms of accomplishing my goals, her lessons were to believe in myself, market myself, always have a Plan B, and, once I make a commitment, to honor it even if I have to march through hell to do so. I did all that, including the march through hell. I persevered. I survived. And I prevailed.

My brother, Paul, incredibly, was also right and didn't lie when he enlightened me about taking the negatives in my life and making them positives in the form of "negative reinforcement."

My wise mentors and second fathers, my father-in-law Dr. Morry Osher, and my Bat-Partner Ben Melniker, set an example for me that nothing is more important than preserving your integrity no matter what the sacrifice. The only thing you get to leave behind and also get to take with you is your own good name.

And the three things I had to learn for myself (like Dorothy having to make her trek to Oz before her ruby slippers could take her home) were: Number One, 90 percent of the competition out there sit on their butts with some sense of entitlement, waiting for the world to come to them, and therefore, my competition was only about 10 percent of the people; Number Two, the only way to succeed, to make my own luck, and to get my foot in any door, was by knocking on those doors, having them slam in my face, picking myself up, knocking again, and knocking again and again until my knuckles bled. The Batman movie franchise was built on my bloody knuckles. Number Three, I don't believe them when they tell me how awful I am and how bad my ideas are, and I don't believe them when they tell me how wonderful I am and how great my ideas are. I just believe in myself and in my work. And that is all that really counts.

And so, after *The Dark Knight,* I became a man on a mission. Thanks to the collegiate reach of Don Epstein and his Greater Talent Network in New York, I have spoken at some sixty colleges and universities, corporations, and charitable organizations, imparting my message. One of the most memorable talks was the keynote address I gave as guest of honor at the New York Comic-Con in 2009, almost forty-five years after my parents took me and Bobby Klein to New York to attend (with 198 other fans) that first comic book convention ever held. And the New York crowd gave me a standing ovation. It was one of those moments when I opened my heart and soul and mind and let thirteen-year-old Michael out to revel in the moment.

I've spoken at the Met and at the Smithsonian, and at the twentieth anniversary screening of *Batman* in L.A., a fantabulous celebration and party, in which noted and knowledgeable *L.A. Times* entertainment reporter and master comic book/movies blogger Geoff Boucher interviewed me before the screening of the pristine print on the big screen. But, the lectures that matter the most to me are the ones at schools. It's my goal every time I speak to impact as many young people as I can with my story and to inspire at least a few of them. But sometimes they inspire me, too, or really make me think. After my speech at Georgetown University (and, yes, I asked everyone there to stop by Georgetown's Law School the next day to check on my waiting list status and let them know I was still patiently

The Uslan Family version of The Fantastic Four: Sarah, David, Nancy, and me as we took the kids onto every Batman movie set since 1989!

checking my mailbox every day), during the Q+A period, a young lady asked me a reflective question, "Your dream of writing Batman comics came true. Then your dream of producing the dark and serious Batman movies came true. What is your dream now?" It was only at that precise moment that I realized that all my dreams today are based upon my children and my family rather than upon my work. What an epiphany for me!

Two memorable talks will forever remain at the top of my life's highlight reel. The first event was the commencement address at my alma mater, Indiana University, before a total of some 34,000 people over two ceremonies. It wasn't all that many years ago I was sitting in the same chairs those graduating students were now in. It was an emotional coming home for me. I spoke from my heart as I wove for them the story of my journey from Bloomington to Hollywood and reminded them that at MY college graduation, neither I nor more than half my friends had a job lined up or even had the prospect of a job. I will never ever forget the standing ovations I received from the assembled graduates and their families as I concluded my address. I choked up. The president of I.U. said it was the first time in the history of Indiana's commencements that the speaker received a standing O. It was an honor that, had my mom been there (physically . . . I was sure she was there otherwise), might have surpassed that "Character Award" as my accomplishment she most prized. In 2009, *USA Today* named my graduation speech at Indiana University one of the "Top Ten Commencement Speeches of All Time." The Web site devoted to such, Graduationwisdom.com, honored my speech in the same way. I know that it's Batman who has given me this forum and creates the opportunity for me to have many, many students turn out to hear what I have to say. Together, we're having such a positive influence on so many young people. "Batman and Michael." It has a very cool ring to it, don'tcha think? Much better than "Batman and Robin." At least, to me.

The second memorable talk, and perhaps the crowning moment of my lecturing, took place in 2009 at West Point. The cadets each year vote for a deserving recipient of their prestigious Cadet's Choice Award. This year, they voted Batman, the Dark Knight, as the character who most represented the code of honor and leadership of West Point, and they invited me to come to accept the award. Nancy and I drove there and were treated like a king and queen, shown around the entire impressive and beautiful campus. I was asked to address the 4,500 cadets at lunchtime for five minutes after receiving the award. I explained that my motivational talk usually runs much longer, but they explained back that lunchtime in total was only fifteen minutes long. What could I say in just five minutes? Then it hit me. I knew exactly what I needed to tell them all.

The Colonel and the cadets ushered Nancy and me into the eating hall, which looked like the eating hall from the Harry Potter movies. The Vikings could have built this place with its massive stonework, vaulted ceilings, flags, and stone balcony ahead at the point. The cadets were all lined up at attention next to their seats at their lunch tables as the awards presentation was made to me on that classic balcony. I then thanked them all and addressed the throng. The words just came out, spur of the moment . . .

"Cadets of West Point, when Bruce Wayne was a boy, he witnessed his parents murdered in the streets before his eyes. On that concrete altar of blood, in the belief that one person CAN make a difference, he sacrificed his childhood and made a life commitment to get the guy who did this and to get all the bad guys, even if it meant having to march through hell in order to honor that commitment. In doing so, he became a leader, an urban warrior. Cadets of West Point . . . YOU are Batman!"

And with that, the hall erupted into a mass of cheering and applauding and whooping and hollering, with some standing on their chairs for emphasis. And that spontaneous outburst went on for minutes, echoing over and over again in the castle-like chamber. I was overwhelmed by their reaction to my words and was so proud to be there and so proud of them. It was the single greatest moment of my career, and Nancy was there to witness what was taking place and share in it.

Possibly the most important moment in my career came when I was invited to speak to the cadets of West Point and receive their 2009 Cadet's Choice Award for *Batman* and *The Dark Knight*! "Cadets of West Point—YOU are Batman!"

A few days later, I received a letter from the mother of one of the cadets. That letter now hangs on the wall of my office. She wrote:

"I'm the mom of a West Point cadet. I thought you should know that your recent visit there REALLY boosted morale! The Corps loved your speech. Apparently, they are all walking around now saying, 'I AM Batman' or 'You ARE Batman' to each other. THANK YOU for leaving them with a wonderful (and fun) concept that they could all embrace during this time when they face such a serious future.

"My son was inspired by the overwhelming cadet reaction to your speech . . . . So you may not realize it, but you have definitely left a legacy for the classes of 2009, 2010, 2011, and 2012. I can picture them running into each other in the field for years to come and exchanging the 'I AM Batman' routine. Thank you again for giving them that!"

It was a humbling letter to receive. But at last, I can believe that in doing what I have chosen to do for a living, I have done something more than merely entertain people for two hours at a time. And that is the big payoff for me in my career.

With that in mind, in looking back, I find my life filled with real versions of what in the craft of writing a movie script we refer to as "set-ups." And as every good screenwriter knows, every "set-up" planted in a film must have a "payoff" . . . and vice versa. My life's screenplay has, indeed, been filled with both. . . .

**THE SET-UP:** In my world of comic books, remember back around 1962 when my prized copy of *Showcase* #4 mysteriously vanished? Of all comics, this was the ridiculously valuable one that introduced not only the Silver Age Flash but the entire Silver Age of Comics itself. Did I say "valuable?" How about $50,000 valuable?

**THE PAYOFF:** Just before my mom died, she sat my dad down and ordered him not to make any emotional and rash decisions after she was gone. She wanted him to remain in our Runyan Avenue house for at least a year before he considered selling it. He stayed there for a year and a half before moving in with us in "Poppy's own wing of the house." But when Pop finally sold our old house, he gave me about forty-eight hours to pack up all the stuff I never ever threw out from the garage, my bedroom, the crawl space, and all my great kid's hiding places. Everything just got thrown into boxes marked "Family," "Grade School," "High School," "College," "Law School," or "Comic Book History." The day finally came in our own house when Nancy went nuts. All boxes from Runyan Avenue were to be gone through and stuff "thrown out," the two most hideous words we collectors and savers ever want to hear. David was home and helped me sort through them, thus joining me in another trip back through time.

The Mother Lode was struck at 3:33 P.M. In the huge "Grade School" box, David found my sixth-grade notebook with the cool picture of Bela Lugosi as Dracula on it. David was captivated by that picture and quickly lifted the notebook out of the box. As he did, four comic books proceeded to fall out of it: *Showcase* #34, introducing the Silver Age Atom (current value: $3,000); *Flash* #105, first Silver Age issue (current value: $15,000); *Detective Comics* #225, introducing J'onn J'onzz, Manhunter from Mars (current value: $10,000); and my elusive, missing-in-action for thirty-three years, *Showcase* #4 (current value: $50,000), for a grand total jackpot of $78,000. David spent the remainder of his summer going through every single piece of paper in every single box. He found lots of cool and historic stuff, but never again struck comic book gold.

**SET-UP #1:** My brother, Paul, became a successful optometrist in Ann Arbor, Michigan, and still is to this day. Of the countless families he has taken care of over the decades, one had a kid who was such a total comic book fanatic that he reminded Paul of me.

**SET-UP #2:** I appeared at my first ever Comic-Con as a pro in Indianapolis circa 1975 and a kid who was a fanatic collector of *The Shadow* made his folks drive him down all the way from near Ann Arbor, Michigan, to hear me speak and get me to autograph the Shadow comics I wrote. I wound up talking to him for twenty minutes after my presentation. Why not? It was the first time I'd ever been asked for an autograph!

**PAYOFF #1:** As a producer, I acquired the rights to the Shadow, the character who started me out as a professional comic book writer and whose driving creative force, Walter Gibson, I had the thrill and pleasure of working with as an advisor on a film project back in the '80s. Jon Levin, one of the great agents in L.A. who also really gets the world of comic books, summoned me to a meeting at the big talent agency CAA. The famed director of the Spider-Man movies, Sam Raimi, wanted to bring the Shadow to the silver screen in a way that would restore the character to the gritty violence of his timeless roots in 1930s New York and would transcend the attempt at a Shadow movie made many, many years previously with Alec Baldwin. Jon was nervous about this meeting. "Now, Michael, Sam Raimi has made Sony billions of dollars, okay?" he stated. "I know you have some definitive ideas as to how to make the Shadow work as a film, but Sam's one of our greatest directors and will probably have his own ideas, too, so please listen to what he has to say, okay?" Jon emphasized. "No problem," I said just as I had learned to say it back in law school. And off I went to meet Sam Raimi and to see if we might partner on the Shadow. Sam is a bright and affable man, and I was immediately impressed with his genuine down-to-earth nature. In this first meeting were two more great people, Josh Donen, son of the legendary director Stanley Donen (his *Singin' in the Rain* is my favorite musical of all time) and FJ DeSanto. FJ started working for Ben and me as an intern from the Tisch School at NYU in the graduate film school program. He had sent in a resume a year previous and had received a reply from me that we had nothing for him but would keep his resume on file. Apparently Ben and I were the only ones in the history of employment that actually meant that, and did so. A year later, we pulled out his resume, called him, and hired him. FJ absorbed everything about the business he could from Ben and me. And, hallelujah, he was a fellow comic book fanboy. FJ learned well and has become both a creative movie/TV producer and comic book writer in his own right.

And so there we were in Sam's sprawling office at Sony about to talk about the Shadow. But Sam had one question for me first. "Uslan . . . Uslan . . ." he mused. "That's a very unusual name." "I know it is," I responded, astounded he could even pronounce it correctly (YOU-slin), as nobody ever gets it right the first time. Sam continued, "Any relation to an optometrist in Ann Arbor, Michigan, Dr. Paul Uslan?" I was stunned. "That's my brother!" I exclaimed. "How do you know my brother?" I wondered, while FJ laughed, knowing just how often these cosmic coincidences happen to me and my family, which includes hundreds of aunts and uncles and thousands of cousins. "Well," said Sam, "when I was growing up just north of Ann Arbor, my mom used to take me to Dr. Uslan to get our glasses." "Wait a minute," I begged as I whipped out my cell phone and called my brother. "Paul, does the name Sam Raimi ring a bell?" I inquired. "Sure!" he offered enthusiastically. "I took care of his whole family. What a nice boy! Whatever happened to that kid?" he asked. "Well," I announced, "I'm sitting here in Hollywood with 'that kid.'" Paul had no idea. But then, again, neither did I, as it turned out. The best and eeriest was yet to come!

**PAYOFF #2:** I went right to the heart of our creative discussion and asked Sam if he saw the Shadow being portrayed on film as he was in the original pulp magazines, or if his vision for it was more in line with the old dramatic radio show interpretation of the character, or if he wanted to try a hybrid approach. Instead, Sam said it was *The Shadow* comic books of the 1970s that he fell in love with and that had made him into a hard-core comic book fanboy. He recounted how he was all set to go on his first boy-girl skiing trip when he read his first *The Shadow* comic book, and literally got off the bus to go back to the comic book shop and find the Shadow issues he had already missed. I asked Sam if there were any stories, incidents, or characters he might like to see in the film. He started mentioning a few things, and I made him stop. I reached into my briefcase and pulled out a couple of Shadow comics from the '70s and verified that many of those bits were from these issues that I had written. "I know. You realize we've met before?" Sam sorta said/asked. I was flummoxed. How could I not recall meeting Sam Raimi? Sam explained it all . . . "Michael, I read in a fanzine that you were speaking at a comic book convention in Indianapolis. I pleaded with my folks to drive me down there from Michigan. I heard your talk and then came up to you afterward to ask you some questions and get you to autograph my Shadow comics for me. You spoke to me for twenty minutes, and I never forgot that. I've followed your career ever since! Now let's have some fun and make this Shadow movie together!" That kid from Michigan? My first autograph ever? Him? Sam Raimi? If I was Dr. Seuss, I'd have asked him, "You are 'Sam'?" And Mr. Raimi would've responded, "Sam I am!" Not just a payoff; not just a double-payoff; but here was a COSMIC payoff!

**THE SET-UP:** The great creators of the world's greatest superheroes from the Golden Age to the Silver Age were disrespected. Many of them were Jewish, and from the 1930s to the 1960s they were shut out of art jobs and writing assignments in the world of Madison Avenue advertising and upper crust New York City publishing circles. But, just as had previously happened with the movie business, no one of wealth and class wanted the comic book or pulp business. It was looked down upon, if not frowned upon. So it was a business the Jews could largely make theirs. But even the people involved in it had no notion of it having lasting value as our mythology or as an American art form. Even Stan Lee at cocktail parties tried to describe himself as a writer of children's stories . . . an editor of magazines . . . anything but comic books. And then came Dr. Wertham accusing them of poisoning the minds and souls of an entire generation of youth. In the early days of comic book fandom, we fans were all looked upon as geeks and freaks with the proverbial screw loose and the opposite of cool. The two hundred of us at the earliest comic book conventions found true camaraderie while we were shunned by everyone else.

**THE PAYOFF:** Today, the San Diego Comic-Con sells out six months in advance, cutting off admissions somewhere around 135,000 conventioneers. Chicago and New York Comic-Cons are hovering around the 100,000 attendance mark. The world's biggest blockbuster movies, hit TV shows, animation, and video games are based on comic books and the genres most closely associated with them. Comic books and graphic novels are now utterly cool. And so are we, the fans. Meanwhile, Eli Lilly funded Indiana University's amazing rare book library, the Lilly Library.

Speaking at San Diego Comic-Con 2010 about my journey to bring Batman to the movies.

When I decided to thank I.U. for giving me my start on the road to making my dark and serious Batman movies by allowing me the opportunity to teach the world's first fully accredited comic book class, I decided to donate some 45,000 comic books and related trade paperbacks, hardbacks, and memorabilia to the Lilly Library. I was quickly asked to work with them to create a notable exhibition of comic books and original art from my collection. It was one of my life's highlights to see on display right next to a Gutenberg Bible my copy of *Batman* #1 from spring 1940. Hanging next to Gilbert Stuart's portrait of George Washington was Bob Kane's drawing for me of his "mysterioso" Batman. I've since spoken about comic books twice at the Smithsonian Institution and worked with the remarkable Montclair Art Museum to mount a massive comic book exhibition, based largely on my collection, which smashed every attendance record in the museum's history. The crown of creation for me was advising the New York Metropolitan Museum of Art's first exhibition devoted to comic book superheroes. This groundbreaking show featured seminal issues of historic comic books mounted under glass on the walls of the Met, many of which were from my collection. It was truly a dream come true to see my comic books on the wall of the Met! The exhibition was an honor and testament to all the artists, writers, editors, and others who have toiled in the comic book industry since 1934. I only wished Otto Binder, C. C. Beck, Julie Schwartz, Sol Harrison, and all the others had been around to witness this!

**THE SET-UP:** I struggled through law school, not wanting to go, but desperately needing a Plan B to get my foot into any open door in Hollywood. Since I had no desire to become a lawyer hanging out a shingle, but had a master plan to receive a legal education and then use it in novel ways, my presence in law school was not embraced by some lawyers-to-be. Making matters even more challenging was my lack of presence on campus as I earned the nickname the Phantom by racing home from school to write the comic book adventures of the Shadow, Beowulf, the Question, and Batman while everyone else was racing to study. But Indiana University School of Law catered to the needs of one student whose unique interests lay with entertainment and communications, and then accommodated those needs, although it meant bending a bunch of rules. Without that legal education, I don't believe I could be doing what I do. It was three years of hard labor with little time off for any behavior whatsoever, but I survived it and it helped me get to where I needed to go.

**THE PAYOFF:** Today, a large percentage of law school students do not become practicing attorneys or remain practicing attorneys, but rather use their legal education for diverse pursuits relating to business and entrepreneurship. And I have appreciated the irony of having been honored by Indiana University's Maurer School of Law for my role as a maverick by being asked to give the commencement address to the law school graduates and of having been awarded the very personally meaningful Hoagy Carmichael Creative Achievement Award honoring the guy who was the first one at Indiana to do what I did. Following in Hoagy Carmichael's footsteps gave me a path to follow rather than one to blaze. He made it easier for me. But perhaps the ultimate irony is that thanks to the kindness of everyone at the law school beginning with deans Lauren Robell and Len Fromm, two of my idols, I was inducted into the prestigious Academy of Law Fellows, causing my portrait to hang permanently in the lobby of the Maurer School of Law . . . which, while cracking up Sully and a nice handful of my law school buddies . . . must gall the shit out of a few former classmates who wouldn't give me the time of day because I didn't actually want to become a lawyer. Oops! My "negative reinforcement" slip is showing!

**THE SET-UP:** In my sandbox of producing movies, there are still favorite toys of my youth I want to play with, and now have upcoming projects in varied stages of development involving crown jewel comic book/comic strip characters I have not only loved since I was a kid, but whose creators or artists and writers I personally knew growing up, including: Batman (Bob Kane, Bill Finger, and my pal, Jerry Robinson); Captain ("Shazam") Marvel (Otto Binder and C. C. Beck); the Shadow (Walter Gibson); and Thunder Agents (Wally Wood). In my other sandbox just used for writing comic books and graphic novels, I was privileged to write characters I also loved as a kid, including: a three-issue story arc for Will Eisner's *The Spirit*, as well as for the very noir feature "The Spirit Black & White"; Mr. Justice, based on MLJ Comics' 1941 supernatural superhero, which, very proudly, I had the opportunity to co-write with my son, David (as my Grandma Miriam would say, "I'm qvelling!"); introductions and histories in hardcover collections of some of DC, Marvel, and Tower Comics' greatest comic books of the Golden Age and Silver Age in their library editions of DC Archives and Marvel Masterworks, many co-written with "the new kid," Bobby Klein; my first hardcover Batman graphic novel, titled *Batman: Detective #27*; and the one comic book character I was always hoping to write one day . . . nope, not Superman or Spider-Man . . . but rather, Archie!

**THE PAYOFF:** I love reading books that weave fictional characters into real events in history, commingling them with real people who lived at the time. I proposed to DC Comics a graphic novel that would allow me to take Bruce Wayne and do the same thing. It would be a creative way to combine my love of Batman, comic books, and history into one great project. Every fan in the world knows that Batman made his debut in the pages of the historic DC comic book *Detective #27* in May 1939. That comic book made additional history when it was auctioned off for $1,100,000.

I was inspired by that title and conceived of an imaginary tale . . . excuse me . . .

I took my passion for American history and New York City history, combined that with my love for Batman, and wrote my first hardback graphic novel, *Batman: Detective #27!*

an "Elseworlds" saga . . . that would unfold starting on the night of Abraham Lincoln's assassination with a plot by the very real Knights of the Golden Circle to topple a major American city seventy-five years in the future . . . in May 1939. In my story, rendered by one of the most imaginative and talented graphic storytellers in the business, artist Peter Snejbjerg, in May of 1939, a twist of fate prevents Bruce Wayne from being inspired by an omen in the form of a bat to become The Batman. Instead, Bruce becomes a member of a secret society of detectives started by Allan Pinkerton himself. The goal of this society is to stop the seventy-five year plot from coming to pass. No one in the society ever uses his real name. Instead, each new detective is assigned a number. Pinkerton is Detective #1, and, in May 1939, Bruce Wayne becomes Detective #27.

I intended to fully explore two things in this graphic novel. The first came out of our first Batman film, in which Tim Burton had the Joker use a catchphrase whose meaning was never, ever, sufficiently explained, "Did you ever dance with the devil in the pale moonlight?" I decided to explain to the world what that question really meant. More importantly, I wanted to resurrect an old Batman villain I loved as a kid, whose secret origin I found in one of those old comic books at Collingwood Auction one Friday night. For a nickel, I bought that copy of *World's Finest Comics* #3 (current value: $6,000) and delved into the world of fear as utilized for evil purposes by the spooky then-new member of Batman's Rogues Gallery, the Scarecrow. In *Batman: Detective #27*, I wanted to examine the role fear plays in society and in good and evil and the ways people in power use it and manipulate it. While it's easy to use fear in a corrupt way as the Scarecrow does, what about the way The Batman uses it against his foes? The fear theme centrally explored in my graphic novel was also explored by Christopher Nolan in *Batman Begins*. As both a brilliant filmmaker and fan, Christopher understood Bruce Wayne/The Batman and what makes him tick. Of course, the New York Yankees fan in me surfaced in time while writing the book, so that Bruce Wayne not only meets Sigmund Freud and F.D.R., but Babe Ruth as well. What fun!

That experience was so wonderful for me, working with Peter and super editor Mike Carlin plus the DC hierarchy of Dan Didio and my fellow–Junior Woodchuck Paul Levitz, that I am now determined to write one more Batman graphic novel with a story I've been aching to tell. Tentatively titled "Batman: Deconstruction," it will explore the notion that the economic recession and the Madoff /Ponzi scheme were the direct results of a new villain close to Bruce Wayne who, after studying every article and detail about The Batman, concludes that Wayne Enterprises is funding his super-expensive technology, including the car. The villain then targets Bruce Wayne's investments and entire financial portfolio and bankrupts him, though bringing down most of the world economy with him in the process. Bruce can no longer afford any of the computers, gadgets, or gizmos. Since the nuclear fuel used in the car costs a minimum of $21,000 every time he uses the car, Batman loses his transportation. Unable to keep his Manor, Bruce also loses the Cave. Finally, The Batman is reduced to the very basics Bruce Wayne started out with . . . his brains, his detective skills, and his fists. Left with nothing more high tech than grappling hooks and some chemicals in the capsules of his belt, Bruce must learn whether or not a Batman deprived of technology and weaponry is still viable. Can The Batman still be The Batman when his greatest superpower now, truly, is his humanity? I think readers everywhere hit by the recession will empathize with this stripped-down version of a very real, very human Batman. I can't wait for the opportunity to plunge into this story one day!

But what a fitting, Disneyesque "Circle of Life" moment when I decided it was time to write an important Archie graphic novel. After all, this was one of the comics I learned to read from, and it formed my notions of what dating and high school would be like. And so, I contacted the venerable Victor Gorelick at Archie Comics. He was there when I was reading every comic in the Archie library in 1980. Victor had started there as a kid in the '60s. He asked me if I had a particular story idea in mind. "Archie gets married," I replied quickly, holding my breath for his response. "You can't do that, Michael!" Victor adamantly exclaimed. "Why not?" I countered. That led to an extraordinary creative discussion, at the end of which Victor was excited about the prospect. I felt that after more than sixty-eight years dating Betty and Veronica, it was about time for Archie's choice. But there were many important themes I wanted to explore in this five-... then six-... then seven-issue story arc.

Conceptually, I was influenced by *It's a Wonderful Life*, *A Christmas Carol*, and *The Wizard of Oz*. But I was directly inspired by a movie, a song, and, in particular, a poem. Gwyneth Paltrow starred in an independent film that had an impact on me, *Sliding Doors*. In that movie, we see what happens when Gwyneth's character in a typical, routine day of living and working in the City fails to make it on board a subway. The film rewinds and then lets us see her do it all again, but this time she just barely makes it onto that subway. And then it follows the two alternative paths of her unfolding life based on making and not making that subway train.

Joni Mitchell wrote a powerful, meaningful song, made famous by Judy Collins's beautiful rendition, "Both Sides Now," in which she looks at life and love from BOTH sides now.

I think I was on the "Most Wanted" list internationally when the world thought I was marrying Archie off to Veronica after sixty-eight years of dating in 2009. The truth is, he married BOTH Betty and Veronica! How? Go read *Archie Marries* . . . !

My favorite poem has been my guiding light through life. "The Road Not Taken" by Robert Frost defines me and may have actually helped mold me. In my life's journey to date, I have found that it is all about the choices we make or fail to make and their consequences. I have often incorporated the poem or its themes into my comic book writing. The three-issue story arc I wrote with FJ DeSanto for The Spirit was titled "Choices." In my graphic novel *Batman: Detective #27*, Bruce Wayne recites it as his favorite poem growing up. And most recently, in the blockbuster addition to the Archie Comics, *Archie Marries*, I use it in its entirety as the heart and soul of the story.

**THE SET-UP:** Nancy is seventeen when we start dating that very first day of college. She's smart and pretty, possessing a great sense of humor but no direction in life as yet, from time to time majoring in education, interior design, business, and nursing.

**THE PAYOFF:** In 2005 while accompanying Jack Hanna's crew filming a documentary in Rwanda, Nancy has a life-changing moment, realizing she needs to do something for the people of this country attempting to heal itself in the aftermath of genocide. She knows the path to healing lies with education. Nancy becomes

Both Sarah and David are now in this same batty business out in Hollywood. David is a producer and at the forefront of the digitization of the comic book industry. Sarah, trained by Bobbi Brown, is a top makeup artist in Beverly Hills and did the makeup for the 2010 Emmy Awards.

the visionary behind the Books and Beyond Project and the founder of the non-profit Friends of the Books and Beyond Project (Friendsofbooksandbeyond.com). The Books and Beyond Project breaks down cultural barriers by bringing three different groups of students from around the globe together, united in the common goal of learning and growing. In 2010, Nancy was a speaker at Indiana University's Women's Colloquium with Meryl Streep, Jane Pauley, and Nobel Prize winner Elinor Ostrom, and she brought down the house with the stunning achievements of Books and Beyond.

**THE SET-UP:** You get married. You have children. You make commitments to bring up those children around your parents and family, to place them in first priority over your work. Then you cross your fingers and stumble through parenthood in the hope that the majority of your decisions, actions, words, example-setting, and attempts to instill values, boundaries, and ideals will be good ones, giving your kids the gifts of roots and wings.

**THE PAYOFF:** Our children, David and Sarah, are now adults, both in the Biz in L.A. Sarah is a top-tier makeup artist, originally trained by Bobbi Brown. And there she was doing the makeup backstage at the Emmy Awards! In 2010, she opened her own business, Luxe Beauty Team (Luxebeautyteam.com). In addition to movies and television, Sarah has been the makeup artist for "A" List actresses and actors at the Oscars, the Golden Globes, and other major red carpet events in Hollywood. David is a producer with movie, TV, animation, and new media deals all over town. Most are either based on cutting edge graphic novels and comic books or on true stories about the Mob. He's also at the forefront of the digitization of comic books that absolutely represents where comic books are heading in the future.

Our now-adult children know who they are, where they come from, and where they are heading. They are loving and caring and have a sense of humor as well as common sense. They have integrity. Nancy and I LIKE them in addition to love them. And I know that wherever their four grandparents are, they have made them proud. They have never forgotten their roots and have truly taken wing.

**THE SET-UP:** It's true. In the temple, on the dais, under the *chuppah*, while I was in the process of marrying Nancy, her rabbi scolded me. Apoplectic that I collected, read, taught, and wrote comic books, and clearly being under the undue influence of Dr. Wertham, Rabbi Goldman looked me in the eye with smiling disdain and said . . . and I quote . . . "And as for you, Michael, remember . . . life is NOT a comic book."

**THE PAYOFF:** It's the night of our premiere screening of the 1989 movie *Batman* in New York. It's a magical, fantastical night for me. Before the picture, I have my few minutes to speak. I talk about all my parents have done for me and how they were always totally supportive of their son who loved Batman. In every way, they made me Me. I then have my mom and my dad stand up. In life, my folks would have told you they had everything they could have hoped for and dreamed of. But the one thing they didn't ever have was a standing ovation. That night, that moment, they got one from the packed audience. Also, I had tracked down Mrs. Stiller and Mrs. Friedman and, in a fantasy I had harbored since eighth grade, sent a limousine for them and brought them to the night's festivities. I told the assembled audience all about them. I spoke of the power and importance and influence a good teacher can have on the lives of her students. And I specified that no one would have been in that theater that night and there would have been no Batman movie but for them and their impact on my life, my work, and my dreams. I had them rise, and they received a standing ovation. They honored me by their presence that night. And in my own attempt to honor them years after that night, I wrote and delivered on behalf of all their students, their eulogies.

People think going to the Oscars is the thrill of a lifetime or that being up on stage receiving a statue at the Emmy Awards is as good as life gets. No. I would trade every Oscar, Emmy, Annie, and People's Choice Award my projects have ever earned . . . if I could grab my brother Paul, find our '56 Packard or 1960 Pontiac Catalina, and pull into just one more family drive-in movie with my mom and my dad. But this moment, able to honor my parents and my teachers, was the best of the best and the crowning memory of my Batman journey and the human endurance contest I saw through to the end.

And now, just before the film that would change my life began to roll, I told the packed theater the story of my wedding ceremony and those infamous words Rabbi Goldman scolded me with . . . "Michael, life is NOT a comic book!" I then said to the SRO audience, "Well, my first dream in life was to write Batman comic books and that dream came true. Since then, my dream in life has been to bring a dark and serious Batman to the movie screen, and tonight, that second dream comes true. And with that in mind, I now say to Rabbi Goldman . . . wherever you are . . . life IS a comic book! And I have lived it!" The place went wild with cheers and stomps and whistles, the lights dimmed, the curtains parted, and the movie *Batman* flickered onto the silver screen.

## ACKNOWLEDGMENTS

Lil and Joe Uslan . . . who not only made me, but made me ME. I loved you for being Mom and Dad, my own personal Super-woman and Superman.

Paul Uslan . . . I love ya for being my brother . . . like the Hang-man was to the Comet. Mom and Dad were right. With them gone, it's just you and me looking after each other.

Nancy Osher Uslan, the girl who enrolled in my comic book course and got an A+ . . . oh, and is also my wife and my children's mom, and the angel to thousands of school children in Rwanda and in Newark, New Jersey, through her amazing, innovative organization The Books and Beyond Project (www.friendsofbooksandbeyond.com) . . . sometimes my Lois Lane, sometimes my Hawkgirl, and the only woman who would know the right thing to say on our wedding day, "Face it, Tiger—You just hit the jackpot!"

Grandma Miriam . . . "Gram," Granny Goodness for real.

Aunt Clara and Uncle Phil, also my Godmother and Godfather in every sense of the words . . . Just like Zor-El and Alura were to Kal-El.

The Uslan, Solomon, Botwinick, and Katz family grandparents (David and Pauline, Sam and Anna), cousins, aunts and uncles, and great aunts and great uncles who taught me "family first". . . my own Marvel Family, led by "Little" Aunt Shirley, my own Doll Girl.

Barry Milberg, Bobby Klein, Marc Caplan . . . my best friends like Robin, Bucky, and Jughead, like Thor's Warriors Three, Volstagg, Fandrahl, and Hogun, and only rarely like Flash's Winky, Blinky, and Noddy.

Anne and Morry Osher, Shaina Rudolph, Georgia Uslan, Bobby and Barb Osher, Sandy Osher, Samantha Uslan and Pov Galecki, Cassie and Shane Malmquist, Jeff and Raz Osher, Jamey and Melissa Osher, Jon Osher and Joanna, Jenny Osher, Jessie Osher, Griffin and Maren Annabelle Osher, Charlie Morris Osher, Ian Duncan, FJ DeSanto, Shirley, Charles, Deanie and the entire Melniker clan, and Rick Rosen (from "Dinosaucers" to WME) . . . all, for me, a combination of The Defenders, The Champions, and The Mighty Crusaders.

That's me all over! I think the key to being a successful producer, writer, or director in Hollywood is no matter how old you get, to never let go of your childhood!

Mom and Dad in the sunset of life with their grandchildren, David and Sarah.

Nancy's I.U. sorority picture. Now you see how a guy can fall in love with the first girl he sets his eyes on in college! We dated four years and are married thirty-eight years . . . possibly a Hollywood record!

Mrs. Eleanor Stiller, Mrs. Rita Friedman, Dr. M. S. Osher, Mr. Benjamin Melniker, Mr. Stan Lee, Mr. Sol Harrison, Mr. Otto Binder, Mr. Dennis O'Neil, Mr. Julius Schwartz, Mr. Irwin Moss, Mr. Dean Stolber, Mr. Joseph Friedman, and Mr. Hal Gefsky . . . my teachers, my mentors, my inspirations, my positive reinforcement, my Guardians of the Universe.

The guys . . . from Ocean Township, from comic book fandom, from Indiana University, from the Sammy House, from *Bloomington Bandstand*, from DC Comics and the Junior Woodchucks, from United Artists, from Archie Comics, from Cedar Grove and Montclair, and from Hollywood. And my teachers, including (but of course, not limited to) Professors Henry Glassie, Irving Katz, and Robert Ferrell; Mr. Jim MacDonald; Mr. Eugene Fogler; Mr. Marty Lefsky; and Mr. George Spillane, collectively my Legion of Super-Heroes.

The girls . . . from Ocean Township, from I.U., from DC, from UA, from Cedar Grove and Montclair, and from Hollywood. Special mention to Ellen Genick (spawn of Abe and Flo); The Big Three: Ronna Berman, Wendy Preville, and Barbara Levine; April Blakeslee; Mary Binder; and my teachers . . . variously (but in NO particular order!): Wonder Woman, Supergirl, Betty, Veronica, the Blonde Phantom, She-Hulk, Ms. Marvel, Catwoman, Batgirl, Duo Damsel, the Wasp, the Black Widow, Nightshade, Night Nurse, Nova Kane, Golden Girl, Marvel Girl, Stargirl, Superteen, Wendy the Good Little Witch, and Dream Girl.

The woman who has guided me on the path from dreams to ideas to words to reality, agent Sandy Choron, a Beautiful Dreamer and, as needed, the Watcher, the Sentry, and Ronan the Accuser.

My editor at Chronicle Books, Emily Haynes, who gets me and gets my story and (Great Caesar's Ghost!) has become my very own Perry White.

The brilliant directors, producers, execs, agents, assorted geniuses, technicians, crews, and actors who made my Batman journey a success, and especially to the creators of the legend that is The Batman: Bob Kane, Bill Finger, Jerry Robinson, and DC Comics' publishers, editors, writers, and artists from 1939 to this coming Wednesday.

And David Miles Uslan and Sarah Rose Uslan . . . my children, my loves, my life, my very own Sugar & Spike, and the two best things I ever produced . . . you two capture all the adjectives I ever learned from comic books: super, fantastic, incredible, amazing, astonishing, uncanny, spectacular, mighty, all-star, ultimate, daring, dynamic, and sometimes even a bit delightfully unusual. You both fill all the comic book nouns as well: wonders, soulgems, and Mom's and my God-given Marvels.

Finally, to every fanboy, Batman fan, comic book collector, and fellow comic book geek . . . let's call ourselves not The Unmen, but rather, collectively, The Supreme Intelligence. Since we were kids, we have endured teasing, taunts, derision, scorn, laughter, finger-pointing, being "date-challenged," and (before the Internet) isolation. But today? Comic books and related genres, sci-fi, fantasy, horror, and animation, account for the biggest blockbuster movies, hit TV shows, video games, DVDs, and new media experiences. They have impacted fashion, art, and music worldwide across borders, cultures, gender, and demographics. Comics are cool. Finally . . . WE WIN!

Michael Uslan,

SECRET WRITING ROOM,
INSIDE THE BRAIN ENCASEMENT SECTION,
MECHANICAL DINOSAUR THAT FOUGHT
BATMAN IN "DINOSAUR ISLAND,"
TROPHY ROOM,
THE BAT-CAVE,
GOTHAM CITY,
EARTH TWO

# IMAGE CREDITS

**PAGE 8:** From *Detective Comics* #33 © DC Comics. Art by Bob Kane & Sheldon Moldoff.

**PAGE 10:** *Batman* #8 cover image © DC Comics. Art by Fred Ray & Jerry Robinson.

**PAGE 12:** From *Action Comics* #1 © DC Comics. Art by Joe Shuster.

**PAGE 16:** *Superman's Girl Friend Lois Lane* #30 cover image © DC Comics. Art by Curt Swan & Stan Kaye.

**PAGE 22:** © The respective copyright holders.

**PAGE 24:** *Fantastic Four* #1. © and ™ Marvel Entertainment, LLC.

**PAGE 28:** © The respective copyright holders.

**PAGE 31:** © The respective copyright holders.

**PAGE 36:** *Strange Adventures* #68 cover image © DC Comics. Art by Ruben Moreira.

**PAGE 36:** *Showcase* #4 cover image © DC Comics. Art by Carmine Infantino & Joe Kubert.

**PAGE 40:** From *Batman* #84 © DC Comics. Art by Sheldon Moldoff & Charles Paris.

**PAGE 42:** © The respective copyright holders.

**PAGE 46:** *Batman* #47 cover image © DC Comics. Art by Bob Kane & Charles Paris.

**PAGE 49:** From *Batman* #1 © DC Comics. Art by Bob Kane & Jerry Robinson.

**PAGE 50:** © The respective copyright holders.

**PAGE 53:** Super-Villains Pin-Up © DC Comics. Art by Carmine Infantino.

**PAGE 54-55:** The Cricket. © Michael Uslan. All Rights Reserved.

**PAGE 56:** From *Batman* #92 © DC Comics. Art by Sheldon Moldoff & Charles Paris.

**PAGE 59:** Movie ad © the respective copyright holders. Batman & Robin © DC Comics.

**PAGE 63:** *Justice League of America* #46 cover image © DC Comics. Art by Mike Sekowsky & Joe Giella.

**PAGE 64:** *Superman's Girl Friend, Lois Lane* #2 cover image © DC Comics. Art by Curt Swan & Stan Kaye.

**PAGE 68:** DC Promotional Superman Pin-Up © DC Comics. Art by Wayne Boring & Stan Kaye.

**PAGE 74:** © The respective copyright holders. Early comic book fandom flyers are the rare place you could find characters from different comic books companies mixed together in one illustration.

**PAGE 77:** Photo courtesy of Bill Schelly.

**PAGE 80:** Photo courtesy of Jean Bails with Bill Schelly and Roy Thomas.

**PAGE 81:** Captain Marvel, Billy Batson, and Mary Marvel © DC Comics. Art by C. C. Beck.

**PAGE 85:** © The respective copyright holders.

**PAGE 87:** © The respective copyright holders. Early comic book fandom flyers are the rare place you could find characters from different comic books companies mixed together in one illustration.

**PAGE 89:** *Marvel Family* #89 cover image © DC Comics. Art by Kurt Schaffenberger.

**PAGE 90:** *Batman* #199 cover image © DC Comics. Art by Carmine Infantino & Murphy Anderson.

**PAGE 102:** From *Amazing World of DC Comics* #3 © DC Comics. Comic Course Cartoon art by Dave Manak.

**PAGE 104:** © 1972 United Press International, Inc. All Rights Reserved.

**PAGE 106:** Photo courtesy of Jack C. Harris.

**PAGE 107:** ® and © 2011 Ripley Entertainment, Inc.

**PAGE 108:** © DC Comics.

**PAGE 118:** From *Batman Annual* #1 © DC Comics. Art by Dick Sprang & Charles Paris.

**PAGE 121:** © *Indiana Daily Student*.

**PAGE 128:** *Detective Comics* #339 cover image © DC Comics. Art by Carmine Infantino & Joe Giella.

**PAGE 130:** *Wonder Woman* #155 cover image © DC Comics. Art by Ross Andru & Mike Esposito.

**PAGE 138:** From *Shadow* #9 © DC Comics. Art by Frank Robbins & Frank McLaughlin.

**PAGE 140:** Top: *Detective Comics* #439. Art by Neal Adams & Dick Giordano; Middle: *Batman* #156. Art by Sheldon Moldoff & Charles Paris; Bottom: *Detective Comics* #327. Art by Carmine Infantino & Joe Giella. All images © DC Comics.

**PAGE 141:** Top: *Batman* #259. Art by Nick Cardy; Bottom: *Batman* #253. Art by Michael Kaluta. All images © DC Comics.

**PAGE 142:** Top: *Detective Comics* #168 cover image. Art by Lew Sayre Schwartz & George Roussos. Bottom: *Detective Comics* # 395 cover image. Art by Neal Adams. All images © DC Comics.

**PAGE 144:** *Shadow* #9 cover image © DC Comics. Art by Joe Kubert.

**PAGE 146:** *Unexpected* #202 cover image © DC Comics. Art by Luis Dominguez.

**PAGE 147:** Top left: *Amazing World of DC Comics* #3 cover image © DC Comics. Art by Joe Kubert. Top right and bottom left: Photos courtesy of Jack C. Harris. Bottom right: From *Amazing World of DC Comics* #3 © DC Comics. Art by Marty Pasko.

**PAGE 148:** *Detective Comics* #460 © DC Comics. Cover art by Ernie Chan and interior art by Ernie Chan & Frank McLaughlin.

PAGE 149: Top left: *Detective Comics* #461. Art by Ernie Chan. Top right: *Detective Comics* #462. Art by Ernie Chan. Bottom: *Shadow* #11. Art by Michael Kaluta. All images © DC Comics.

PAGE 151: *Beowulf* #1 © DC Comics. Cover and interior art by Ricardo Villamonte.

PAGE 164: *Life With Archie* #158 Cover image ™ & © Archie Comic Publications, Inc. All Rights Reserved.

PAGE 170: Previously unpublished Congorilla story © DC Comics. Art by Marc D. Nadel.

PAGE 174: *Batman* #227 cover image © DC Comics. Art by Neal Adams.

PAGE 176: *World's Finest* #172 cover image © DC Comics. Art by Curt Swan & George Klein.

PAGE 178: Photo courtesy of Deanie and Charles Melniker.

PAGE 187: *The Shining* © Warner Bros. Inc. All Rights Reserved.

PAGE 188: *Detective Comics* #27 cover image © DC Comics. Art by Bob Kane.

PAGE 190: *Batman* #91 cover image © DC Comics. Art by Winslow Mortimer.

PAGE 193: Batman © DC Comics. Art by Bob Kane.

PAGE 201: Batman © DC Comics. Art by Bob Kane.

PAGE 202: *Swamp Thing* #68 cover image © DC Comics. Art by John Totleben.

PAGE 204: © 1982 Swampfilms, Inc. All Rights Reserved.

PAGE 214: © Sony Pictures Television.

PAGE 223: Batman and the bat logo are © and ™ DC Comics.

PAGE 224: *Batman* #251 cover image © DC Comics. Art by Neal Adams.

PAGE 226. *Batman* #20 cover image © DC Comics. Art by Dick Sprang.

PAGE 236: Photo by Eric Bartelt. Courtesy of and © Pointer View.

PAGE 242: *Batman: Detective* #27 cover image © DC Comics.

PAGE 244: *Archie Marries* . . . cover image ™ & © Archie Comic Publications, Inc. All Rights Reserved.

THANK YOU for the photos, art, and images bringing to life *The Boy Who Loved Batman*:

Robert Klein; Marc Caplan; Michael Morris, Becca Cohen, Erin Thacker, and Emilie Sandoz of Chronicle Books; Mark McNabb; Jay Kogan, Thomas King and Allan Asherman of DC Comics; Dan Buckley and Gregory Pan of Marvel Comics; Jon Goldwater and Victor Gorelick of Archie Comics; Bob Kane; Sherri Ralph and Julie Heath of Warner Bros.; Sandy Bressler and Jack Nicholson; Edward Zimmerman and Joanne Mazzu of Sony Pictures; Andrea Pereira of UPI; Angela Johnson of Ripley Entertainment; John Sullivan; Jebb Dykstra, Esq.; Bill Schelly; Roy Thomas; Jean Bails; Vincent Zurzolo of Metropolis Collectibles; Jack C. Harris; Paul and Mary Lou Hyman; Ronna Berman; Mark D. Nadel; Deanie, Charles, Heather and Harvey Melniker and family; the officers, cadets, and families of West Point; Curt Simic, Brad Hamm and Ron Johnson of Indiana University.

And a thank you from my heart to the real places more magical than anywhere you'll find in comic books . . . the places where the dreams I dared to dream really did come true—Bayonne, New Jersey, Ocean Township, New Jersey, Asbury Park, New Jersey, and Bloomington, Indiana.

When in Bloomington, Indiana, visit
The Michael E. Uslan Comic Book Collection
at the Lilly Library.

I shall be telling this with a sigh
Somewhere ages and ages hence:
Two roads diverged in a wood, and I—
I took the one less traveled by,
And that has made all the difference.

—From *The Road Not Taken,* by Robert Frost